The Political Economy of International
Reform and Reconstruction

Ludwig von Mises

Selected Writings of Ludwig von Mises

The Political Economy of International Reform and Reconstruction

Edited and with an Introduction by
Richard M. Ebeling

LIBERTY FUND INDIANAPOLIS

Introduction, translation © 2000 Hillsdale College. All rights reserved.

Licensed by Hillsdale College.

© 2000 The Estate of Ludwig von Mises. All rights reserved.

Published in the United States of America

Frontispiece photograph courtesy of Bettina Bien Greaves.

04 03 02 01 00 C 5 4 3 2 1
04 03 02 01 00 P 5 4 3 2 1

Library of Congress Cataloging-in-Publication Data

Mises, Ludwig von, 1881–1973.
   The political economy of international reform and reconstruction/
Ludwig von Mises; edited and with an introduction by Richard M. Ebeling.
      p.   cm.   (Selected writings of Ludwig von Mises; 3)
   Includes bibliographical references and index.
   ISBN 0-86597-270-2 (alk. paper).
   ISBN 0-86597-271-0 (pbk.: alk. paper)
   1. Europe—Economic policy.   2. Europe—Economic conditions—1945–
3. Free enterprise—Europe.   4. Capitalism—Europe.   5. Socialism—
Europe.   I. Ebeling, Richard M.   II. Title.   III. Series: Mises, Ludwig von,
1881–1973.   Selections.   2000; 3.
HB101.V66A25   2000 vol. 3
[HC240]
330.15′7 s—dc21
[338.94]   99-16126

Liberty Fund, Inc.
8335 Allison Pointe Trail, Suite 300
Indianapolis, Indiana 46250-1684

Contents

ACKNOWLEDGMENTS

Preparation of this volume would have been impossible if not for the enthusiastic assistance and support of several individuals. First and foremost was Foundation for Economic Education Resident Scholar Bettina Bien Greaves, who kindly made available and provided the permission to bring into print these previously unpublished essays by Ludwig von Mises.

Dr. Grete Heinz of Monterey, California, prepared the translation of "A Draft of Guidelines for the Reconstruction of Austria." Some suggestions about terminology in this chapter were also provided by Hillsdale College Professor of Marketing Wolfgang Grassl.

Preparation of the annotated footnotes for the essays would have been much more difficult if not for the timely and professional assistance of the Hillsdale College library staff, especially Mary "Squeak" Barnett, Judy Leising, and Janet Ryan. They not only handled numerous interlibrary loan requests and helped with finding material in the Hillsdale College library collection but also hunted down obscure references and historical information through computer searches.

Carol Kratzer and Pia York retyped the essays for uniformity of style and format.

The staff and trustees of Liberty Fund, most especially President George B. Martin and Director of Publications David A. Bovenizer, have underwritten and overseen the publication of Mises's papers. In terms of time, expertise, and resources, their generosity has been unstinting.

Mr. and Mrs. Quinten E. Ward, Mrs. Mildred Dunn, Mr. Sheldon Rose, and Dr. John Sheridan have also provided major financial support that will enable Hillsdale College to share this volume with a wide audience.

Finally, my wife, Anna, is the centerpiece around which all my personal and professional activities revolve, the partner in all that I have done, and the source of the greatest inspiration and support. It is to her that I owe the greatest thanks.

RICHARD M. EBELING

Ludwig von Mises Professor of Economics
Hillsdale College
February 2000

INTRODUCTION

Ludwig von Mises: The Man and His Ideas

All except one of the essays in this volume were written by Austrian economist Ludwig von Mises in the four years immediately after his arrival in the United States in the summer of 1940 as a refugee from war-torn Europe. Half of them were delivered as lectures. The others were prepared as monographs on special topics. Their general theme is the problem of international reconstruction and reform in the era succeeding the Second World War.[1]

In the Europe he had left behind, Ludwig von Mises had been one of the most celebrated—and controversial—economists of his time. Over the preceding thirty years, he had acquired an international reputation as one of the leading contributors to the Austrian School of economics and as possibly the foremost critic of the collectivist trends of the early twentieth century. In the 1920s, when the appeal of socialism in its various forms was at its zenith, Mises boldly challenged the feasibility of a fully centralized planned economy. He also questioned the long-term stability of an interventionist or mixed economy as a sustainable "middle way" between a free market system and a socialist, centrally planned economy. And he forcefully argued that only a system of *laissez-faire* capitalism—of genuine capitalism—could successfully assure freedom and prosperity.

At the same time, he developed his analysis of alternative systems of social and economic order in the wider context of a philosophical and methodological approach that ran counter to the Marxist, positivist, and historicist prejudices of the time. He insisted that social analysis had to have as its starting point a general theory of individual human action and choice. It could not be successfully constructed on the basis of mythical racial, class, or nationalistic aggregates.

An understanding of Mises's arguments on these subjects, as well as his

---

1 Two other previously unpublished papers from 1943 by Mises on the related topics of "Autarky and Its Consequences" and "Economic Nationalism and Peaceful Economic Cooperation" were included in an earlier collection; see Richard M. Ebeling, ed., *Money, Method, and the Market Process: Essays by Ludwig von Mises* (Norwell, Mass.: Kluwer Academic Press, 1990), pp. 137–65.

work as an influential economic policy analyst in the Austria between the two world wars, is essential if one is to appreciate his ideas on postwar reconstruction and reform. In 1920, Mises published "Economic Calculation in the Socialist Commonwealth,"[2] which he expanded into a comprehensive treatise on *Socialism* in 1922.[3] In 1927, he published *Liberalism*,[4] which was followed two years later by *Critique of Interventionism*.[5] In these important books, he offered a detailed and consistent defense of free-market capitalism in opposition to the regulated economy and socialism.

For Mises, one of the greatest accomplishments of mankind has been the discovery of the higher productivity arising from a division of labor. The classical economists' analysis of comparative advantage—under which specialization in production increases the quantities, qualities, and varieties of goods available to all participants in the network of exchange—is more than merely a sophisticated demonstration of the mutual gains from trade. As Mises was to later express it, the law of comparative advantage actually is the law of human association: The mutual benefits resulting from specialization of activities constitute the origins of society and the development of civilization.[6]

The rationality of the market economy lies in its ability to allocate the scarce means of production in society for the most efficient satisfaction of consumer wants in a complex system of division of labor—that is, to see to

2 Ludwig von Mises, "Economic Calculation in the Socialist Commonwealth," [1920] in F. A. Hayek, ed., *Collectivist Economic Planning* (London: Routledge & Sons, 1935), pp. 87–130.

3 Ludwig von Mises, *Socialism* (Indianapolis: Liberty Fund, [1951] 1981); on Mises's critique of socialism and its relation to earlier criticisms of central planning, see Richard M. Ebeling, "Economic Calculation under Socialism: Ludwig von Mises and His Predecessors," in Jeffrey M. Herbener, ed., *The Meaning of Ludwig von Mises* (Norwell, Mass.: Kluwer Academic Press, 1993), pp. 56–101.

4 Ludwig von Mises, *Liberalism in the Classical Tradition* (Irvington-on-Hudson, N.Y., and San Francisco, Calif.: Foundation for Economic Education and the Cobden Press, [1927] 1985).

5 Ludwig von Mises, *Critique of Interventionism* (Irvington-on-Hudson, N.Y.: Foundation for Economic Education, [1929] 1996).

6 Ludwig von Mises, *Socialism*, pp. 258–61; *Human Action, A Treatise on Economics* (Irvington-on-Hudson, N.Y.: Foundation for Economic Education, 4th rev. ed., 1996), pp. 157–66.

it that the means at individuals' disposal are applied to the most highly valued uses, as expressed in the free choices those individuals make in the marketplace. Of course, this requires some method of discovering the alternative uses for which scarce means might be employed and their relative value in their competing uses. Mises explained that competitively determined market prices, in an institutional setting of private ownership over the means of production, provide the only reliable method for solving this problem. On the market for consumer goods, buyers express their valuations for commodities in the form of the prices they are willing to pay. Similarly, on the market for producer goods, entrepreneurs express their appraisals of the relative future profitability of using factors of production in manufacturing various goods through the prices they are willing to pay.

Market prices, expressed through the common denominator of money, are what make economic calculation possible. The relative costs and expected revenues from alternative productive activities are compared and contrasted with ease and efficiency. The competitive processes of the market tend to assure that none of the scarce factors of production is applied for any productive purpose for which there is a more highly valued use (as expressed in a rival entrepreneur's bid for their hire). The value of the goods desired by consumers is imputed back to the scarce means of production through the competitive rivalry of entrepreneurs. Thus the means available in society are applied to best serve people's ends.

Mises's crucial argument against all forms of socialism and interventionism is that they prevent the effective operation of this market process and thus reduce the rationality of the social system. The triumph of socialism—with its nationalization of the means of production under government control and central planning—meant the *irrationalization* of the economic order. Without market-based prices to supply information about the actual opportunity costs of using those resources (as estimated by the competing market actors themselves) decision-making by socialist central planners is inevitably arbitrary and "irrational." The socialist economy is, therefore, fundamentally *anti-economic*.

Interventionism does not abolish the market economy. Instead, it introduces various forms of onerous controls and regulations that deflect production from the paths that would have been followed if entrepreneurs, in the search for profits through the best satisfaction of consumer demand, had been left free to fully follow their own judgments concerning the use and disposal of the factors of production under their control. Price controls, in particular, distort competitively determined relationships between selling prices and cost prices, resulting in severe misallocations of resources and misdirected production activities.

One other major contribution by Mises during his years in Europe was his pioneering work on monetary theory and policy. Before the First World War he published *The Theory of Money and Credit* (1912).[7] In this book, he applied the Austrian theory of marginal utility to the problem of explaining the value of money on the basis of individuals' demands for holding cash balances. He also developed a dynamic sequence analysis, enabling him to explain the process by which changes in the quantity of money bring about redistributions of wealth, relative price changes that modify the allocation of real resources among various sectors of the market, as well as how monetary changes introduced through the banking system can distort interest rates in such a way as to generate business cycles. One of the conclusions that Mises reached in his analysis of monetary processes is that business cycles are *not* a phenomenon inherent in the market economy. Rather, they are caused by government mismanagement of the monetary and banking system. He later restated and refined his arguments relating to monetary policy in *Monetary Stabilization and Cyclical Policy.*[8]

A wider theme of Mises's writings in the period between the world wars is the philosophical and methodological foundations of economic science. In a series of essays written in the 1920s and early 1930s he argued that economics belongs to a more general science of human action, which he came to call "praxeology." He stated that economics begins with the concept of intentionality and purposefulness, and that this makes economics—and its methods of analysis—different from the approaches followed for the study of the physical sciences. At the same time, the logic of action and choice, which economists take as their starting point for analy-

7 Ludwig von Mises, *The Theory of Money and Credit* (Indianapolis: Liberty Fund, 3rd revised ed., [1924; 1953] 1980).

8 Ludwig von Mises, "Monetary Stabilization and Cyclical Policy," [1928] in Percy L. Greaves, ed., *On the Manipulation of Money and Credit* (Dobbs Ferry, N.Y.: Free Market Books, 1978); see Richard M. Ebeling, "Ludwig von Mises and the Gold Standard," in Llewellyn H. Rockwell, Jr., ed., *The Gold Standard: An Austrian Perspective* (Lexington, Mass.: Lexington Books, 1983), pp. 35–59; and Richard M. Ebeling, "Variations on the Demand for Money Theme: Ludwig von Mises and Some Twentieth Century Views," in John W. Robbins and Mark Spangler, eds., *A Man of Principle: Essays in Honor of Hans F. Sennholz* (Grove City, Pa.: Grove City College Press, 1992), pp. 127–38.

sis of market phenomena, has universal properties and characteristics concerning the human condition from which the general laws of economics can be derived. As a result, Mises strongly opposed the highly popular positivist and historicist ideas of his time. The essays in which he developed these ideas on the methodology of the human sciences were published as a collection in 1933.[9]

Besides his writings on capitalism, socialism, interventionism, and the monetary order, Mises also attempted to influence the course of events in Austria as a policymaker. Beginning in 1909, he was employed in the department of finance at the Vienna Chamber for Commerce, Trade, and Industry as an economic analyst. In this capacity he evaluated and made recommendations about various legislative proposals in the areas of banking, insurance, monetary and foreign-exchange policy, and public finance. In the years between the two world wars, he was a senior secretary with the Chamber, enabling him to argue with some authority on the economic policy issues confronting the Austrian government.[10]

A review of documents and memoranda he prepared for the Vienna Chamber of Commerce during the 1920s and early 1930s shows his consistent emphasis on the desirability of freeing the Austrian economy of high taxes and tariffs, foreign-exchange controls, industrial regulation and price controls, and the excessive power of special interest groups, especially trade unions to control labor markets. The general consensus of economists and others who knew Mises during this period is that he was extremely influential in moderating collectivist and inflationary policies in Austria. For

---

9 Ludwig von Mises, *Epistemological Problems of Economics* (New York: New York University Press, [1933] 1976); for an exposition and analysis of Mises's ideas on the logic of human action and his comparative study of capitalism, socialism, and interventionism, see Richard M. Ebeling, "A Rational Economist in an Irrational Age: Ludwig von Mises," in Richard M. Ebeling, ed., *The Age of Economists: From Adam Smith to Milton Friedman*, Champions of Freedom Series, Vol. 26 (Hillsdale, Mich.: Hillsdale College Press, 1999), pp. 69–120; Mises's theory of human action was influenced by the phenomenological method of Edmund Husserl and the sociological approach of Max Weber; see Richard M. Ebeling, "Austrian Subjectivism and Phenomenological Foundations," in Peter J. Boettke and Mario J. Rizzo, eds., *Advances in Austrian Economics*, Vol. 2A (Greenwich, Conn.: JAI Press, 1995), pp. 39–53; and Richard M. Ebeling, "Expectations and Expectations Formation in Mises' Theory of the Market Process," in Peter J. Boettke and David L. Prychitko, eds., *The Market Process: Essays in Contemporary Austrian Economics* (Brookfield, Vt.: Edward Elgar, 1994), pp. 83–95.

10 Ludwig von Mises, *Notes and Recollections* (South Holland, Ill.: Libertarian Press, 1978), pp. 71–92.

example, he was instrumental in preventing the full nationalization of the Austrian economy by a socialist government immediately after the end of the First World War. He successfully helped to redirect public and political opinion to bring the Great Austrian Inflation to an end in 1922. And in the aftermath of this monetary disaster, he played an important role in the writing of the statutes and by-laws of the National Bank of Austria, which was reconstructed under the auspices of the League of Nations in 1923.

Mises's early activities at the Chamber were interrupted in 1914 when his reserve unit in the Austro-Hungarian army was called up for active service in the First World War. For part of the next four years, he served as an artillery officer on the Russian front. Three times he was decorated for bravery under fire. Following the signing of the Treaty of Brest-Litovsk between imperial Germany and Lenin's new Bolshevik government that ended the war on the Eastern front in March of 1918, Mises was appointed the officer in charge of currency control in Austrian-occupied Ukraine. His headquarters were in Odessa. Later in the same year he was transferred to duty in Vienna to serve as an economic expert for the Austrian General Staff. In this role he was responsible for preparing memoranda on inflation, war industry, war finance, and related issues. With the end of the war, Mises returned to civilian life. Besides his duties with the Vienna Chamber of Commerce, he was appointed in late 1918 as director of the League of Nations Reparations Commission for the settlement of prewar debts and war claims. He held this position until 1920.

In 1913, Mises had been granted the right to teach at the University of Vienna as a *Privatdozent,* or unsalaried lecturer; in 1918, he was promoted to the title of Professor Extraordinary. Except during the war, he taught a course at the university almost every semester until 1934, thus influencing a new generation of young Viennese and foreign scholars. He also cofounded and served as vice president of the Austrian Economic Society. In 1920, Mises began a *Privatseminar,* or private seminar, that normally met twice a month from October to June at his Chamber office. This seminar brought together a group of Viennese scholars in economics, political science, philosophy, sociology, and law, many of whom went on to become world-renowned scholars in their respective fields.[11] Almost

11 Mises, *Notes and Recollections,* pp. 93–100.

to a man, the participants recalled that the seminar was one of the most rigorous and rewarding experiences of their lives.[12]

One other singularly important activity of Mises during this period was his founding of the Austrian Institute for Business Cycle Research in 1926. With the future Nobel laureate, twenty-seven-year-old Friedrich A. Hayek, as the first director, the Institute was soon internationally recognized as a leading center for economic forecasting and policy analysis in Central Europe.[13] Shortly after it was founded the Institute began to be commissioned by the League of Nations to prepare reports and studies on the economic situation in Central and Eastern Europe. When, in 1931, Hayek accepted an appointment at the London School of Economics, another young Austrian economist, Oskar Morgenstern, assumed the position of Institute director. Morgenstern remained the director until 1938, when Nazi Germany annexed Austria. Mises served as the Institute's vice president until 1934.

In March of 1934, William E. Rappard, cofounder and director of the Graduate Institute of International Studies in Geneva, Switzerland, wrote to Mises in Vienna inquiring if he would be willing to accept a visiting professorship in international economic relations.[14] Mises accepted the appointment and assumed his responsibilities at the Graduate Institute in October of 1934. Shortly after arriving in Geneva, he began a project he had in mind for many years, namely the writing of a comprehensive treatise on economics. Apart from his light teaching responsibilities (one course and one seminar a semester), most of his time during the next six years was devoted to this project. In May of 1940, as Europe was falling under the dark cloud of Nazi occupation, this monumental work, *Nationalökonomie*, was published in Switzerland.[15] It served as the basis for his later English-language treatise, *Human Action*, published in 1949.

12 For recollections of Mises's *Privatseminar* by former members, see the appendix in Margit von Mises, *My Years with Ludwig von Mises* (Cedar Falls, Iowa: Center for Futures Education, 2nd ed., 1984), pp. 199–211; see also Earlene Craver, "The Emigration of the Austrian Economists," *History of Political Economy*, Vol. 18, No. 1 (1986), pp. 1–32.

13 See Richard M. Ebeling, "Friedrich A. Hayek: A Centenary Appreciation," *The Freeman* (May 1999), pp. 28–33.

14 See Richard M. Ebeling, "William E. Rappard: An International Man in an Age of Nationalism," *The Freeman* (January 2000), pp. 39–46.

15 Ludwig von Mises, *Nationalökonomie: Theorie des Handelns und Wirtschaftens* (Munich: Philosophia Verlag, [1940] 1980).

In June of 1940, Mises resigned from his position at the Graduate Institute. On July 4, he left Geneva for the United States. After a harrowing
journey across France and Spain to Lisbon, Portugal, he embarked on an
ocean liner on July 24, and he arrived in New Jersey on August 2, 1940.

Mises's first years in the United States—the period when the essays in
this volume were written—were not easy ones. He experienced great difficulty in finding a permanent teaching position, partly because of his age
(he was fifty-nine years old when he arrived) and partly because of the intellectual climate that then prevailed. His was a voice for an older classical liberalism and free-market capitalism that was out of step with the
popular trends of socialism, interventionism, and Keynesian economics
embraced by a large majority of American academics and policymakers.

However, Mises was supported through research grants generously
supplied by the Rockefeller Foundation as well as an affiliation with the
National Bureau of Economic Research. He completed two works that
were both published in 1944: *Omnipotent Government: The Rise of the
Total State and Total War*[16] and *Bureaucracy*.[17] A third book, written shortly
after his arrival in the United States, *Government and Business*, remained
unpublished until just recently, when it appeared under the title *Interventionism: An Economic Analysis*.[18]

Not until 1945 was Mises appointed to an academic post as a visiting
professor in the Graduate School of Business at New York University, a
position he retained until his retirement in 1969 at the age of eighty-eight.
During almost a quarter of a century of teaching in the United States, he
was able to train a new American generation of "Austrian" economists.[19]
He also published a number of significant books, including *Planning for*

16 Ludwig von Mises, *Omnipotent Government: The Rise of the Total State and Total War*
(Spring Mills, Pa.: Libertarian Press, [1944] 1985).

17 Ludwig von Mises, *Bureaucracy* (Spring Mills, Pa.: Libertarian Press, [1944] 1983).

18 Ludwig von Mises, *Interventionism: An Economic Analysis* (Irvington-on-Hudson, N.Y.:
Foundation for Economic Education, 1998).

19 On the history and ideas of the Austrian School of economics, see Ludwig M. Lach-
mann, "The Significance of the Austrian School of Economics in the History of Ideas,"
[1966] in Richard M. Ebeling, ed., *Austrian Economics: A Reader*, Champions of Freedom Series, Vol. 18 (Hillsdale, Mich.: Hillsdale College Press, 1991), pp. 17–39; and
Richard M. Ebeling, "The Significance of Austrian Economics in Twentieth-Century Economic Thought," in Richard M. Ebeling, ed., *Austrian Economics: Perspectives on the Past
and Prospects for the Future*, Champions of Freedom Series, Vol. 17 (Hillsdale, Mich.:
Hillsdale College Press, 1991), pp. 1–40.

Freedom,[20] *The Anti-Capitalistic Mentality,*[21] *Theory and History: An Interpretation of Social and Economic Evolution,*[22] *The Ultimate Foundation of Economic Science,*[23] and *The Historical Setting of the Austrian School of Economics.*[24]

When Ludwig von Mises died on October 10, 1973, at the age of ninety-two, there is no doubt that he left a profound and lasting legacy as an economic theorist and a champion of liberty.

Economic Nationalism in the Period Between the Two World Wars

The catastrophe of the Second World War was, in Mises's view, the logical culmination of the political and economic policies of the 1920s and 1930s. Having after 1914 abandoned the principles and practice of economic liberalism and free trade, Europe (and the world in general) had created a political environment in which social conflict within countries and war between nations was almost inevitable.

In a social setting of free-market capitalism, in which governments basically confined themselves to the equal protection of each person to his liberty and property before the law, sectional and national conflicts were practically nonexistent. Directed by the incentives of market opportunities, every individual found his place in the social system of division of labor. Labor, capital, and commodities migrated to those places offering the most attractive returns. Production and employment were localized where market profitability suggested the greatest productive advantage.

Moreover, in such a free-market setting, rivalries between competitors

---

20 Ludwig von Mises, *Planning for Freedom* (South Holland, Ill.: Libertarian Press, 4th ed., 1980).

21 Ludwig von Mises, *The Anti-Capitalistic Mentality* (Spring Mills, Pa.: Libertarian Press, [1956] 1990).

22 Ludwig von Mises, *Theory and History: An Interpretation of Social and Economic Evolution* (Auburn, Ala.: Ludwig von Mises Institute, [1957] 1985).

23 Ludwig von Mises, *The Ultimate Foundation of Economic Science: An Essay on Method* (Kansas City, Kans.: Sheed Andrews and McMeel, [1962] 1978).

24 Ludwig von Mises, "The Historical Setting of the Austrian School of Economics," [1969] in Bettina Bien Greaves, ed., *Austrian Economics: An Anthology* (Irvington-on-Hudson, N.Y.: Foundation for Economic Education, 1996), pp. 53–76.

were private affairs in which their only weapons were cheaper and better products to capture more consumer business. With governments limited to the protection of life and property, national boundaries were merely administrative lines on maps with no economic significance. Men, money, and goods moved freely and unhindered by politically imposed barriers.

In the generally free-market order before 1914, most of the world's monetary system was based on a market-based commodity: gold. Though governments through national central banks relegated to themselves control over the money supply, they managed the monetary system by the "rules" of the gold standard. The quantity of money was determined by the profitability of gold mining based on the demand for gold for monetary as well as commercial uses. The purchasing power of money was set by the market forces of supply and demand, and only to a relatively limited extent by the manipulations of governments pursuing various and sundry political goals.

It is always easy to look back at earlier times and to picture them nostalgically as "golden ages" from which the present represents a tragic fall. In fact, however, the period before the First World War possessed many of the characteristics summarized in Mises's conception of a world of free trade and free markets.[25] It is true that even before the First World War destroyed this epoch of classical liberalism, the world had been returning to policies of governmental intervention and trade restrictions, with imperial Germany in the lead.[26] Nonetheless, the era before 1914 was a world characterized by what Gustav Stolper called the epoch of the "three freedoms": freedom of movement for men, for goods, and for money.[27] In addition, the world enjoyed an unprecedented level of peace. Conflicts and even wars did occur, but, under the classical liberal ideal of individual freedom, private property, and limited government, wars — especially in Europe — were

---

25 See Mises, *Omnipotent Government*, pp. 95–96; also John Maynard Keynes, *The Economic Consequences of the Peace*, in D. E. Moggridge, ed., *The Collected Works of John Maynard Keynes* (New York: Macmillan Co., [1919] 1971), pp. 5–7.

26 See Hermann Levy, *Economic Liberalism* (London: Macmillan Ltd., 1913), p. 1; Wilhelm Röpke, *German Commercial Policy* (London: Longman, Green and Co., 1934); and Gustav Stolper, *German Economy, 1870–1940* (New York: Reynal and Hitchcock, 1940), pp. 60–92.

27 Gustav Stolper, *This Age of Fable: The Political and Economic World We Live In* (New York: Reynal & Hitchcock, 1942), pp. 7–8.

few in number, short in duration, and restrained in their damage to life and property.[28]

The First World War ushered in an era of economic planning, price and production controls, foreign-exchange regulations, restrictions on international trade, capital movements, and migration, and a flood of paper-money inflations to cover the costs of war. When the war ended on November 11, 1918, the world had to reconstruct the political and economic landscape. The political map of Europe was radically redrawn, with the German, Austro-Hungarian, and Russian empires carved up to make a tapestry of new and differently shaped nation-states in Central and Eastern Europe. But with the emergence of political nationalism came the rise of economic nationalism.[29] Each of the new successor states imposed tariff barriers and artificially stimulated the creation of greater agricultural or industrial sectors in their economies. These policies were enacted through subsidies, monopoly rights of production and sale, import and export regulations and quotas, tax incentives, foreign exchange controls, and restrictions on the free movement of capital and labor.[30]

Each of these nations of Europe considered that political independence required a corollary: economic independence. The ideal of "autarky" —economic self-sufficiency—increasingly became the basis upon which the governments of these countries judged the appropriateness of any economic policy.[31] Domestic and foreign economic policies by one country became the cause for suspicion and planned counter-policy by its neigh-

28 See Richard M. Ebeling, "World Peace, International Order and Classical Liberalism," *International Journal of World Peace* (December 1995), pp. 47–68.

29 See T. E. Gregory, "Economic Nationalism," *International Affairs* (May 1931), pp. 289–306; Lionel Robbins, "The Economic Consequences of Economic Nationalism," *Lloyds Bank Limited Monthly Review* (May 1936), pp. 226–39; William E. Rappard, "Economic Nationalism," in *Authority and the Individual, Harvard Tercentenary Conference of Arts and Sciences* (Cambridge, Mass.: Harvard University Press, 1937), pp. 74–112; Michael A. Heilperin, *Studies in Economic Nationalism* (Geneva: Librarie E. Droz, 1962).

30 See Leo Pasvolsky, *Economic Nationalism of the Danubian States* (New York: Macmillan Co., 1928); Antonin Basch, *The Danubian Basin and the German Economic Sphere* (New York: Columbia University Press, 1943); Frederick Hertz, *The Economic Problems of the Danubian States: A Study in Economic Nationalism* (London: Victor Gollancz, 1947).

31 See A. G. B. Fisher, *Economic Self-Sufficiency* (Oxford: Clarendon Press, 1939); and Leo Grebler, "Self-Sufficiency and Imperialism," *Annals of the American Academy of Political and Social Science* (July 1938), pp. 1–8.

bors. Nor did the countries of Western Europe fully return to the freer policies that prevailed before 1914; they, too, retained various forms of the controls that had been implemented during the war. Consequently, a climate of antagonism, fear, and economic warfare came to dominate the arena of international politics.

Furthermore, whereas the gold standard had formed the basis of the monetary system of virtually all major countries before the First World War, in the postwar era monetary nationalism joined economic nationalism as the new currency order of the world.[32] Under the prewar gold standard, a unit of each nation's currency was fixed as a certain quantity of gold, exchangeable on demand at that ratio at any representative bank. Through this common gold connection, the national currencies of the world were bound into a unitary and international monetary order.[33]

After the monetary chaos of the immediate postwar period, during which some currencies, like Germany's, were literally destroyed by hyperinflation, there was an attempt to return to monetary stability and a weaker form of the gold standard.[34] Most governments, however, were unwilling or unable to follow the "rules of the game" required under the gold standard. Money was no longer a market-based medium of exchange through which were facilitated the domestic and global transactions of private trade and investment. Instead, money was increasingly viewed as a tool of national economic policy. Money's domestic purchasing power and external foreign-exchange value were things to be manipulated by governments to further "national purposes." With the advent of the Great Depression in 1929, these tendencies merely continued and intensified.[35]

There were half-hearted attempts to restore international trade and

32 See F. A. Hayek, "Monetary Nationalism and International Stability" [1937] in Stephen Kresge, ed., *The Collected Works of F. A. Hayek, Vol. VI: Good Money, Part II* (Chicago: University of Chicago Press, 1999), pp. 27–100; and Lionel Robbins, *Economic Planning and International Order* (London: Macmillan Ltd., 1937), pp. 280–301.

33 See Wilhelm Röpke, *International Order and Economic Integration* (Dordrecht, Holland: D. Reidel Publishing Co., 1959), pp. 75–77; also T. E. Gregory, *The Gold Standard and Its Future* (New York: E. P. Dutton, 1935), pp. 1–21; and Moritz J. Bonn, "The Gold Standard in International Relations," in William E. Rappard, ed., *Problems of Peace*, 8th Series (Freeport, N.Y.: Books for Libraries, [1934] 1968), pp. 163–79.

34 See Leland B. Yeager, *Experiences with Stopping Inflation* (Washington, D.C.: American Enterprise Institute, 1981), pp. 45–98.

35 See Frederic Benham, "The Muddle of the Thirties," *Economica* (February 1945), pp. 1–9.

monetary order in the 1920s and 1930s, but they all failed.[36] The forces of political and economic nationalism, the emerging idea of economic planning, the pragmatic politics of interventionist policies to foster the special interests of domestic groups, and the formal abandonment of the gold standard in favor of purely fiat monies exacerbated the disintegration of the international economic order.[37] In the 1930s, governments increased their subsidies and protectionist supports to industry and agriculture, their interference in the management and control of private enterprise, their monetary and fiscal manipulations to influence domestic output and employment, their taxing policies to modify the distribution of wealth, and their regulation of foreign trade and foreign-exchange rates.[38] The benefits of a free international economic order were forgotten.[39]

With the growth of political and economic nationalism came political

36 See William E. Rappard, *Post-War Efforts for Freer Trade* (Geneva: Geneva Research Centre, 1938) and "The Common Menace of Economic and Military Armaments," [1936] in *Varia Politica, Republication of Essays by William Rappard on the Occasion of His Seventieth Birthday* (Zurich: Editions Polygraphics, 1953), pp. 76–100; Jacob Viner, "International Economic Relations and the World Order," in Walter H. C. Laves, ed., *The Foundations of a More Stable World Order* (Chicago: University of Chicago Press, 1940), pp. 42–45; *Commercial Policy in the Interwar Period: International Proposals and National Policies* (Geneva: League of Nations, 1942); and Ragnar Nurkse, *International Currency Experience: Lessons of the Inter-war Period* (Princeton, N.J.: Princeton University Press, 1944).

37 See Ludwig von Mises, "The Disintegration of the International Division of Labor," [1938] in Richard M. Ebeling, ed., *Money, Method, and the Market Process*, pp. 113–36; and Wilhelm Röpke, *International Economic Disintegration* (Philadelphia, Pa.: Porcupine Press, [1942] 1978).

38 See Moritz J. Bonn, "Introductory Address," in *The State and Economic Life, A Record of a First International Study Conference* (Paris: International Institute of Intellectual Co-operation, 1932), pp. 7–15; J. B. Condliffe, "Vanishing World Trade," *Foreign Affairs* (July 1933), pp. 645–56; Lionel Robbins, *The Great Depression* (London: Macmillan Ltd., 1934); Gustav Stolper, "Politics versus Economics," *Foreign Affairs* (April 1934), pp. 357–76; P. W. Martin, "The Present Status of Economic Planning: I. An International Survey of Governmental Economic Intervention," *International Labour Review* (May 1936), pp. 619–45; Henry J. Tosca, *World Trade Systems* (Paris: International Institute of Intellectual Co-operation, 1939); Margaret S. Gordon, *Barriers to World Trade: A Study of Recent Commercial Policy* (New York: Macmillan Co., 1941); and Richard M. Ebeling, "Liberalism and Collectivism in the 20th Century," in Alexsandras Shtromas, ed., *The End of "Isms"? Reflections on the Fate of Ideological Politics After Communism's Collapse* (Cambridge, Mass.: Blackwell Publishers, 1994), pp. 69–84.

39 See J. B. Condliffe, "The Value of International Trade," *Economica* (May 1938), pp. 123–37.

and economic tyranny. Dictators emerged all across the face of Central and Eastern Europe. Freedom was under attack as never before in modern times.[40] Political and economic nationalism in Europe finally culminated in the barbarism and destruction of World War II.

International Reconstruction and Reform after the Second World War

Even before the worst carnage of the war had occurred, economists, political scientists, historians, sociologists, and men of practical politics had begun to ask themselves how the world had reached such a state of disorganization and chaos and how the era to come after the war could be made better. At first, when the outcome of the war was still uncertain, the analysis often focused on what the alternative international orders might look like were the postwar world to be primarily totalitarian or democratic, or if there were to be a division of the globe between the two rival political systems.[41] As the war progressed, it became clear that the Western democracies would triumph, with fascist and Nazi totalitarianism unconditionally defeated. Accordingly, the world was faced with the serious need to reconstruct the international political and economic order. A general consensus existed, especially among economists, that the world required a reversal of the economic nationalism and protectionism that had plagued the interwar period. There was plenty of evidence that such policies only

40 William E. Rappard, "Nationalism and the League of Nations Today," in *Problems of Peace*, 8th Series (New York: Books for Libraries Press, [1934] 1968), pp. 17–19; also by Rappard, *The Crisis of Democracy* (Chicago: University of Chicago Press, 1938); and William Henry Chamberlin, *Collectivism: A False Utopia* (New York: Macmillan Co., 1938).

41 See J. B. Condliffe, *The Reconstruction of World Trade: A Survey of International Economic Relations* (New York: W. W. Norton & Co., 1940); Michael A. Heilperin, "Totalitarian Trade," *World Affairs Interpreter* (January 1941), pp. 1–8; Lewis L. Lorwin, *Economic Consequences of the Second World War* (New York: Random House, 1941); Douglas Miller, *You Can't Do Business with Hitler* (Boston: Little, Brown and Co., 1941); Thomas Reveille, *The Spoil of Europe: The Nazi Technique in Political and Economic Conquest* (New York: W. W. Norton, 1941); Howard Ellis, "The Problems of Exchange Systems in the Postwar World," *American Economic Review* (May 1942), pp. 195–205; Frank Munk, *The Legacy of Nazism: The Economic and Social Consequences of Totalitarianism* (New York: Macmillan Co., 1943); and Jacob Viner, *Trade Relations Between Free Market and Controlled Economies* (Geneva: League of Nations, 1943).

led to economic disaster and political tension. The postwar world would desperately need the benefits of free trade and the advantages of an international division of labor.

There were some who forcefully called for a revival of classical liberal ideals for domestic and international economic reconstruction and reform.[42] But such voices for a return to pre–World War I classical liberalism were in a small minority. The general view among proponents of a new international economic order was that an unregulated and unplanned market economy was a thing of the past—and would be undesirable even if it were feasible. Under the influence of Keynesian economics and the apparent "advantages" of wartime planning, the majority of economists expected that, in peacetime, governments would still extensively intervene in and regulate the market economy. They asserted with confidence, in the words of Howard Ellis, that "governments have definitely accepted welfare economics as a basic policy; and it is altogether unlikely that any nation will again leave to the vagaries of unregulated international competition the crucial matter of total effective demand for its products and its manpower."[43] As Charles E. Merriman, a supporter of this new consensus, said: "Planning is coming. Of this there can be no doubt. The only question is whether it will be democratic planning of a free society, or totalitarian in character."[44]

The ideal was the so-called "middle way" between *laissez-faire* and a totally planned economy.[45] But a middle way necessarily involved a pre-

---

42 See Henry Simons, "Trade and the Peace," in Seymour E. Harris, ed., *Postwar Economic Problems* (New York: McGraw-Hill Book Co., 1943), pp. 141–55; also Benjamin M. Anderson, "The Road Back to Full Employment," in Paul T. Homan and Fritz Machlup, eds., *Financing American Prosperity: A Symposium of Economists* (New York: Twentieth Century Fund, 1945), pp. 9–70.

43 Howard Ellis, "Removal of Restrictions on Trade and Capital," in Seymour Harris, ed., *Postwar Economic Problems*," p. 345; see also Richard M. Ebeling, "The Global Economy and Classical Liberalism: Past, Present, and Future," in Richard M. Ebeling, ed., *The Future of American Business*, Champions of Freedom Series, Vol. 24 (Hillsdale, Mich.: Hillsdale College Press, 1996), pp. 9–60, especially pp. 18–23, on the relationship between domestic intervention and "demand management," and regulation of international trade.

44 Charles E. Merriam, "The Place of Planning," in Seymour E. Harris, ed., *Saving American Capitalism: A Liberal Economic Program* (New York: Alfred A. Knopf, 1948), p. 161.

45 See Eugene Staley, *World Economy in Transition: Technology vs. Politics, Laissez Faire vs. Planning, Power vs. Welfare* (Port Washington, N.Y.: Kennikat Press, [1939] 1971), pp. 127–200 and 225–326, and "The Economic Side of Stable Peace," *Annals of the American*

eminent position for governments in regulating prices and production, and in managing domestic aggregate employment and output and the price level through various monetary and fiscal methods. If a world economic order were to be reconstructed, governments would have to be the overseers and coordinators, meshing their internal plans with any intergovernmental policies for international trade, investment, and exchange-rate stability.[46]

International organizations, therefore, became the vehicle for intergovernmental planning and coordination: the International Monetary Fund, the International Trade Organization, the International Bank for Reconstruction and Development, the World Bank, and numerous agencies surrounding the United Nations.[47] The creation of these organizations involved a radically different ordering of international economic relationships. Before 1914, international trade and investment were mostly private matters of business and commerce, with the leading governments securing the political and legal framework within which private enterprises went about their market-oriented affairs.[48] After the Second World War, the new

---

Academy of Political and Social Science (July 1945), pp. 27–36; and J. B. Condliffe, *Agenda for a Postwar World* (New York: W. W. Norton, 1942).

46 See Jacob Viner, "The International Economic Organization of the Future," in Ernest H. Wilkins, ed., *Toward International Organization* (New York: Harper & Brothers, 1942) and "International Economic Cooperation," in William B. Willcox and Robert B. Hall, eds., *The United States in the Postwar World* (Ann Arbor, Mich.: University of Michigan Press, 1947), pp. 15–36; also J. B. Condliffe and A. Stevenson, *The Common Interest in International Economic Organization* (Montreal: International Labor Organization, 1944).

47 See H. W. Arndt, *The Economic Lessons of the Nineteen-Thirties* (London: Oxford University Press, 1944), pp. 295–302; Murray Shields, ed., *International Financial Stabilization: A Symposium* (New York: Irving Trust Co., 1944); Michael A. Heilperin, *International Monetary Organization: The Bretton Woods Agreements* (Washington, D.C.: American Enterprise Association, 1945); Nathaniel Weyl and Max J. Wasserman, "The International Bank, An Instrument of World Economic Reconstruction," *American Economic Review* (March 1947), pp. 93–107; Raymond F. Mikesell, "Quantitative and Exchange Restrictions under the ITO Charter," *American Economic Review* (June 1947), pp. 351–68; Philip Cortney, *The Economic Munich: The I.T.O. Charter, Inflation or Liberty, The 1929 Lesson* (New York: Philosophical Library, 1949); Henry Hazlitt, *From Bretton Woods to World Inflation: A Study of Causes and Consequences* (Chicago: Regnery Gateway, 1984).

48 However, on the extent to which governments did attempt to influence for political or economic reasons the private patterns of foreign loans and investments in the nineteenth and early twentieth centuries, see Jacob Viner, "Political Aspects of International Finance," *Journal of Business* (April and July 1928), pp. 141–73 and 324–63.

international order was to be based on planned, regulated, and intergovernmentally managed trade.[49]

It is true that, for the first two decades after the end of the Second World War, the Western world experienced a degree of economic prosperity and stability unknown in the period between the world wars.[50] Freer trade was the hallmark of postwar international commerce in comparison to the aggressive economic nationalism of the interwar era. But it was governments, through the international organizations established after the war, that determined the degree and form that trade and investment patterns assumed.[51] Additionally, the apparent stability of foreign-exchange rates and the international monetary order were punctuated with periods of crisis and disorder because of national inflationary policies.

The period following the Second World War was also deeply affected by the protracted tensions and conflicts of the Cold War. Communism and central planning became the new ideals of the emerging Third World countries. Consequently, some feared that freedom and democracy would perish in the ideological contest with Marxism around the globe.[52] Even Western economists looked at the trends of growth in Gross National Product in the United States and the Soviet Union in the 1950s and 1960s and concluded, by extrapolation, that before the end of the century the revolutionary center of communism might very well outstrip the world's bastion of capitalism in production and standards of living.[53]

The world has turned out differently from what many had either anticipated or feared in the 1960s and 1970s. Notwithstanding the regime in China, communism officially died in 1991 with the collapse of the Soviet Union. The former Soviet-bloc countries are implementing some market-style reforms through privatization. Western and Central Europe

49 Henry Hazlitt, "The Coming Economic World Pattern," [1944–45] in *From Bretton Woods to World Inflation: A Study of Causes and Consequences*, pp. 127–42.

50 See Gottfried Haberler, "The Liberal International Economic Order in Historical Perspective," [1979] in Anthony Y. C. Koo, ed., *The Liberal Economic Order*, Vol. I (Brookfield, Vt.: Edward Elgar, 1993), pp. 354–55; and Jagdish Bhagwati, *Protectionism* (Cambridge, Mass.: MIT Press, 1988), pp. 1–15.

51 See Jan Tumlir, *Protectionism: Trade Policy in Democratic Societies* (Washington, D.C.: American Enterprise Institute, 1985).

52 Jean-François Revel, *Why Democracies Perish* (Garden City, N.Y.: Doubleday, 1984).

53 Paul Samuelson, *Economics* (New York: McGraw-Hill, 7th ed., 1967), pp. 790–92; and Campbell R. McConnell, *Economics: Principles, Problems, and Policies* (New York: McGraw-Hill, 10th ed., 1987), p. 904.

are moving toward economic integration. Third World countries have begun turning away from central planning and have entered the epoch of market-oriented industrialization and computerization. But bureaucrats and politicians still manipulate the global marketplace. The welfare state still remains entrenched in the Western world. Through central banks, monetary central planners still control and manipulate the currencies of every country. Economic crises due to governmental mismanagement of monetary, fiscal, and foreign-exchange institutions still erupt. Much of the world still subscribes to the policies of the interventionist state and the mentality of the social engineer.

Mises's Proposals for International Economic Reconstruction and Reform

In the first five essays in this collection—delivered as lectures at Yale University, New York University, and Columbia University—Ludwig von Mises explored the causes of Europe's decline into war and destruction in the years between the two world wars, and the general ideological and policy changes that were needed for a return to peace and prosperity in the postwar period. He argued that the reconstruction of the international economic order could be fully successful only if the nations of the world abandoned the ideology of economic nationalism. There could be neither domestic nor international peace as long as governmental policy had as its objective the bestowing of privileges and favors on some at the expense of others. Mises explained that economic nationalism is the foreign policy corollary of internal interventionism for the purpose of bestowing such privileges and favors.

Generally speaking, less efficient producers who are unable to devise ways of meeting the competition of their more efficient rivals in the domestic market turn to the government for protection and financial assistance to maintain their market position and to limit or prohibit the ability of their rivals within the country to compete against them. In the arena of international trade, less efficient producers turn to their respective governments to limit or prohibit foreign rivals from competing in their domestic market. The purpose of economic nationalism is to impose "harm" on foreign producers who otherwise would have profited from better satisfying the wants of consumers than some domestic manufacturers and suppliers.

By politicizing the market rivalries of private producers, international trade becomes one of "affairs of state." Foreign producers and investors came to be viewed as "enemies" to defeat or take advantage of through political means. The tools of "economic warfare" between countries guided by economic nationalism are tariffs and import quotas, export subsidies, foreign-exchange controls and manipulations, and taxes and regulations on foreign investors. The results, insisted Mises, are international tensions and hostilities that narrow or even destroy the international division of labor. Finally, he warned that actual war can grow out of economic nationalism if one of the "combatants" in these trade conflicts believes he is strong enough to defeat an opponent and capture his resources, raw materials, and markets. Mises pointed out that the distinctive feature of economic nationalism in Germany under the Nazis was the German political leadership's confidence it could use military force to conquer *Lebensraum* ("living-space") for the German people—living space in terms of resources, land, markets, and military security in a world in which other nations were also attempting to close off their markets for the exclusive advantage of their own citizens.[54]

Mises was not surprised that in the 1930s collective security had failed to frustrate the territorial ambitions and conquests of Europe's tyrants. Considering that the various nations of Europe viewed each other as rivals and even "enemies" in the arena of economic warfare, it was unlikely that they could successfully unify their political and military efforts to prevent Nazi, fascist, and Soviet aggrandizement.

Furthermore, as Mises explained, political and economic problems in Central and Eastern Europe contained a distinctive quality not present to the same extent in Western Europe. Almost all the countries in the eastern half of Europe were made up of "mixed" populations of diverse linguistic, religious, and ethnic backgrounds. Interventionist policies in these countries were frequently used as tools for discrimination against minorities. Taxing, regulatory, licensing, and trade policies were often applied as devices to impose economic disadvantages upon some of these national

---

54 The term and concept of *Lebensraum* apparently was first coined and argued for by the German author Moeller van den Bruck (1876–1925), after the First World War; see Frank Munk, *The Economics of Force* (New York: George W. Stewart, 1940), pp. 23–24.

minorities for the economic benefit of more politically influential groups. Social peace within the borders of these nations was impossible as long as economic nationalism was the prevailing ideology.

Antagonisms in Central and Eastern Europe were reinforced by the politics of national self-determination, according to which countries coveted territories belonging to their neighbors on the basis of the idea that all peoples speaking the same language should be unified within the same nation-state. But precisely because linguistic and ethnic groups in this part of Europe were so intermingled within geographic areas, no redrawing of boundaries could successfully separate peoples in such a way that nationalistic tensions could be eliminated or even significantly minimized. The only answer, Mises declared, was a return to the political philosophy of classical liberalism and a consistent free-market capitalism, under which social and economic relationships would be depoliticized.

Mises warned that the end of the Second World War would find Europe economically destroyed. Capital would have been consumed and ill maintained as a result of the war. The infrastructure of the society—roads, bridges, railways, housing—would be ruined or in a state of disrepair. The quantity and quality of the work force would be weakened due to the conflict, lowering the productivity of labor. Agriculture would be less productive. Postwar Europe would be much poorer than before the conflict. In such a setting, Europe would no longer be able to afford the politics of redistribution and the economics of intervention and nationalism.

Work, savings, investment, and capital formation would be essential. A reconstitution and reintegration of Europe within the global division of labor would be imperative. For this to happen, Mises wrote, three changes needed to occur in the European mentality. The first required change concerned the attitude that economic policy was only about achieving short-run goals. Practical politics in the earlier decades of the twentieth century had been geared to providing immediate benefits to various groups that could be satisfied only by undermining the long-run prospects and prosperity of society. In the new postwar era, Mises argued, taxes could no longer be confiscatory. International debts could no longer be repudiated or diluted through currency controls or foreign-exchange rate manipulations. Foreign investors could no longer be viewed as victims to be violated or plundered through regulation or nationalization.

The countries of Europe would have to think about and design their economic policies from a long-term point of view. To avoid reliance solely on internal savings, Europe would desperately need infusions of foreign capital. But attracting private foreign investors—which in the postwar period primarily meant private American investors—would require a secure system of property rights, strict enforcement of market contracts for both domestic and foreign businessmen, low and stable taxes, reduced and limited government expenditures and balanced budgets, and a stable, noninflationary monetary system. Only then would governments have done everything in their power to create the political and economic environment most conducive for participants in the market to begin and achieve economic recovery. Consistent with a leading theme expressed in many of his writings, Mises emphasized that the prime movers in the social system of division of labor were the entrepreneurs—the creators and coordinators of the market process—whose central role needed to be appreciated and given unrestricted freedom of action. The ideology of anticapitalism, therefore, had to be rejected in its entirety.

The second change required of European thinking, Mises wrote, concerned the attitude that politics should be geared toward special interest groups. Earlier in the twentieth century, governments had increasingly used their regulatory and fiscal powers to prevent the market forces of supply and demand (and the market forces of profit and loss) from determining success and failure in the economy. Instead, government interventions had maintained less efficient producers by placing barriers in the way of new and innovative entrepreneurs, by fixing prices at nonmarket-determined levels, and by imposing tariff and other trade walls against foreign competitors. Economic reconstruction required the acceptance that such short-sighted "producer policies" are counter to the economic well-being of the society. The essential function of market competition is to continuously discover each participant's comparative advantage and, therefore, most economically appropriate place in the system of division of labor. Market prices are the mechanism through which the opportunity costs of using resources (including labor) and the relative profitabilities of alternative lines of production are discovered for purposes of assuring the greatest satisfaction of consumer demands.

Mises warned that postwar Europe would be too poor to afford the waste and misuse of its scarce factors of production. The purpose of production is consumption. The use and value of the means has to reflect the importance and value of the ends for which they are applied. This requires a "consumer-oriented" policy in which production would be constantly adjusted to actual and changing demand and supply conditions in the market. The only rational policy for reconstruction and rising standards of living, therefore, is unhampered free-market competition.

The third of Mises's recommendations for a change in European thinking concerned the ethics of the redistributive state. Mises emphasized several times in these first essays that Europe's problem at the end of the Second World War would be moral and spiritual. The "dependency state" had become the ideal and demand of large segments of the European population. Governments had been expected to be the guarantor of employment and profits, and the provider of income and security. The redistribution of wealth, rather than its creation, had become the hallmark of "progressive economic policy." But, in truth, he wrote, governments can supply none of these in the long run. Employment and profits arise out of savings, investment, work, and intelligent direction of production to serve consumer demands by market-selected entrepreneurs. Governments can provide and secure income for some only by taxing and redistributing the income and wealth of others. Such redistributive policies weaken incentives, retard the formation of capital, and consume the private wealth accumulated in the past. The inevitable results from such policies are stifled growth and a diminished standard of living.

Europe's moral and spiritual decay, in the early twentieth century, was due to a declining sense of individual responsibility, a loss of the understanding that the truly "social" requires relationships of peaceful and voluntary cooperation through the market, and a growing illusion that society can long endure in a setting of plunder, confiscation, group conflict, and war. Consequently, Mises wrote, the revival of prosperity and a sustainable future of material and cultural improvement could not be imported from or subsidized by foreign sources. In other words, the economics, politics, and ethics of the free and prosperous society could only come from within each nation—from a change in the minds and ideas of each nation's citizens.

Government-to-government aid and loans or government-subsidized and government-guaranteed investments to private enterprise would merely perpetuate the interventionist myths of the past that had brought so much misery, poverty, crises, and war. International organizations for intergovernmental cooperation in matters of money, finance, and trade, Mises concluded, are unworkable in the long run if the member governments continue to function on the basis of interventionism and economic nationalism. His reasoning was that each nation would try to use governmentally directed organizations to further its own "interests" at the expense of other countries. If, on the other hand, each nation were to adopt and follow the precepts of classical liberalism and economic liberty in domestic and foreign trade policies, such international organizations would be unnecessary. If the major nations of the world were to practice free trade in both their domestic and foreign affairs, international order would emerge out of the peaceful and mutually beneficial relationships of private transactors in the marketplace. Intergovernmental agreements and international bureaucracies, Mises concluded, are not a substitute for sound policies of economic freedom at home.

The various proposals for intergovernmental monetary coordination during the war years, eventually instituted through the Bretton Woods Agreement and the establishment of the International Monetary Fund and related organizations, were viewed by Mises, therefore, as misplaced solutions to the fundamental problem of international monetary order. His reasons for this view and his alternative proposal are presented in "A Noninflationary Proposal for Postwar Monetary Reconstruction" and "The Main Issues of Present-Day Monetary Controversies."

The interwar period had seen the demise of an international monetary system. The gold standard that prevailed prior to the First World War had been destroyed by governments wishing to use the printing press to finance their wartime expenditures. The half-hearted attempts to reconstruct the gold standard in the 1920s had been a failure because governments were no longer willing to allow the supply and value of money to remain outside of their direct and discretionary control. Whether to finance current expenditures to satisfy special interest groups or to inflate the general level of prices to influence employment and production in the domestic economy, monetary manipulation was a vital tool in the quest for the attainment of short-run policy goals.

If the world after the Second World War was to once again have a sound monetary system, each country would have to begin the process "at home." The determinates behind the quantity and value of money would have to be put beyond the immediate reach of governments. Historically, the only monetary regime that had succeeded to any great extent in doing this was the gold standard. Therefore, Mises proposed a return to a gold standard.

The first step toward a sound monetary system for any country, Mises argued, would be to balance the government's budget, so that the pressure to increase the money supply to cover current expenditures would be re-

lieved. The second step would be the adoption of a 100 percent gold
reserve system. The existing money supply would be frozen, and any ad-
ditions to the supply of money in the form of currency or bank demand deposits would occur only through a new deposit of a sum of gold. The ratio
of currency or bank deposit money to be issued on the basis of a new gold
deposit would be temporarily set by the market price between dollars and
gold plus a margin of 10 percent. The third step, instituted at the same
time as the second, would be the abolition of all restrictions on a free market for gold and foreign-exchange dealings. The fourth and final step would
occur after a period of time during which foreign-exchange markets would
have established a fairly stable rate of exchange between, for example, dollars and gold. At that point, a new gold parity for the dollar would be legally
fixed between gold and the total quantity of currency and bank deposit
money in the U. S. economy. After that, dollars would be fully redeemable
on demand in gold. Currency and deposit money would be fully backed,
dollar for dollar, with a sum of gold held as a 100 percent reserve at
currency-issuing and deposit-issuing institutions.

Mises was not unique or alone in proposing a 100 percent reserve
banking system. In the 1930s, a number of economists proposed such an
institutional change.[55] However, these proponents advocated a 100 percent fiat money system managed and controlled by the government. The
government would have the task of consciously changing the total quantity of money in circulation to maintain a particular policy target—usually
price-level stabilization. Mises's proposal, in contrast, had the precise goal
of removing government from the monetary process except for the initial
role in establishing the monetary "rules of the game": a 100 percent gold
reserve requirement on all banking institutions, redemption of all currency and deposits by those institutions on demand at the specified gold
parity, and a free foreign-exchange market on the basis of the gold stan-

55 See Henry Simons, *Economic Policy for a Free Society* (Chicago: University of Chicago Press, 1948), pp. 62–65 and 160–83; Irving Fisher, *100% Money* (New Haven: City Print-ing Co., 1945); James W. Angell, "The 100 Per Cent Reserve Plan," *Quarterly Journal of Economics* (November 1935), pp. 1–35; and Frank D. Graham, "Partial Reserve Money and the 100 Per Cent Proposal," *American Economic Review* (September 1936), pp. 428–40; also Milton Friedman, "A Monetary and Fiscal Framework for Economic Stability," [1948] in *Essays in Positive Economics* (Chicago: University of Chicago Press, 1953), pp. 135–36, and *A Program for Monetary Stability* (Bronx, N.Y.: Fordham University Press, 1960), pp. 65–76; and Lloyd W. Mints, *Monetary Policy for a Competitive Society* (New York: McGraw-Hill, 1950).

dard. The quantity of money and its value (or purchasing power) over goods would be determined by the market forces of supply and demand, not by government.[56] Mises's reasoning was that government simply could not be trusted with control over a monopoly printing press. Furthermore, as these two essays demonstrate, he did not believe that it was in government's power or ability to successfully manage the monetary system or stabilize any "targets" such as the general price level. Mises's ultimate ideal for a monetary order most consistent with a free society was for a system of free banking based on a market-selected commodity like gold. But he considered the establishment of this ideal system to be possible only far off in the future, when there would have been a complete renunciation of socialist and interventionist ideas.[57]

Mises knew that a sound monetary system did not require international agreements or intergovernmental monetary organizations. Any country could adopt such a gold-based monetary order independent of what other nations might do. If international agreements attempted to restrain member countries from following inflationary paths in an ideological environment in which national governments had the desire to continue abusing their monetary powers, the result would be tensions, conflicts, crises, and a final collapse of the intergovernmental monetary system. The disintegration in 1971 of the Bretton Woods system of fixed exchange rates under a system of national currencies open to governmental manipulation strongly suggests that Mises was correct in his judgments.

The one essay in this collection written by Mises before his arrival in the United States is "A Draft of Guidelines for the Reconstruction of Austria." It was prepared in May of 1940 for Otto von Habsburg, former archduke of Austria, shortly before Mises's departure from Geneva. It diagnoses the reasons for Austria's political and economic problems in the 1920s and 1930s and presents the reforms and policy changes that would have to be implemented for Austria's rebirth and revival as a prosperous and inde-

---

56 For a defense of a 100 percent gold reserve system by a student of Mises's, see Murray N. Rothbard, "The Case for a 100 Percent Gold Dollar," in Leland B. Yeager, ed., *In Search of a Monetary Constitution* (Cambridge, Mass.: Harvard University Press, 1962), pp. 94–136.

57 Mises, *The Theory of Money and Credit*, pp. 434–38; "Monetary Stabilization and Cyclical Policy," pp. 138–40, 145–46, 156; and *Human Action*, pp. 443–48; also Lawrence H. White, "Mises on Free Banking and Fractional Reserves," in John W. Robbins and Mark Spangler, eds., *A Man of Principle*, 517–33.

pendent nation in the postwar period. Because Austria is a small country with various economic disadvantages in comparison with other, larger nations better endowed with resources and fertile land, Mises recommended that the country adapt to the international trade environment. Austria should find its place in the global system of division of labor and acquire through imports the food, raw materials, and capital it needed from other countries by exporting those industrial goods for which it had a comparative advantage.

But, Mises asked, given the inevitable state of postwar poverty under which Austrians would be living, how would the incentives be created to begin the process of economic recovery? The answer is that domestic regulations would have to be abolished, labor markets would have to be freed from trade-union domination and control, government expenditures and redistributionist policies would have to be drastically cut back, nationalized industries would have to be privatized, Austrian businessmen driven from their homeland by anti-Semitism and Nazi policies would have to be invited back and made welcome in their own country, the multiple levels of bureaucratic administration throughout the country would have to be reduced and streamlined, the monetary system would have to be based on gold, and international economic relations would have to be guided by the idea of free trade. The only permissible trade restrictions would be retaliatory tariffs against specific countries that might discriminate against or prohibit Austrian goods from being sold in their markets.

Crucial to Austrian recovery and reconstruction, Mises wrote, would be fiscal policy. The fostering of savings, investment, and capital formation would be imperative. He proposed the end of all direct income taxation. Instead, the primary sources of all government revenues would be, first, general consumption taxes, including: (a) excise taxes on alcoholic beverages and tobacco products, (b) sales taxes, but only on final goods sold to the consuming public, and (c) a playing-card stamp tax. Second, there should be wealth taxes on consumption, including: (a) a progressive tax on higher consumption levels, based on housing expenditures (excluding those in the lower-income housing categories), (b) a tax on ownership of higher-priced automobiles for private use, and (c) a tax on lottery winnings. Third, there should be business and employment taxes, including: (a) a moderate tax on net profits paid out to shareholders of corporations and partners in limited partnerships, when the annual disbursements exceed six percent of capital assets, (b) administrative fees for patent rights, registration of brand names, and other official stamps, and (c) a wage tax paid by employers to cover social insurance programs, but which would not be deducted from wages. Mises stressed that, except for the wage tax and the net profits tax, all earnings would be exempt from direct taxation. This would create the fewest disincentives to income and wealth creation.

Such, he concluded, is the path to economic recovery for a small country like Austria. But Mises pointed out there were problems unique to Central and Eastern Europe because of their mixed populations of numerous linguistic, ethnic, and religious groups. The essay "An Eastern European Democratic Union: A Proposal for the Establishment of a Durable Peace in Eastern Europe" is Mises's suggestion for solving these problems in a world still in the grip of political and economic nationalism.

In two of his earlier works, *Nation, State, and Economy*[58] and *Liberalism*,[59] Mises dealt extensively with the problem of nationality and national self-determination. He emphasized that among the principles of classical liberalism is the right of self-determination and freedom of association. In classical liberal thought, this means the *self-determination of the individual.* Each individual has, in principle, the right to decide of which political entity he will be a member. But, because of administrative constraints, the practical meaning of this principle is that the citizens within districts and regions, and even towns and villages, should have the right of plebiscite to express their preference to remain part of the nation-state to which they presently belong, to join some other nation-state, or to form a new state of their own.

Unfortunately, during the nineteenth and twentieth centuries this idea had been distorted to mean "national self-determination," that is, that all peoples belonging to the same linguistic or ethnic group should belong to the same nation-state, regardless of the actual wishes of the individual residents within a geographical area. This idea of national self-determination has been the cause of many of the tensions, antagonisms, and conflicts within and between nations in Europe. And it served as the rationale for Hitler's insistence on the annexation of parts of countries adjoining Nazi Germany that contained German-speaking peoples.[60]

58 Ludwig von Mises, *Nation, State, and Economy: Contributions to the Politics and History of Our Time* (New York: New York University Press, [1919] 1983), pp. 9–56.

59 Mises, *Liberalism*, pp. 105–24.

60 See Richard M. Ebeling, "World Peace, International Order, and Classical Liberalism," pp. 59–62, and "Nationalism and Classical Liberalism," "Nationalism: Its Nature and Consequences," "National Conflicts, Market Liberalism, and Social Peace," and "Social Conflict, Self-Determination, and the Boundaries of the State," in Richard M. Ebeling

Mises noted that the problem of nationalist antagonisms is exacerbated in an ideological setting of interventionism. Governments become the tools for linguistic and ethnic groups seeking to use the power of the state for their own benefit through discriminatory laws and policies against others. The only way to protect against such a political environment is to create a vast political and economic union. Mises proposed such a union for all the countries of Eastern Europe from the Baltic Sea to the Aegean Sea, including Estonia, Latvia, Lithuania, Poland, Czechoslovakia, Austria, Hungary, Romania, Yugoslavia, Bulgaria, Albania, Greece, and the part of Germany east of the Oder-Neisse Rivers. Only such a union, Mises reasoned, would have the combined strength to repel military aggression against these countries by either Germany or Russia. More important, such a union would diminish the ability of the member governments to use their domestic power to discriminate against national minorities and threaten war on their neighbors in the name of political or economic nationalism.

Mises proposed that political authority and legislative power would be reserved to a single parliamentary chamber that would have the only power to tax and upon which the member states would be dependent for disbursement of funds for administrative expenditures. The member states would retain their flags, symbols, anthems, and even embossed coins and stamps, but they would no longer have the power to pass legislation or impose laws that could infringe on a regime of private property and free trade within their jurisdictions and between the member states. Discriminatory laws against linguistic, ethnic, or religious groups would be forbidden. There would be for all citizens the freedom to move, live, and work within the boundaries of the union, and the same rights would apply to foreigners who chose to live, work, and invest in any part of this Eastern European Union.

In Mises's view, under such a regime of free markets and free trade, no individual would or could be abused by national political power. All persons would be free to pursue the trade, profession, and occupation of their choice without political restraint and to speak and educate their children in the language and customs of their own choice. Schools would be primarily private and eligible for receiving lump-sum per-pupil tax revenues

---

and Jacob G. Hornberger, eds., *The Failure of America's Foreign Wars* (Fairfax, Va.: Future of Freedom Foundation, 1996), pp. 327–48.

as long as they were in compliance with certain basic rules and standards specified by the central government of the union.

Mises was not so naive as to expect to see the immediate acceptance and establishment of a broad political and economic union along the lines he recommended. But he believed that movement toward this goal was the only way to introduce restrictions on the interventionist power of national governments. And, indeed, the only rationale for such a union was to bring about the implementation of the ideals of the free market and free trade. Unless a union were constituted for this purpose, its existence would be impossible to justify.

Under the sponsorship of the School of Economics at the National University of Mexico, Mises spent January and February of 1942 lecturing in Mexico City and other Mexican cities. In June of 1943 he prepared for an association of Mexican businessmen a detailed report, "Mexico's Economic Problems," in which he recommended policies that would most likely assist in fostering Mexican economic development and industrialization.[61]

In this report, Mises maintained that the war-related trading opportunities that Mexico was enjoying with the United States were likely to end with the cessation of the conflict. Mexico, therefore, must look forward to an agenda of postwar market-oriented reforms for further economic improvement. Free trade is essential to the country's future, he wrote, and in this context he emphasized that the benefit from trade comes from the imports obtainable at prices less costly than those incurred by alternative domestic production. Exports are the means for acquiring those imports and not an end or a good in themselves.

Anticipating one of the major schemes proposed by postwar development planners, Mises strongly criticized what he labeled the "closed door method of industrialization," which became more widely known and popular in Third World countries after 1945 as the "import-substitution method" for development. According to this method, industrialization is to be forced through trade restrictions and high tariff barriers behind which domestic industries will be stimulated at artificially high prices far above those in the general global market. He pointed out that countries implementing this method inevitably make their own people poorer and less productive.

---

61 This report has been translated into Spanish and published in Mexico for the first time as a monograph fifty-five years after it was originally written under the title *Problemas Economicos de Mexico: Ayer y Hoy* (Mexico City: Instituto Cultural Ludwig von Mises, 1998).

To the extent that imports are reduced so, too, Mises wrote, are exports. Potential foreign buyers of Mexican goods would lose the means of earning the Mexican revenue that would have provided them with the financial wherewithal to purchase Mexican exports. This would bring about a misdirection of Mexican production inconsistent with a most efficient use of the country's resources. Mexico would be locked out from maximizing the income it could earn from exporting those goods for which it had the greatest comparative advantage in the international market. And consumers would have to pay the cost of such a method of "hothouse" industrialization through a lower standard of living due to the higher prices and lower quality of the domestic substitutes they would be forced to purchase on the Mexican market. Import-substitution methods of economic development merely represent a modern version of the eighteenth-century mercantilist fallacies.

Equally disastrous for Mexican development would be any attempt to raise Mexican wages to comparable United States levels through either government legislation or trade-union pressure. Mexico in the 1940s, Mises added, was a capital-poor country with a relatively large supply of labor. This necessarily meant that labor productivity was far lower than that of American workers. The only way that Mexican labor could compete with American labor and other competitors in the global market would be to take advantage of those opportunities in which it could be a lower-cost producer in labor-intensive lines of production. The standard of living in Mexico could permanently rise only through the normal processes of market-directed capital formation over time and through migration of a part of the labor force to other countries where wages and the marginal productivity of labor were higher. Since the latter method was generally closed off, due to immigration barriers in the United States and other countries, only the former method was available to Mexico under prevailing international conditions, Mises reasoned. Raising wages above market-determined levels could only condemn a part of the Mexican labor force to permanent unemployment or more primitive lines of employment.

Since Mexico had long practiced protectionist, interventionist, and socialist policies, the country would have to make a transition to a regime of free markets and free trade. Those familiar with Mises's apparently "intransigent" and "dogmatic" advocacy of *laissez-faire* economics may be surprised that he proposed a series of "gradualist" policies for Mexico. For example, because a number of industries had been long protected behind high tariff walls, Mises suggested a transition to free trade over a period of years during which tariff levels would be reduced by 10 percent a year. (In this, Mises merely followed in the tradition of many of the earlier classical economists who also called for a gradual shift to free trade so as to minimize the severity of the economic adjustment.)[62]

While generally critical of government-sponsored and supported cooperative movements,[63] Mises argued that full land privatization in Mexico should be supported for the poor peasantry through government assistance in forming farm-producer cooperatives and even limited but temporary state subsidies to help them get started. In the area of privatization, Mises argued that the most desirable course of action was full denationalization. But, given the ideological climate in Mexico, Mises proposed that the national railway system, for instance, be transformed into a government-owned but independent corporation; management of the rail system would operate on a for-profit basis.

Crucial and central to any economic reform project in a country such as Mexico, Mises again emphasized, would be the establishment and the strict enforcement of property rights and contract, for both Mexican and foreign investors alike. Inflationary monetary policies would have to be renounced, and a policy of free trade would have to be practiced.

Conclusion

Ludwig von Mises's purpose in preparing the lectures and writing the monographs included in this volume was to restate fundamental truths at a time when many of the most important premises of sound economic thinking seemed to have been forgotten or rejected. He realized that in a world dominated by socialist and interventionist ideas this was often a thankless task. But he believed that no real change for the better was possible unless the truth was spoken.

Mises was determined to explain why, after the Second World War, economic liberty was both desirable and essential if the world was to avoid the mistakes of the past. Yet he was aware that ways had to be found to en-

---

62 For example, see Adam Smith, *The Wealth of Nations* (New York: Modern Library, [1776] 1937), Book IV, Ch. II, p. 438; Jean-Baptiste Say, *A Treatise on Political Economy* (New York: Augustus M. Kelley, [1821] 1971), p. 170.

63 See Ludwig von Mises, "Observations on the Cooperative Movement," [1947] in Richard M. Ebeling, ed., *Money, Method, and the Market Process*, pp. 238–79.

courage a rebirth of the ideal and practice of market freedom. The first task was to explain how the world had arrived in its present state and why previous ideologies and policies had led to disaster. Next, the logic and benefits of the free-market order had to be articulated once again. Finally, specific policies had to be formulated to begin the process of international reconstruction and reform.

Today the world is searching for a new international economic order, just as it was searching for one in the mid-1940s. The former communist bloc countries, including the former Soviet Union, are groping with varying degrees of success toward the establishment of a market order and democratic political regimes. The countries of Asia, Africa, and Latin America are trying to escape from socialist and neo-mercantilist experiments of previous decades. The Western industrial democracies are looking for ways to overcome the burdens of the welfare state and the regulated economy.

The world at the third millennium abounds with proposals for economic and monetary unions, international trading agreements and intergovernmental rules for investment and capital movements. But what is lacking in many, if not most, of these proposals is a clear statement of first principles and a clear conception of where any particular policies implemented should be leading in terms of a long-run vision of the free and prosperous society. Many in the public arena praise and endorse the idea of a global free-market order. But beneath the rhetoric of some alleged free-market proponents are variations on the old interventionist theme. These proponents are merely proposing islands of market activity in an ocean of regulations, controls, and political redistributions of wealth.

This is not the meaning of the free market as it was understood by Ludwig von Mises.[64] He chose to call things by their real names and explain them in terms of their real meanings. Anything less, he believed, would be a betrayal of truth and understanding. It is perhaps appropriate, therefore, to conclude by recurring to Mises's own thoughts on this point, which ended his lecture on "The Fundamental Principle of Pan-European Union":

> It is a thankless job indeed to express such radical and "subversive" [free-market] opinions and to incur the hatred of all supporters of the old

---

64 See Richard M. Ebeling, "The Free Market and the Interventionist State," in Richard M. Ebeling, ed., *Between Power and Liberty: Economics and the Law*, Champions of Freedom Series, Vol. 25 (Hillsdale, Mich.: Hillsdale College Press, 1998), pp. 9–46.

[interventionist] system that has amply proven its inexpediency. But it is not the duty of an economist to be fashionable and popular; he has to be right. Those timid souls who fear challenging spurious doctrines and superstitions because they have the support of influential circles will never improve conditions. Let them call us "orthodox"; it is better to be an intransigent orthodox than an opportunist time-server.

Richard M. Ebeling

Ludwig von Mises Professor of Economics
Hillsdale College

February 2000

The Political Economy of International
Reform and Reconstruction

CHAPTER I

Postwar Reconstruction[1]

We are witnesses to the most frightful and phenomenal occurrence in human history: the decay of Western civilization. London, one of the centers of this civilization, the city of the most eminent representatives of this culture, is almost completely destroyed. The buildings of the Parliament of Westminster are in ruins; the House of Commons holds its assemblies in the catacombs.[2] Every day brings us the news that some eminent contemporary has been killed in his home by enemy action. One of the most distinguished economists of our day, Lord Stamp, met with this fate.[3] The theater of war is spreading, and the day seems not distant when peace will have lost its last refuge.[4] It is a moral and material collapse without precedent. The horsemen of the apocalypse are riding roughshod.

And all this comes only a few years after the great Wilsonian experiment of the League of Nations[5] and after the outlawing of war by the

1 [This paper was delivered as a lecture at the Yale Economic Club at New Haven, Connecticut, on May 22, 1941.—Ed.]

2 [The German air force bombed London seventy-one times between September of 1940 and May of 1941, dropping almost nineteen thousand tons of bombs.—Ed.]

3 [Lord Josiah Stamp (1880–1941) was a leading expert on the British taxation system; beginning in 1919, he was a member of Royal Commission on Income Tax, and in the 1920s he became a member of the Dawes and Young Committees on German war reparations. He died in a German air raid on April 16, 1941.—Ed.]

4 [At the time this essay was written in May of 1941, the United States was still a neutral power in the Second World War.—Ed.]

5 [The League of Nations was formed in 1919 after the First World War as an international organization to promote peace and security. It was dissolved in 1946 and replaced by the United Nations. It was originally sponsored by President Woodrow Wilson, but the U. S. Senate rejected American membership.—Ed.]

Kellogg-Briand Pact.[6] It is a terrible failure and a painful disillusionment. It is obvious that people seek the causes of this catastrophe and that they are asking the question how mankind may find an order which could make the world safe for peace.

The problem of economic and social reconstruction cannot be dealt with without a thorough understanding of the causes that led to the present situation. To gain it we have necessarily to resort to an historical analysis of the development of the forces that have determined the course of events.

Since time immemorial, humanitarians, philanthropists, and philosophers have raised their voices in favor of an eternal peace. They would approach the kings and address them in this way: "Of course, war and conquest are very advantageous for you. By war and conquest you increase your power and your wealth. But think, what a price your subjects have to pay for your glory. Consider the pain you inflict on the widows and orphans and on the mutilated, consider the terrible destruction and material losses of every kind. Be merciful and charitable, renounce the profits which you may derive from war and the glory of military success. It is more decorous for a king to be known as the benevolent father of his subjects than to be called a conqueror and hero. Don't you know the commandment, 'Thou shalt not kill'? God will reward you in heaven for your noble behavior and your subjects will praise your benevolence. Feel pity!"

These were the ideas implied in the old humanitarian and utopian pacifism. It failed completely. The kings did not disarm and did not renounce conquests. Their acquisitiveness and their ambition for glory brought wars again and again. Frederick the Second of Prussia frankly admitted that the incentives of his actions were only the desires for glory and wealth. He considered it shameful for a king not to take advantage of every opportunity to increase both his realm and his fame. History rewarded the cynic by giving him the epithet the "Great."[7]

Then, beginning in the eighteenth century, a radical change in the

6 [The Kellogg-Briand Pact, signed in Paris in 1928 by fifteen nations and eventually ratified by sixty-two countries, was intended for countries to settle all conflicts by peaceful means and renounced war as an instrument of national policy.—Ed.]

7 [Frederick the Great (1712–86), King of Prussia from 1740 to 1786, was victorious in the War of the Austrian Succession (1740–48) and the Seven Years' War (1756–63). He was a prime mover in the first Partition of Poland (1772), which greatly increased the territory of Prussia.—Ed.]

reasoning concerning war and peace took place. A new philosophy, liber-alism, took possession of men's minds.[8] Its immediate political program called for the replacement of the rule of kings by a government of the peo-ple. In this new democratic order, war lost its appeal. The individual citi-zens were not interested in conquest. For them it was immaterial whether the boundaries of the nation included a greater or a smaller territory. They could not improve their own lot by the conquest of a province. They were peaceful because they could not derive any advantage from war. What was needed to make the world peaceful was to eliminate autocracy. Once this was accomplished, there would be no more wars. The dawn of democracy meant the abolition of war.

But democracy means not only abolition of external wars, it means at the same time the cessation of internal strife, civil wars, and revolutions. When in an autocratic country the people wish to replace an unsatisfac-tory system of government by a better one or undesirable administrators by more desirable men, they have no other means than the appeal to vio-lence. But in a democracy, the adjustment of the system of government and of the administrative personnel to the wishes of the people is provided for through peaceful processes. The decision of the voters eliminates peacefully the unpopular system and its supporters. There is no function left for violence.

The reasoning of the old liberals can be condensed in one sentence: War is useless in a liberal world. This theorem is absolutely correct, but we must not forget the condition, "in a liberal world." Both Norman Angell, the outstanding representative of contemporary pacifism, and President Woodrow Wilson overlooked this condition.[9]

8 [Throughout this essay and the others in this volume, Mises uses the term "liberalism" in its nineteenth-century classical sense. Mises, *Human Action: A Treatise on Economics*, (Irvington-on-Hudson, N.Y.: Foundation for Economic Education, 4th rev. ed. 1996), p. vii: "First, I employ the term 'liberal' in the sense attached to it everywhere in the nineteenth century and still today in the countries of continental Europe. This usage is imperative be-cause there is simply no other term available to signify the great political and intellectual movement that substituted free enterprise and the market economy for the precapitalistic methods of production; constitutional representative government for the absolutism of kings and oligarchies; and freedom of individuals for slavery, serfdom, and other forms of bondage." —Ed.]

9 [Norman Angell (1872–1967), an internationally renowned British peace advocate, gained fame with *The Great Illusion* (1910), in which he argued that the growing eco-nomic interdependency among nations and the high cost of armaments races increasingly made war counterproductive for both the potential victors and the vanquished. After the

Mr. Angell still holds to the belief that the individual citizen cannot improve his position by conquest. Of what advantage to the German citizen was the conquest in 1871 of Alsace-Lorraine?[10] He had to pay for it with his blood, but he gained simply nothing. This is true. But is it in the same way true today?

President Wilson was fully convinced that the German nation was peaceful and that it had been pushed to war by the Kaiser [Wilhelm II][11] and the Junkers.[12] What was necessary to avoid a new war was the replacement of German absolutism by democracy. Today, the British stubbornly believe that the German masses are essentially peaceful and that they are forced to fight by a dictator who seized power by deception. In the first months of the war, they repeated the old slogan used by the armies of the French Revolution: "We are not fighting the German masses, we are fighting their oppressor only."

But, unfortunately, we are no longer living in a world of *laissez-faire, laissez-passer*; in a world of free trade, private ownership, capitalism, and goodwill among the nations. Our world is very different, and in this world you cannot say that war is useless. It is not true that the individual citizen cannot derive any advantage from a victorious war.

In the utopia of the old liberals, the government concerns itself with the protection of life, health, and private property against force or fraud. The state ensures the smooth working of the market economy by the weight of its coercive power. It refrains, however, from any interference with the freedom of action of the people engaged in production and distribution so long as such actions do not involve the use of force or fraud against the life, health, or property of others. This very fact characterizes such a community as a market or capitalist economy.

First World War, he actively worked for international cooperation and peace. He was knighted in 1931 and awarded the Nobel Peace Prize in 1933.—Ed.]

10 [Alsace-Lorraine is the northeast region of France bordering on the Rhine River. It was annexed by Germany following the Franco-Prussian War (1870–71), and it was returned to France after the First World War.—Ed.]

11 [Kaiser Wilhelm II (1859–1941), emperor of imperial Germany (1888–1918), attempted to make Germany the dominant political and military power on the European continent, resulting in events that led to the First World War. He abdicated in November 1918 and took refuge in the Netherlands, finally settling on his estate at Doorn, where he died in 1941.—Ed.]

12 [The Junkers were the large estate-owning nobility of the eastern regions of Prussia. —Ed.]

In this world of capitalism there are neither trade barriers nor migration barriers. Goods and men can freely cross the frontiers. Everyone is free to move to the place where he wishes to live, to earn, and to work. The laws and the authorities treat citizens and foreigners in the same way; there are no laws discriminating against foreigners. Under these conditions, boundaries do not have any importance for the individual. It is immaterial for the individual whether the night watchman bears a cockade in white-blue or red-white.

Of course, this liberal utopia was never completely achieved. But the liberals were fully convinced that conditions were developing toward this goal, that social and economic evolution must necessarily lead to it, and that no return to the obsolete system of government interference with private life was possible. On this faith, they based their optimism concerning the disappearance of violence. War was doomed like other remnants of a dark past, like religious intolerance, superstition, slavery, and tyrannical government.[13]

The optimism of Bentham,[14] Cobden,[15] and Bastiat[16] was not justified. History went another way. Today we are living in a world of government interference with business and, in some countries, of socialism. There are everywhere trade barriers and migration barriers. In domestic policy, the governments are anxious to interfere in order to benefit some groups at the expense of other groups. "Nationalism" is the characteristic feature of modern foreign policy.

---

13 [On the classical liberal conception that free trade would diminish and even, perhaps, eliminate the causes of war, see Edmund Silberner, *The Problem of War in Nineteenth-Century Economic Thought* (Princeton, N.J.: Princeton University Press, 1946). —Ed.]

14 [Jeremy Bentham (1748–1832), an English philosopher, jurist, and political theorist, was the founder of utilitarianism. His contributions to political economy are contained in *Jeremy Bentham's Economic Writings*, Werner Stark, ed., 3 vols. (London: George Allen and Unwin, 1952). —Ed.]

15 [Richard Cobden (1804–65) was a leader of the British free trade movement and one of the managers of the Anti–Corn Law League that helped bring about the end of protectionist trade restrictions in Great Britain in the 1830s and 1840s. As a member of Parliament, Cobden negotiated the "Cobden Treaty" for reciprocal tariff reductions with France in 1859–60. —Ed.]

16 [Frederic Bastiat (1801–50), a French political economist, was referred to by Joseph Schumpeter as "the most brilliant economic journalist who ever lived" in defense of free trade and *laissez-faire*. His best known works are *Economic Sophisms*, *Selected Essays on Political Economy*, and *Economic Harmonies*. —Ed.]

The term is used in a very inexact sense. I suggest the term "economic nationalism" be applied to a policy that intends to improve the conditions of some groups of citizens by inflicting evils on foreigners.[17] Nationalism is exactly a policy of discrimination against foreigners. Foreign goods are excluded from the domestic market or only permitted after an import duty has been paid. Foreign labor is disbarred from competition on the domestic labor market. Foreign capital is liable to confiscation. Similar discriminatory measures are applied against citizens who belong to a racial, linguistic, or religious minority.

In this world of ours—that is, in this world of state interventionism, socialism, and economic nationalism—it is simply not true that the individual citizen cannot derive profit from a victorious war and from conquest. I do not wish to discuss the problem of whether these measures of economic nationalism really benefit the citizens of the country that applies them, but there can be no doubt that they hurt the material interests of the citizens of foreign countries. The abolition of such measures would therefore improve the conditions of those injured by them.

I wish to emphasize that it is not my intention to discuss all aspects of the war policies of the aggressor nations. I wish to clarify the facts in order to make the antiwar policies of the future more successful than those of the past. The first step toward this end has to be the critique of the erroneous belief that under present conditions the individual citizen is not personally interested in victory and conquest.

Let us consider the migration barriers. Today, practically no country of the world is open to immigration. The result is that natives of countries that offer less favorable natural conditions of production are prevented from moving into the areas where the national resources are more favorable. In relatively overpopulated countries, there are many millions of peasants who have to till land that is far less fertile than many millions of acres of unused soil in better endowed countries. These peasants cannot go to the countries where their labor could give them greater returns. There are many millions of workers who are forced to remain in countries where the marginal productivity of labor is lower than in better endowed countries.

17 [On the history of the meaning and practice of economic nationalism, see T. E. Gregory, "Economic Nationalism," *International Affairs* (May 1931), pp. 289–306; William E. Rappard, "Economic Nationalism," in *Authority and the Individual: Harvard Tercentenary Conference of Arts and Sciences* (Cambridge, Mass.: Harvard University Press, 1937), pp. 74–112, and Michael A. Heilperin, *Studies in Economic Nationalism* (Geneva: Libraire E. Droz, 1962).—Ed.]

They could earn higher wages in countries where the marginal productivity of labor is higher. At the same time, the outflow of a considerable number of hands would make wages rise for those who do not immigrate. In a world of mobility of labor, there prevails a tendency toward an equalization of wages for the same quality of labor all over the world. In a world of migration barriers, there is a tendency toward a stabilization of the differences in wages and standards of living.[18]

I am fully aware of the fact that the laws hindering immigration are not motivated solely by considerations of labor policy. The racial, linguistic, and cultural factors involved must not be overlooked. But I am not concerned here with addressing this very complicated question.

Let me incidentally make some remarks about the Marxian view of this problem. A consistent Marxian who is eager to explain every "ideology" as a superstructure of selfish class interests would have to consider all these ideological justifications of the immigration barriers as nothing other than a disguise of class interests. Of course, the Australian capitalists are economically not interested in the maintenance of the laws hindering immigration to Australia. These laws result in higher wages. An open door policy would lower wages and would therefore be harmful to Australian labor. When the Japanese arm and prepare for a war against the British empire in order to obtain the right for their citizens to immigrate into this dominion, the consistent Marxian would have to say that this imperialistic war is a war of Japanese labor versus Australian labor. The consistent Marxian would have to say that modern imperialism is the superstructure of trade unionism and labor class interests.

I make these remarks only in order to demonstrate how foolish are the current Marxian doctrines on imperialism, even from the Marxian point of view. I do not wish to dwell on this subject. My distinguished friend, Professor Lionel Robbins of the London School of Economics,[19] and my

18 [On the topic of international migration and wage rates, see Mises, "The Freedom to Move as an International Problem," [1935] reprinted in Richard M. Ebeling and Jacob G. Hornberger, eds., *The Case for Free Trade and Open Immigration* (Fairfax, Va.: Future of Freedom Foundation, 1995), pp. 127–30; and Mises, *Liberalism in the Classical Tradition* (Irvington-on-Hudson, N.Y., and San Francisco, Calif.: Foundation for Economic Education and Cobden Press, [1927] 1985), pp. 136–42.—Ed.]

19 [Lionel Robbins, *The Economic Causes of War* (New York: Howard Fertig, [1939] 1968) and *The Economic Basis of Class Conflict, and Other Essays in Political Economy* (London: Macmillan Ltd., 1939), pp. 3–28. Lord Robbins (1898–1984) was a leading British economist at the London School of Economics who formalized the definition of economics as the logic of choice: the allocation of scarce means among competing ends ranked in order

former colleague at the Graduate Institute of International Studies in Geneva, Professor Eugene Staley, now connected with the Fletcher School of Law and Diplomacy [at Tufts University], have examined these Marxian fallacies in the most brilliant way.[20]

Neither do I wish to criticize the errors and contradictions contained in the Nazi theories that I shall now present to you. A full refutation of the fallacies of the Nazi doctrines would require more time than that of a brief lecture. In my course at Geneva dealing with the economic and sociological doctrines in modern political thought, I used to devote many hours to this task.[21] I venture to say that for the present audience a mere presentation of these theories will be sufficient and that no further criticism of them will be needed.

I shall start with the German doctrine of the *Lebensraum*, or "living space."

"We Germans," say the Nazis, "were injured in the distribution of the world. Of course, it was our own fault. In those centuries in which the British, the Spaniards, and the Portuguese conquered the newly discovered territories there was virtually no German empire. Germany was divided and weak. The Germans fought each other and missed the opportunity to colonize overseas countries. The result is that they are now forced to crowd together in an overpopulated area. They are prevented from exploiting idle resources in countries that nature has better endowed for production. They have to be content with a standard of living much lower than the standard of living in Anglo-Saxon countries. Every German suffers from the present state of things and every German citizen's lot could be improved by changing it."

"And," says the Nazi, "we will change it. Today we are united and thereby strong. We are ninety millions and we are courageous fighters. We

---

of their importance to the individual decisionmaker. In the 1930s, he was a strong proponent of the Austrian School of economics and a critic of various forms of government intervention and socialist central planning. — Ed.]

20 [Eugene Staley, *War and the Private Investor* (New York: Howard Fertig, [1935] 1967), and *Foreign Investment and War* (Chicago: University of Chicago Press, 1935). Eugene A. Staley (1906–89) was a specialist in international trade theory and the economics of developing nations. On the same theme, see Walter Sulzbach, *"Capitalistic Warmongers,"* A *Modern Superstition* (Chicago: University of Chicago Press, 1942). — Ed.]

21 [Before coming to the United States, Ludwig von Mises taught at the Graduate Institute of International Studies in Geneva, Switzerland, from 1934 to 1940. — Ed.]

do not agree with your doctrine that the historical age of wars and conquests is gone forever and that the present distribution of resources is inviolable and has to be maintained for all time to come. This is the mentality of the 'haves,' which we 'have-nots' will never accept. You are enforcing your migration laws and your tariff system by the police forces and by armed customs officers. We are strong enough to smash these guardsmen. This is not aggression. We are not aggressors. The aggressors are you, because you started the use of violence against the peaceful Germans, Italians, and Japanese, who wished nothing else than to work or to sell products in the countries whose doors you have closed."

"Of course," says the Nazi further, "we are unfortunately not yet strong enough today for the conquest of New Zealand or Canada. But we are not too weak for the conquest of Poland or of Czechoslovakia. We are sorry for the Poles and the Czechs. But we cannot help it. They are for us what the Indians and the natives of Australia were for the British settlers—peoples who, unfortunately, are living in a country that we are strong enough to conquer. Our claims are not worse than the claims of British and Latin settlers in America and Australia: force and violence. Our arguments are the same that they used: arms."

This is the meaning of the *Lebensraum* theory. The have-nots are still too weak to attain the ultimate goal of their policies; for the time being they have to content themselves by installments and to limit their conquests to the countries which are included in their living space.[22] Thus the Germans attacked Czechoslovakia and Poland, but not yet Canada and Brazil. Thus the Italians attacked Albania and Abyssinia,[23] but not yet Egypt and Argentina. Thus the Japanese attacked Manchukuo[24] and China, but not yet Australia and the Dutch East Indies.[25]

The most popular fallacy concerning Nazism is the belief that its ideas

---

22 [For critiques of the "Lebensraum" doctrine, see Norman Angell, *This Have and Have-Not Business: Political Fantasy and Economic Fact* (London: Hamish Hamilton, 1936), and C. Bresciani-Turroni, "'Living Space' Versus an International System," *Revue Al Qanoun Wal Iqtisad*, No. 1–2 (Cairo, Egypt: 1940), pp. 35–68.—Ed.]

23 [Abyssinia was the name for Ethiopia.—Ed.]

24 [Manchukuo was a Japanese "puppet state" established in Manchuria, the northeast region of China, between 1931 and 1945.—Ed.]

25 [The Dutch East Indies was the name for Indonesia while it was under the control of the Netherlands until 1949; it was occupied by the Japanese during the Second World War.—Ed.]

and its program are in any way new and different from the ideas and program of the German nationalists of the Kaiser's time. This is absolutely wrong. The Nazi ideology was completely laid out by writers who published their books and articles in the last thirty years of the nineteenth century. Nothing is new in the books of Hitler and Rosenberg,[26] not even the poor style. Everything had been said by earlier authors. Hitler and Rosenberg only repeated; they did not add a single idea or a single point. Nazism differs from German pre–World War I ideology only in one respect: The Nazis are more energetic in the prosecution of their plans.

The time assigned to my lecture is too limited to give me the opportunity of providing you with ample evidence of my statement. I wish only to mention two facts in order to demonstrate that the far-reaching plans of world conquest and world domination were long supported not only by the radical wing of German nationalism, the *Alldeutsche Partei* [Pan-German Party], but that they met with the approval of the most representative men of German political thought. From the early eighties of the nineteenth century until the First World War, the chairs of economics at the University of Berlin were occupied by Gustav von Schmoller[27] and Adolph Wagner.[28] The influence and the prestige that these men enjoyed is comparable to the united authority of Professor John Dewey[29] and Justice Felix Frankfurter[30] in present-day America. They were at the same

26 [Alfred Rosenberg (1893–1946) was a German Nazi leader whose racist ideas in *The Myth of the Twentieth Century* (1930) were incorporated into National Socialist doctrine by Adolf Hitler. He was responsible for Nazi atrocities in Eastern Europe after 1941. Rosenberg was convicted at the Nuremberg trials as a war criminal and hanged.—Ed.]

27 [Gustav von Schmoller (1838–1917) was a prominent University of Berlin economist in imperial Germany who led the "Socialists of the Chair" and who defended and glorified Prussian political and military power. He was also founder of the *Verein für Sozialpolitik* (Association for Social Policy) and a prominent spokesman for the German Historical School.—Ed.]

28 [Adolph Wagner (1835–1917) was another well-known University of Berlin economist in imperial Germany. He was an advocate of "state socialism," which called for the transformation of liberal capitalism into a state-interventionist welfare system.—Ed.]

29 [John Dewey (1859–1952), an American philosopher and educator, developed a philosophy of "instrumentalism" related to pragmatism, which held that truth is relative to the problems requiring solutions and is subject to change. Dewey is also considered a founder of "progressive" education.—Ed.]

30 [Felix Frankfurter (1882–1965), an associate justice of the U. S. Supreme Court, was one of the founders of the American Civil Liberties Union and a supporter of Franklin D. Roosevelt's New Deal policies, which strengthened executive power.—Ed.]

time the shapers of public opinion in all economic, social, and moral matters; the oracles of the intellectuals and of members of parliament; and the chief advisors of the imperial government. About forty years ago, both men edited a book in two volumes with the collaboration of almost all the eminent German professors of economics.[31] The aim of the book was to support the plans of the Kaiser and of Admiral von Tirpitz[32] to make the German navy more powerful.

Professor Schmoller, in his own contribution to this symposium, bases his enthusiasm for the naval armament on the consideration that there is a lot of work to be done by the German navy. He contents himself, however, with referring to only one instance because the limited space of his article forbids him to cite more. And what is this example? At any rate, says Schmoller, sooner or later Germany will have to conquer a great part of Brazil. And, of course, for this adventure a strong navy would prove very useful.

Professor Wagner was still more enterprising. In his standard book on German protectionism, published in the first years of the present century, he speaks of Germany's impending war for more space. And he adds, "Vain pretensions like the Monroe Doctrine are for us not insurmountable obstacles."[33]

The students of these teachers are the Nazis of our day.

In the world of state interventionism, the territorial expansion of his own state and nation is of the utmost importance to each individual citizen. Every benefit that he derives from his own government is the more valuable the larger its territory is. Every new conquest further restricts the area in which discrimination is applied against him. This fundamental fact is completely overlooked by Norman Angell.

---

31 [Gustav Schmoller, Adolph Wagner, and Max Mering, eds., *Handels- und Machpolitik, Reden und Aufsätze im Auftrage der Freien Vereinigung für Flottenvorträge* (*Commerce and Power Politics: Speeches and Essays Commissioned by the Independent Association for Naval Lectures*), 2 vols. (Stuttgart: Cotta, 1900). —Ed.]

32 [Alfred von Tirpitz (1849–1930) was the architect of the imperial German navy that fought in World War I. He later entered politics and founded the Fatherland Party, serving as a nationalist member of the German Reichstag, or Parliament, from 1924 to 1928. —Ed.]

33 [Adolph Wagner, *Agrar- und Industriestaat: die Kehrseite des Industriestaates und die Rechtfertigung agrarischen Zollschutzes: mit besonderer Rucksicht auf die Bevölkerungsfrage* (*The Agrarian and Industrial State: The Disadvantage of the Industrial State and the Justification of Agrarian Tariff Protection, with Special Consideration to the Population Question*), 2nd ed. (Jena: Gustav Fischer, 1902), p. 83. —Ed.]

It would be a great mistake to believe that this militant nationalism is peculiar to big nations like Germany, Italy, and Japan. I will try to give you a description of the conditions in that part of the world where the two world wars arose. Eastern Europe includes all the countries and nations between the eastern boundaries of Germany and Italy and the western borders of Russia. It reaches from the shores of the Baltic to those of the Black Sea and Aegean Sea. If you ask men of these many small nations what they consider would be a fair determination of the boundaries of their own country, and if you mark these boundaries on a map, then you will discover that the greater part of this territory is claimed by two nations and that a considerable part is even claimed by three nations. Every nation knows how to justify its claims with linguistic, racial, historical, geographical, economic, social, or religious arguments. Not one is prepared to renounce even one of its claims for reasons of expediency. Every nation is ready to resort to arms in order to satisfy its pretensions. Every nation therefore considers its immediate neighbors as mortal enemies and relies on its neighbors' neighbors for armed support of its own claims against the common foe. Every nation tries to profit from every opportunity to satisfy its claims at the expense of its neighbors. The newspapers provide us every day with new proofs of the correctness of this description.

It is impossible to draw boundaries in Eastern Europe which would clearly separate linguistic groups. A great part of these territories are inhabited by men using different languages. Every territorial division would therefore necessarily leave minorities under foreign rule. These minorities are the bearers of permanent unrest, of Irredentism,[34] and hatred.

The League of Nations has tried two different systems to dispose of the problem of minorities in a peaceful way. Both methods failed because they did not take into account the economic problems involved.

One method was the protection of minority rights by international law. I do not have to elaborate on the purely legal aspects of this system. The economist has to recognize the fact that this system could be successfully applied only in a world of an unhampered market economy. It must necessarily fail, and it did fail in a world of government interventionism. A law cannot protect anybody against measures dictated purely by considerations of economic expediency. If a law in one of these countries discriminated

---

34 [Irredentism refers to the advocacy of the recovery of territory that is culturally and historically related to one nation and that is presently subject to the control of a foreign government. — Ed.]

against the members of the minority group—for instance, by refusing them educational opportunities—the international tribunal could interfere. But, if the government injures a minority, by economic measures that make no specific mention of minority distinctions but whose effect is virtually discriminatory, the international provisions are in vain. If, for instance, members of the minority are alone engaged in a specific branch of business, the government can ruin them by means of customs provisions. In other words, they can raise the price of essential raw materials and machinery. In these countries, every measure of government interference—taxes, tariffs, freight rates, labor policy, monopoly and price control, foreign exchange regulations—was used against the minorities. If you wish to build a house and you use the services of an architect from the minority group, then you find yourself beset by difficulties raised by the departments of building, of health, of fire. You will wait longer to receive your telephone, gas, electric, and water connections from the municipal authorities. The department of sanitation will discover some irregularities in your building. If members of your minority group are injured or even killed for political reasons, the police are slow in finding the culprit. Against such obstacles all provisions of minority protection are useless. Think of the assessment of taxes. In those countries, Chief Justice Marshall's dictum "The power to tax is the power to destroy" was practiced against the minorities.[35] Or think of the power that [occupational] licensing gives to a government.

The second method suggested is the exchanging of minorities. It was applied in the case of Greece and Turkey and in the case of the Assyrians.[36] This method would be excellent in a world where all regions offer the same opportunities for production. In our actual world, it is absolutely inadequate. It can only aggravate and stabilize the inequalities already existing, those very inequalities that are the economic causes of war. When Hitler recently withdrew German minorities from Eastern countries, he did so because he had conquered more valuable land for them.[37] No seri-

---

35 [John Marshall (1755–1835) was the fourth chief justice of the U. S. Supreme Court. His actual words, "The power to tax involves the power to destroy," appeared in his majority decision in *McCulloch v. Maryland*, March 6, 1819.—Ed.]

36 [During and after the Greco-Turkish war of 1922–24, almost 1.4 million Greeks were transferred from Turkey to Greece, and about four hundred thousand Turks were expelled from northern Greece to Turkey.—Ed.]

37 [Between 1939 and 1941, 1.2 million Poles and three hundred thousand Jews were expelled from those parts of western Poland formally annexed as part of Nazi Germany and forcibly moved to the territory of the "General Gouvernement" in the central part of Nazi-

ous economist can fail to realize the impracticability of this alleged solution.

Now we may understand why the Treaty of Versailles[38] and the League of Nations were bound to fail. In a world of socialism and interventionism, there is only one possible way to attain permanent peace: the conquest of all countries by one nation. This is the peace forced on the world by a victorious conqueror and not a peace like the liberal democrats wished to attain: a peace of nations that do not fight because there is no incentive to do so.

What the founders of the League intended was to provide for the lack of a peace ideology by the establishment of a bureau and a bureaucracy. In the midst of conditions on all sides predisposed to war, they hoped to ensure peace by the construction of an expensive palace in Geneva and by the appointment of a staff of lawyers, economists, and statisticians.[39]

A bureaucracy cannot create a new ideology. There is one great task in our age: to revive and to spread the economic and social mentality that makes war useless and peace durable. But, in the face of the fact that our contemporaries are far from such a mentality, we have to answer the question of what can be done to protect civilization after the war. We have to emphasize that a really lasting peace can be attained only with the universal acceptance of an ideology that could lead us to a perfect free market economy. Under the rule of such a mentality, and with all nations placed on a free trade footing, there would be peace even without a spe-

---

occupied Poland. Almost five hundred thousand Germans were resettled into those parts of western Poland, one hundred thousand of them being ethnic Germans from various countries in Eastern and Southern Europe. By 1943, as many as one million Germans had been moved into these Polish areas.—Ed.]

38 [The Treaty of Versailles was signed in May of 1919, ending the First World War. It imposed heavy reparations payments on Germany, to be paid to the Allied Powers; limited the size of the German armed forces; restored Alsace-Lorraine to France; transferred Prussian Poland, most of West Prussia, and part of Silesia to the new state of Poland; made Danzig a free city; transferred Germany's African and Asian colonies into mandates of the League of Nations; placed the Saarland under French administration; called for plebiscites in various territories formerly controlled by Germany and Austria-Hungary; and required the demilitarization of the German Rhineland. In 1935, Hitler unilaterally abrogated most of the terms of the Treaty of Versailles.—Ed.]

39 [For a history of the failure of the League of Nations in preserving peace and security in the interwar period, see William E. Rappard, *The Quest for Peace, Since the War* (Cambridge, Mass.: Harvard University Press, 1940).—Ed.]

cial bureau in Geneva. Under the rule of interventionism and socialism, peace cannot be maintained by treaties and institutions. What can be done under present conditions is only to reduce the dangers a little, not to remove them. Within these limitations I wish to try to review briefly the possible alternatives.

The first possibility is a victory of the totalitarians. The victors will exterminate or enslave the conquered nations. Later, they will fight each other over their respective shares in the spoils. The ultimate victor will rule the whole earth in the same way as Hitler rules Poland today.

The second possibility is a smashing British victory. If they exterminate the Nazis, they will no longer be in danger of being attacked again by Germany. This would solve the German problem, but it would not abolish other factors making for war.

The supposition of Clarence Streit's "union" project is that the victors do not exterminate the conquered Germans and therefore have to be ready to defend themselves again against new totalitarian aggressions.[40] The idea is sound on this supposition. Those menaced have to unite in order to repel possible attack. But of course this does not mean peace. It means only better conditions for the democracies in the Third World War.

It is the general belief today that the sovereignty of the small nations has proved its impracticability and that they have to disappear as independent states. This is true under present conditions. But we have to add that, in the face of the aggressive attitudes of the Axis, even the United States must be reckoned among these "small" nations. Without allies, it would be very hard for the United States to defend itself alone against the united forces of continental Europe, Japan, and the African colonies of the Axis.

I believe that the only thing that the Western democracies can do is to form a union for defense. The success of Hitler was due only to the fact that he had to fight every adversary singly. If all the fourteen or sixteen countries that he has invaded had been united on the first day of the war, Hitler and Mussolini would today enjoy the company of the Kaiser at Doorn.[41]

---

40 [Clarence Streit (1896–1986) was a League of Nations correspondent for the *New York Times*. He proposed a federal union among fifteen democratic nations, including Great Britain and the United States. He developed this idea in *Union Now: A Proposal for a Federal Union of the Democracies of the North Atlantic* (New York: Harper and Brothers, 1939) and *Union Now with Great Britain* (New York: Harper and Brothers, 1941).—Ed.]

41 [See footnote 11.—Ed.]

I do not see any other reasonable solution for the postwar problem than a closer political and military union between the menaced democracies.

Should this union go further and abolish business and economic nationalism? I wish to emphasize that this too could be achieved only with a universal *laissez-faire* ideology. If you abolish the economic meaning of frontiers within the Union, then all non-American countries have all the consequences of free trade. They are no longer protected against the most effective competition, that of the most highly productive industry and agriculture. If the Belgian motorcar producer has no protection against Ford and General Motors, he is no longer interested in any protection at all.

On the other hand, free trade and free migration do not create economic unity if the different governments have all the other means of interventionism at their disposal. They could, by these other means of governmental intervention, completely counteract the effects of free trade. Under the conditions of interventionism or socialism, economic unity can be achieved only by a strong, strictly centralized government. This is the reason why in all federative nations, with the progress of interventionism, the importance of the member states declines in comparison to that of the central government. If Mr. Streit's union should strive for economic unity, the members would lose their sovereignty. If America and Great Britain join it under these conditions, the president of the United States and the prime minister of Great Britain would be reduced to the rank of provincial governors. I do not believe that either the Americans or the British would like this.[42]

In my opinion, the weakness of the Streit proposal is that it does not say anything about Eastern Europe. The military prospects of the Western democracies could be vastly improved by the creation of a second big union including all the small nations of Eastern Europe. One cause of the breakdown of the system of Versailles was that these Eastern nations were unable to defend themselves or to contribute anything to the struggle for their own independence. What is wanted is to create a big Eastern European union, which, with about 150 million people, could counterbalance Germany and Italy and resist Russia.[43]

42 [See Mises, "Super-National Organization Held No Way to Peace," *New York Times* (January 3, 1943), p. 8E. — Ed.]

43 [See Chapter IX, "An Eastern Democratic Union: A Proposal for the Establishment of a Durable Peace in Eastern Europe," in this volume. — Ed.]

It is necessary to realize that such a union could never be achieved in the form of a federation. In the United States, there is a strong feeling in favor of federal government. Federalism has succeeded in a wonderful way in America. But it could succeed only in a homogeneous nation. If there were linguistic or racial discrepancies between the populations of the individual member states, the union could not work. Federal government presupposes a strong feeling of national unity.

A federation of the Eastern European nations could neither solve the minority problem nor the boundaries problem. All the factors which make these nations fight one another would remain and would shatter the union. The only possible constitution for such an Eastern Union would be a strictly centralized organization. But this, too, presupposes the absence of all kinds of economic intervention. If the government is limited to the preservation of security, it could avoid measures that some linguistic groups consider prejudicial.

The politicians and statesmen of these Eastern nations are united today on only one point: the rejection of this proposal. They do not realize that the only other alternative is the partition of their territories among Germany, Russia, and Italy. They do not believe it because they firmly rely on the invincibility of the British and the American forces. They do not imagine that the "American boys" have any other task in this world than to undertake an expedition to Europe every few years in order to fight for them.

The mentality of many Europeans concerning America is really naive. For the solution of every economic difficulty, the average European knows a very easy way out: American loans. They say loans, but they mean gifts. They are not bothered about interest payments and much less about repayment of the principal.

America and Great Britain could force Eastern Europe to unite by a clear declaration that they will not fight for them in a Third World War. Then Eastern Europe would have to replace the anarchy of a dozen or more states, ready at any moment to plunder their immediate neighbors, with a durable system of cooperation.

There are only two methods to achieve lasting peace. The first method is the maintenance of free trade, the abolition of government interference with business, the abandonment of economic nationalism. Under these conditions the assumptions of Norman Angell are correct. No individual citizen can derive any profit from war and conquest; war is useless and nonsensical. The second method is the conquest of all countries by one nation, the new order according to the ideas of Comrade Stalin or Herr Hitler. But no durable peace is thinkable in a universe where independent sovereign interventionist or socialist governments exist.

Everybody agrees that economic nationalism is responsible for the revival of the spirit of war and conquest. But people fail to grasp the essence and meaning of nationalism. Nationalism is neither hatred, nor chauvinism, nor a superiority complex. Nobody in Switzerland hates the Americans or the Danes; no Swiss citizen believes in the superiority of his own race as compared with those in America or Denmark. Nevertheless, the Swiss government discriminates against American and Danish commodities and labor. It is a sad fact that the average German imagines Paris not as the city of Renan,[44] Pasteur,[45] and Bergson,[46] but as a city of nightclubs. And it is similarly unfortunate that Frenchmen apply the term, *"le vice allemand,"*[47] to a particular human depravity. But these facts have nothing to do with the wars between Germany and France. The peoples of Eastern Europe call cockroaches "Swabiens," which means "Germans" in their languages; and the Germans call the same insects "Russians." This fact was not responsible for the First World War, and today it does not hinder the cooperation between Russia and Germany.[48] Some German professors declared that the last wars between Germany and France were wars of Kant[49] and Hegel[50] versus Descartes[51] and Voltaire,[52] that the German "he-

44 [Ernest Renan (1823–92) was a French philologist, historian, and critic.—Ed.]

45 [Louis Pasteur (1822–95) was a French scientist noted for his studies of fermentation and bacteria. Pasteurization is named after him.—Ed.]

46 [Henri Bergson (1859–1941) was a French philosopher, noted for his works *Time and Free Will* (1889) and *The Creative Mind* (1934).—Ed.]

47 [The term "le vice allemand," or "the German vice," refers to homosexuality.—Ed.]

48 [When this essay was written in May of 1941, Nazi Germany and the Soviet Union were still bound by an unofficial alliance under the terms of the Nazi-Soviet Nonaggression Pact signed in August of 1939. On June 22, 1941, Nazi Germany invaded the Soviet Union, bringing the USSR into the Second World War on the side of Great Britain.—Ed.]

49 [Immanuel Kant (1724–1804) was a German philosopher and one of the most important figures in the history of metaphysics.—Ed.]

50 [Georg Wilhelm Friedrich Hegel (1770–1831) was a German philosopher known for his concept of dialectic development of an "absolute spirit."—Ed.]

51 [René Descartes (1596–1650), a philosopher, mathematician, and scientist, developed analytical geometry. He wanted to extend the mathematical method to all areas of human knowledge.—Ed.]

52 [François Marie Arouet de Voltaire (1694–1778) was a French philosopher and one of the main contributors to Enlightenment thought in the eighteenth century.—Ed.]

roes" are fighting the English "shopkeepers," and that the true issue in this great world revolution is Teutonic "idealism" versus Anglo-Saxon "materialism."[53] They call the appetite for raw materials "idealism."

Nationalism is a policy of discrimination against foreigners. It is the corollary of a domestic policy of government interference with business. Of course, the greater part of the measures of government interference with business would be in vain if foreigners were not prevented from competing on the domestic market. Economic nationalism cannot disappear without a return to what people call *laissez-faire.*

In a world of nationalism, it is hopeless to abolish war. All that can be done is to make aggression more risky for the aggressors. It was a terrible mistake of the Covenant of the League of Nations to look with disfavor on alliances between individual groups of nations. In this world of ours, such alliances are the only means to prevent war. This is why the union as proposed by Mr. Streit and supplemented by an Eastern European union, as I suggested, is the only reasonable program for the defense of civilization and for a reconstruction of Europe and the whole world.

---

53 [The contrast between British "shopkeepers" and German "heroes" was made by Werner Sombart, *Händler und Helden: Patriotische Besinnungen (Shopkeepers and Heroes: Patriotic Reflections)* (1915). Sombart (1863–1941), a professor at the University of Berlin after 1917, was a prominent proponent of the German Historical School. At first, he was sympathetic to the Marxian critique of capitalist society. By the 1930s, he had become an apologist for the Nazi regime in Germany.—Ed.]

CHAPTER II

Postwar Economic Reconstruction of Europe[1]

Western civilization is a civilization of industrial countries, as distinguished from agricultural countries. The characteristic feature of an industrial country is that it imports raw materials and foodstuffs and that it exports manufactured goods, which are, for the most part, manufactured from imported raw materials.

What made the countries of Western and Central Europe industrial countries was not so much their natural resources as accidental historical factors. Western Europe has developed political and economic ideas that have given rise to an organization in which modern capitalism can flourish. Economic liberalism[2] and its corollaries, capitalism and political democracy, had their origin in the West, and from there, in the course of the nineteenth century, slowly spread to other parts of the world. The headstart thus gained by Western Europe explains why these Western countries, up to the outbreak of the First World War, were by far the richest. Their capital had already begun to accumulate at a time when other countries were still following backward methods in government and production.

It is important to realize that the advantage thus gained by Western and Central Europe was temporary only, and that it was doomed to be overtaken by the development of natural resources in other parts of the world. Viewed from our present state of geographical and geological knowledge, the cradle of modern capitalism indeed must appear poorly endowed. There are many varieties of raw materials and foodstuffs that

1 [This paper was delivered as a lecture at the Banking Seminar of the School of Business at Columbia University on November 7, 1940. —Ed.]

2 [On Mises's use of the term "liberalism" in the classical nineteenth-century sense, see Chapter I, "Postwar Reconstruction," footnote 8. —Ed.]

cannot be produced at all in these countries, and there are many others that can be produced only with a greater expenditure both of capital and labor than is required elsewhere. With the realization of these disparities of natural endowment, and with the practical adoption of modern methods of government and production by the backward countries which nature had better endowed, capital and labor concomitantly migrated from Europe.

This transfer of capital and labor, by which Western Europe gave and all the rest of the world only received, was the greatest historical event of the most glorious epoch in human history so far. It made North America, great parts of Latin America, Australia, and a large area of South Africa the Europeans' home. It transformed the economic and social structure of Japan, China, and India. It left no part of the world untouched. It made international the outer trappings, the paraphernalia of modern civilization.[3] We may deplore the fact that this internationalization did not concurrently include the political and moral ideas of English and French nineteenth-century liberalism, and that, far from eradicating the innate propensities to violence, it only provided the non-European nations with

---

3 [On the political, economic, and cultural achievements of nineteenth-century classical liberalism in creating a peaceful and prosperous international order, see C. F. Bastable, *The Commerce of Nations* (London: Methuen and Co., 1899), pp. 1–4; John Maynard Keynes, "The Economic Consequences of the Peace," in D. E. Moggridge, ed., *The Collected Writings of John Maynard Keynes*, Vol. II (London: Macmillan [1919] 1971), pp. 5–7; Gustav Le Bon, *The World in Revolt* (New York: Macmillan Co., 1920), pp. 35–46; C. Delisle Burns, *A Short History of International Intercourse* (New York: Oxford University Press, 1924), pp. 114–42; Felix Somary, *Changes in the Structure of World Economics Since the War* (London: P. S. King & Son, 1931), pp. 34–39; Benedetto Croce, *History of Europe in the Nineteenth Century* (New York: Harcourt Brace and Co., 1933), pp. 351–52; William Henry Chamberlin, *Collectivism: A False Utopia* (New York: Macmillan Co., 1936), pp. 1–3; William E. Rappard, *The Crisis of Democracy* (Chicago: University of Chicago Press, 1938), pp. 29–116; Joseph A. Schumpeter, "An Economic Interpretation of Our Time," [1941] in *The Economics and Sociology of Capitalism* (Princeton, N.J.: Princeton University Press, 1991), pp. 339–40; Gustav Stolper, *This Age of Fable: The Political and Economic World We Live In* (New York: Reynal and Hitchcock, 1942), pp. 3–18; Wilhelm Röpke, *International Order and Economic Integration* (Dordrecht, Holland: D. Reidel Publishing Co., 1959), pp. 72–79; Oskar Morgenstern, *International Financial Transactions and Business Cycles* (Princeton, N.J.: Princeton University Press, 1959), pp. 17–22; and Richard M. Ebeling, "World Peace, International Order, and Classical Liberalism," *International Journal of World Peace* (December 1995), pp. 47–68. —Ed.]

more efficient and terrible instruments. But this failure is only to be as-
cribed to the replacement of these liberal ideas, today stigmatized and
laughed at as "orthodox," by so-called more realistic doctrines of power
politics.

But the transfer of capital and labor has long since stopped. It was this
"Realpolitik"[4] that brought the period of *laissez-faire* and *laissez-passer* to
an end. Today, international migration is practically impossible, and it may
be that, in the not too distant future, migrations will even be hindered
within the boundaries of every country by the same factors that have already reduced international migration figures.

The mobility of labor had created a tendency toward an equalization
of the marginal productivity of labor. The great disparities in wages and
standards of living among different areas of the world gradually diminished. Today, labor is practically country-bound. This fact has the tendency
not only to perpetuate but to aggravate the inequalities in standards of living and civilization among different nations. Wages are today much higher
in the United States and in the British Dominions than even in England;
in Europe wages are lower the farther we go eastward and southward from
England.

No less changed is the situation with respect to the supply of capital.
Foreign investment was based on the assumption that the rights of private
property would be respected. Precisely the opposite was the case. We may
safely say that today expropriation of the rights of foreign investors and the
repudiation of foreign loans are considered a regular means of economic
and financial policy. It is an accepted and generally tolerated practice of
governments to use their sovereign powers for the sake of the nationalization of enterprises held by foreigners. It is a common rule to establish foreign exchange regulations in order to nullify the claims of foreign creditors.[5]

Looking back over the history of foreign investment and international
credit, we may observe that but for the United States and the British Dominions, capital marched on a one-way route. Only rosy optimists could
believe that the fate which the foreign investors and creditors will meet in

4 ["Realistic" or pragmatic politics.—Ed.]

5 [For examples of expropriation and nationalization of foreign investment property and
repudiation of foreign loans before and after the Second World War, see Harold M. Flem-
ing, *States, Contracts, and Progress: Dynamics of International Wealth* (New York: Oceana
Publications, Inc., 1960).—Ed.]

China and British India[6] will differ essentially from what has befallen them in Russia, Germany, and the Balkans.

Until the outbreak of the First World War, Western and Central Europe financed their purchases of imported food and raw materials to a great extent through the interest on foreign loans and by the earnings of foreign investment. This will no longer be the case. That part of foreign assets which has not already been lost by repudiation has been confiscated by governments of the creditor nations and used for the financing of war expenditures. The present war will leave Europe without foreign assets.[7]

This makes the situation that the Western countries of Europe will have to face critical. On the one hand, an industry without adequate equipment: machinery used up and not properly replaced, and machinery for the production of arms and military necessities that cannot be used for the production of goods that buyers in peacetime demand. On the other hand, no way to provide the capital required. It is unlikely that the American investor, after all the experiences he has had with foreign stocks and bonds, and with the unpleasant memory of foreign exchange restrictions, will be anxious to run the risk anew. But, even if he should be ready, his government will hinder him. It is nowadays one of the items on the labor program of creditor countries to stop the outflow of capital in order to render higher the domestic level of wages.[8]

This state of affairs spells the doom of European labor. Men will have

6 [British India, a part of India comprising seventeen provinces that was a British colony and subject to British law. It gained independence in 1947 and was divided between India and Pakistan.—Ed.]

7 [As one example, between September of 1939, when the war in Europe began, and November of 1940, when this essay was written, Great Britain spent almost $5 billion in purchases of war materiel from the United States by selling off investments of British citizens in the U. S. and draining dollar reserves held by the British government. The remaining $2 billion in gold and foreign assets held by the British government or its subjects was not at that point sufficient to pay for half of the supplies and goods that Britain still had on order from the United States; see Winston Churchill, *Memoirs of the Second World War* (Boston: Houghton Mifflin Co., 1959), pp. 384–86; also, Mises, "British Postwar Problems," *New York Times* (July 25, 1943), p. 10E. By 1945, Great Britain had liquidated £1,118 million of overseas investments, but still had an external debt of more than £3,000 million at the close of the war.—Ed.]

8 [In the postwar period, Marshall Plan aid by the United States to European countries stipulated that a large percentage of the dollars provided under the aid program had to be spent on American goods and often carried on American ships, to generate a stimulus for U. S. industry and employment; see Tyler Cowen, "The Marshall Plan: Myths and Reali-

to work in factories whose equipment is much poorer than the equipment of the competing plants abroad. The European entrepreneur will have to pay on the world market the same price for raw materials as his competitors overseas, who produce under more favorable conditions. He will, moreover, have to sell his products at a lower price than his competitor, who will be sheltered in his home market by protective import duties. The result will be low wages for industrial workers, which will depress their standard of living to something like Japanese levels.

These conditions—a comparatively unfavorable state of material resources for production, an extreme scarcity of capital, the impossibility of emigration for the excess population, and trade barriers in the foreign markets—will make it impossible to continue the prewar economic policies. These policies were characterized by a disregard of vital necessities and by ignorance of the principal requirements of business. What people are accustomed to call a progressive socioeconomic policy consisted mainly in measures resulting in a reduction of output and in the consumption of capital. Modern labor policy was designed to reduce hours of work, to raise wages above the level which industry could bear, and to confiscate a part of the capital invested in order to spend it. The most outstanding instances of this policy are unbalanced budgets and the practice of embarking upon public works regardless of the profitability of the enterprise. It represented a misguided "class" policy that did not understand the meaning of profitability within the framework of a capitalistic society. If capital is withdrawn from branches of business where it could pay and invested in activities where it does not pay, the result is waste of capital and the creation of a privilege for minority groups. If capital is consumed or wasted, it is not only the entrepreneur and the capitalist who pay the bill. Other things being equal, more capital means a higher marginal productivity of labor and, therefore, higher wages. All the measures of modern social legislation, which effectively restricted the quantity of capital available and productive output, were, in the last analysis, measures against the masses, both as wage earners and as consumers.

For policies of this type there will be no room left in postwar Europe. This, let us say, "Victorian" policy was one of taking away something from the entrepreneur and the capitalist. Where there is a tremendous shortage of capital and where the entrepreneur lacks the means for acquiring

ties," in Doug Bandow, ed., *U. S. Aid to the Developing World: A Free Market Agenda* (Washington, D.C.: Heritage Foundation, 1985), pp. 70–72.—Ed.]

better equipment for his plant, for the purchase of raw materials and for the payment of wages, nobody can tax him or interfere with his management, if the wheels of the mills are to continue turning. Under such conditions, there is no field where trade unions can operate. There will be left no other taxpayer than the wage-earner and the consumer. Everybody will easily understand the problems involved and the somewhat metaphysical aphorism, "The state should pay this or that," will lose its undeserved prestige. Where all the taxes must necessarily be paid by labor, because there are no rents and business profits to tax, every increase in public expenditure will immediately decrease labor's capacity to consume. The budget will be based on something like head taxes on great masses of extremely poor workers. The old slogan, "Tax the rich, subsidize the poor," is void of meaning where everybody is a "have-not" and where the only goal of a reasonable economic policy has to be to facilitate the accumulation of capital. The labor policy of the traditional type and the activities of trade unions will become obsolete.

The same will hold true for the prewar agrarian policy. In the industrial countries of Europe, high import duties, the quota system, and rigid prohibitions of imports, on the one hand, and subsidies and tax exemptions, on the other hand, made the farmer live at the expense of the consumer. Domestic food prices were often at least three times higher than world market prices. It will be impossible to maintain this system to the disadvantage of an extremely impoverished nonagrarian population. This means the disappearance of the greater part of agricultural production in these countries.

Nor will conditions be better for urban real estate. An impoverished people will hardly be able to pay rents sufficient for the maintenance of the buildings. With the decline in value of real property and the income derived from it, mortgages will be defaulted. Savings banks and insurance institutions will go bankrupt because their assets will depreciate.

Of course there is no doubt that, notwithstanding the military and political result of the war, all bank assets will be valueless. Their foreign assets have been expropriated by the government. Their holdings of commercial paper, of loans on collateral, of government bonds and debentures, and of mortgages will likewise lose their value.

The day after the cessation of hostilities will therefore mark the beginning of a long and deep depression. Total war will result in total bankruptcy. It would be wrong to attempt to refute this by citing the armistice day of 1918. At that time there were not only many European countries that had not suffered at all, but even in the belligerent countries the structure of the apparatus of production was unshattered. And a very important difference is this: The Jews have been practically eliminated from business. What this means no American can realize. In Central and Eastern Europe, virtually everyone who is business-minded has been removed, and those remaining expect every improvement from the action of a metaphysical entity, the state. The quick reconstruction of economic life in Europe after 1918 was the work of businessmen, among whom in Central Europe more than 50 percent and in Eastern Europe more than 90 percent were Jews.[9]

This dark prospect becomes still worse if we consider the mentality of the people involved. They will not be ready to face stark reality and to understand that nothing else can lead them back to prosperity than restless work. They will look for some artificial remedy, for some magic wand to change dust into food and clothes. Decades of demagogy have given them the conviction that there is some panacea against all economic ills. They believe that it is the duty of the government to discover it. They believe superstitiously in the power of financial artifices, be it stamp money, social credit, or anything else. They believe in everything but in what they call orthodox economics. If someone explains that capital can be accumulated only by saving, they call his advice an example of the "dismal science."

There is no doubt that after the war Europe will have to go through a long period of extreme poverty. Until new capital is accumulated, the masses will live on a level not better than that of the infancy of modern capitalism. One consequence of this relapse will be an increase in the difference in the level of life and civilization between Europe and America.

It is obvious that the economic decline of Europe will affect America,

9 [The *American Jewish Yearbook for 1933* estimated the total Jewish population in Europe to be approximately 9.5 million, with most European Jews living in Eastern or Central Europe. Poland had the largest Jewish community in Eastern Europe, numbering about 3 million. The Romanian Jewish population was 980,000, and the three Baltic states contained around 255,000 (155,000 in Lithuania, 95,000 in Latvia, and 5,000 in Estonia). In Central Europe, Germany had the largest Jewish population, with 565,000; there were 445,000 Jews in Hungary, 357,000 in Czechoslovakia, and 250,000 in Austria. Between 1933 and 1940, about 432,000 Jews emigrated from Germany and territories at that time occupied by Nazi Germany (including 282,000 from Germany and 117,000 from Austria). In 1950, the Jewish population in Europe was estimated at only 3.5 million. Only 45,000 remained in Poland, 280,000 in Romania, 37,000 in Germany, 155,000 in Hungary, 17,000 in Czechoslovakia, and 18,000 in Austria.—Ed.]

too. Europe will no longer be able to buy the quantities of American raw materials, food, and other products that it used to buy. Irrespective of the result of the war, the American farmer will suffer a disappointment. The demand for wheat, lard, cotton, tobacco, and other farm produce in Europe will be curtailed. In any case, the international division of labor will be restricted, not because of government-established trade barriers but because of a retrogression in European production. There still are, today, some branches of production where Europe is supreme, that is, optical instruments in Germany, watchmaking in Switzerland, fashions in Paris, cloth in Great Britain. And there is no reason why the production of these articles should not receive an impetus in the United States, which has the advantage of being the biggest market for their consumption.

What is true for North America is no less true for Latin America. Impoverished Europe will not fulfill the hopes of those South American politicians who expect to find an outlet for their raw materials and foodstuffs. The fantastic plans for a German penetration of Latin America will fail.

The most important question seems to be whether the United States will be able to contribute to a better and quicker reconstruction of Europe. It is unlikely that the American trade unions will in the near future lose their influence or change their minds as regards immigration. On the other hand, we may assume that the American investor will not be hindered by the government from investing his capital where he likes. But the problem is whether the reasonable investor would want, again, to risk his capital in Europe. It seems indubitable that all kinds of foreign investment and loans to foreigners are doomed if the present state of international law concerning these matters continues to prevail. This legal state of affairs is characterized by the following features:

(1) Every government is free to repudiate its obligations or to tax as it likes the yield from its bonds.

(2) Every government is sovereign as far as its currency is concerned. It may *ad libitum* devalue its currency, it may make unilateral changes in the value of the money which it owes. It has the right by means of foreign exchange regulations to rob all foreign creditors of their principal and interest.

(3) Every government has the right to expropriate [the property of] foreigners directly or through taxation. Even undisguised discrimination against foreigners is tolerated if it is presented to the public as a measure against capital and big business.

Of course, it is clear that only countries which will be ready to abdicate their sovereignty in these matters have a chance to attract foreign capital. The most important financial provision in the new constitution of the League of Nations will, therefore, have to be the transfer to the League of the competence to legislate on these matters, and the establishment of an efficient tribunal to adjudicate all disputes arising therefrom.

It is obvious that a satisfactory state of international relations that would keep the world at peace would require many more encroachments on national sovereignties. But under the present state of prevailing ideologies, it is simply utopian to demonstrate that peace and goodwill among the nations is possible only in a world of free trade and private property. It will take some time until mankind will be ripe again for this practice. We have to realize that postwar reconstruction will have to be accomplished in a much less perfect milieu.

Our contemporaries have the strange belief that economists and bankers may discover some magic power which can rebuild the ruins at no expense to society. In the presence of these beliefs, it is the duty of honest economists to repeat again and again that, after the destruction and the waste of a period of war, nothing else can lead society back to prosperity than the old recipe—produce more and consume less. This is the only way for Europe to reconstruct its economic machinery, as far as it still can be rebuilt.

This reconstruction cannot be undertaken from without, it must come from within. It is not simply a matter of economic technique, still less of engineering; it is a matter of social morale and of social ideologies. It can succeed only on the basis of a return to capitalism and to the economic methods of the nineteenth century. Of course, many contemporaries believe that there is an alternative, that is, socialism. It is not within the scope of this essay to discuss the pros and cons of both these systems of social cooperation. The analysis of the theoretical side of this question would lead us far afield. I wish only to emphasize that the experience both in Russia and in Germany is not conducive to a favorable judgment of socialist methods. What is wanted is to secure for Europeans something better than the Russian mode of life.

The first and immediate consequence of the armistice and the demobilization of millions of soldiers will be a tremendous amount of unemployment. Probably some quacks will recommend, as a remedy, public works, labor camps, and compulsory labor service. But who should pay for these expenditures? The problem is not busy work, but work which can produce the commodities which the producers of raw materials and food in non-European countries are ready to accept as payment. No government and no socialist management ever could produce such commodities for export. For this production, entrepreneurs are needed.

The spirit of enterprise and the initiative of business has, in the last two hundred years, transformed Europe from a continent of barefooted and half-starved masses into a world of mass consumption of goods once unknown or considered as luxuries. If there is any hope for a new upswing, it rests with the initiative of individuals. Let us not forget that the nationalist parties of Europe have destroyed their civilization in the name of a fight against individualism and liberalism.

The entrepreneurs will have to rebuild what the governments and the politicians have destroyed.

CHAPTER III

Europe's Economic Structure and the Problem of Postwar Reconstruction[1]

It is customary in this country to call the free enterprise system the "American system." This appellation is appropriate insofar as the marvelous achievements of America are an accomplishment of its economic freedom and capitalist individualism. But it would be a serious blunder to interpret this term in such a way as to underrate the feats of European capitalism.

It is quite right to call Europe an old country and America a young or new country. However, Europe's economic system as it existed on the eve of the present war was no less an achievement of nineteenth-century liberalism, individualism, and capitalism than the economy of this country.[2] We must not fall prey to what may be called the sightseer's fallacy. The average tourist admires in Europe the medieval cathedrals and castles and very often neglects to see the modern factories. For instance, in Nuremberg he visits the city of Meistersinger with its old churches and with its famous museum. He rarely goes beyond the walls that enclose this narrow region and separate it from what is one of the most important centers of German manufacturing.

On the eve of the Industrial Revolution, Europe was already long since completely colonized. There were no empty spaces of virgin soil left. Every spot was used to the extent possible under the prevailing methods of exploitation. And there were neither highways nor canals; primitive roads, furrowed by the wheels of carts, were the only facilities of transportation. The dwellings of the burghers and peasants were, from the point of view

---

1 [This paper was delivered as a lecture before a luncheon meeting of the New York University Men in the Finance Club on December 21, 1944.—Ed.]

2 [On Mises's use of the term "liberalism" in the classical nineteenth-century sense, see Chapter I, "Postwar Reconstruction," footnote 8.—Ed.]

of our modern standards, hardly better than slums. The palaces of the aristocracy lacked all that equipment which no American of modest means would like to miss in his home. There were neither factories nor machines. All these things only came later as an achievement of the industrial era.

But European capitalism had not only to provide for the needs of the very dense population that already peopled the countries at the end of the eighteenth century. It had, moreover, to make provisions for an unprecedented increase in their numbers. In the period from 1800 to 1925, the population of the four main European nations—outside of Russia, that is—Great Britain, France, Germany, and Italy, increased by one hundred and seven million. In the same period the population of the United States increased by one hundred and nine million. This means: These four old completely colonized European countries with a total area considerably smaller than that of the five largest states of the Union had to provide the means of subsistence for an additional population of almost the same magnitude as the United States.

While America had millions of square miles of practically empty land at its disposal, these European nations were under the necessity of cramming the increment of additional population into the narrow space of already overpopulated areas.

Europe, outside of Russia, has a population of about four hundred million, that is, three times the population of the continental United States.[3] But Europe's soil is poor in natural resources. It does not produce any cotton, rubber, coffee, tea, copra, or jute. Its capacity to produce wool and many basic metals is insignificant. In 1937, the European production of crude petroleum was 56 million barrels, namely, 52 million in Romania and 4 million in Poland. In the same year, the United States produced 1,279 million barrels, twenty-two times more. Moreover, the outcome of the present war will give these European oil wells to Russia.[4]

The predominantly industrial countries of Europe can neither feed nor clothe their citizens out of domestic resources. In order to acquire the

3 [This population figure for Europe refers to the mid-1940s.—Ed.]

4 [Many of the oil fields in pre–World War II southeastern Poland were in that portion of the country annexed by the Soviet Union as part of the joint Nazi-Soviet division of Poland in September of 1939. As part of the Yalta Conference agreements in February of 1945, this area was retained by the Soviet Union in the post–World War II period. Since 1991, it has been part of the independent Republic of Ukraine. Romania was one of the Soviet-bloc countries in the postwar period.—Ed.]

badly needed foodstuffs and raw materials, they must export manufactures, most of which are produced out of imported raw materials. One of the main export industries of Europe, for instance, was the cotton goods industry. The raw material was imported primarily from this country, with smaller quantities from Egypt and British India.[5]

The vital strength of Europe was its export trade. The economic background of nineteenth-century European civilization, which begot Pasteur,[6] Darwin,[7] Verdi,[8] Wagner,[9] Ampère,[10] and Freud[11] was capitalism. The flowering of the European nations was an achievement of free enterprise. It was surely not an outcome of government policies and the activities of politicians.

But capitalism in Western and Central Europe did even more than that. It provided the greater part of the capital needed for the development of the natural resources in the economically backward areas of Russia, southeastern Europe, Asia, Africa, Australia, and Latin America. Almost all railroads outside of Europe were built by European capital. Even in this country the early history of railroad construction was to some extent a record of European investment.[12]

In dealing with the specific economic problems of Europe, I want to disregard Russia, Sweden, Spain, and Portugal. The Soviet empire is, properly speaking, not a part of Europe. It is the most vast empire history has ever seen. It covers one-sixth of the earth's surface. Its territory is much

5 [See Chapter II, "Postwar Economic Reconstruction of Europe," footnote 6. — Ed.]

6 [See Chapter I, "Postwar Reconstruction," footnote 45. — Ed.]

7 [Charles Darwin (1809–92) was the English naturalist who developed the theory of organic evolution. He was also the author of *The Origin of Species* (1859). — Ed.]

8 [Giuseppe Verdi (1813–1901) was a prominent Italian operatic composer best known for *Rigoletto, La Traviata,* and *Aïda.* — Ed.]

9 [Richard Wagner (1813–83), the leading composer of German Romanticism, was best known for his operas *Der Fliegende Hollander (The Flying Dutchman)* and *Der Ring des Nibelungen (The Ring Cycle).* — Ed.]

10 [André-Marie Ampère (1775–1836) was a French physicist, mathematician, and natural philosopher. The basic unit of electric current, "ampere," is named for him. — Ed.]

11 [Sigmund Freud (1856–1939), an Austrian psychiatrist, was the founder of psychoanalysis. — Ed.]

12 [By 1914, foreign investment outside Europe by Great Britain was $20 billion; by France, $8.7 billion; and by Germany, $6 billion. See Herbert Feis, *Europe, The World's Banker, 1870–1914* (Clifton, N.J.: Augustus M. Kelley, [1930] 1974). — Ed.]

better endowed by nature than any other part of the world. It is very thinly populated. It is, in any economic regard, just the opposite of Europe. Sweden, too, is different from the rest of Europe. Its population is small and its natural resources, iron ore and lumber, are immense. Spain and Portugal have economic problems of their own. In a brief lecture, it would be impossible to deal adequately with these questions.

Now, in Europe proper there are two different zones: the predominantly industrial Western and Central area, and the predominantly agricultural Southeast. The predominantly industrial part can live only by exporting manufactures. It must sell these products on the open world market in competition with products of countries in which the natural conditions for manufacturing are much more favorable. It must leap over trade barriers towering to the skies. It has only one means to compensate for the handicaps set by nature and foreign trade barriers: low wages and a low standard of living.

The predominantly agricultural section of the Southeast entered the scene of the world market in the second part of the nineteenth century, when the railroads gave them the opportunity for shipping their excess production to Western and Central Europe. With the intensification of competition provided by overseas countries, the conditions for Southeastern Europe became worse and worse. Its soil is fertile when measured by Western European standards; it is poor when compared with the fields of Canada and other countries. Here, too, the only way out is low wages and a low standard of living.

Foreign observers sometimes make the mistake of blaming European enterprises for alleged economic backwardness. But what they call backwardness is precisely the adjustment of technical methods to unfavorable conditions beyond the control of business. Natural resources are poorer and capital is more scarce than in America; on the other hand, there is plenty of labor available. In such a state of affairs, many mechanical devices which can be used profitably in this country would not pay in European manufacturing. European farming does not use some of the machines known in this country, but it employs more fertilizers. Its average yield per acre, in spite of the comparative poverty of the soil, is greater than outside of Europe. The large estates in Germany, Czechoslovakia, and Hungary were certainly not less skillfully operated than any other agricultural outfit on the earth.

The capital consumption caused by the war is enormous. Homesteads and factories have been destroyed. Industrial equipment worn out by the intensified production has not been properly replaced.[13] But even worse is the fact that the spirit of free enterprise has vanished. The governments and political parties are firmly resolved not to go back to the system to which Europe owed its well-being in the past. They are committed to the ideas of totalitarian economic management. They are fascinated by the alleged success of German and Russian planning.[14]

13 [As an indication of the degree of wartime destruction in 1945 resulting from the Second World War in Europe, please note: Throughout Europe, huge sectors of some cities were totally destroyed. Others, such as Berlin and Warsaw, were almost completely demolished. In France, two million houses were destroyed or severely damaged; in Holland, the number was almost five hundred thousand; in Italy, two million; in Great Britain, four million; and in Germany, ten million. Many roads were also closed to traffic. In the western part of Germany, seven hundred and forty river bridges out of nine hundred and fifty-eight were unusable; in Sicily, no permanent bridge remained on the road between Catania and Palermo. In France, nine-tenths of the trucks were undrivable. Throughout Europe, the railway system was in ruin. In France, four thousand kilometers of track were out of commission; in Germany twelve thousand; and in Yugoslavia and Greece, two-thirds of the entire railway system was destroyed. In Czechoslovakia, moreover, one-quarter of the railway tunnels were blocked. And everywhere, there were few locomotives in working order: only 50 percent in Germany, 40 percent in Belgium and Poland, 25 percent in Holland, and less than 20 percent in France. Only 509 kilometers of French rivers and canals were open out of a total of 8,460 kilometers of normally navigable waterways. Elsewhere, rivers, canals, and harbors were blocked with debris and sunk ships and barges. To make matters worse, European coal production was only 40 percent of its prewar level. The German Ruhr region, which before the war produced four hundred thousand tons of coal a day, was extracting only twenty-five thousand tons a day in 1945. Electricity output in Italy was only 65 percent of its 1941 level. Industrial production in Germany was only 5 percent of its prewar level; in Italy, production was only 25 percent; in Belgium, France, Greece, Holland, Yugoslavia, and Poland, it was 25 percent. European fertilizer production had also fallen to 20 percent. Not surprisingly, in 1945, European farm yield per acre was 75 percent, and the wheat crop was 40 percent of its prewar level.—Ed.]

14 [On the similarities and differences between the Nazi and Soviet forms of planning, see Mises, *Omnipotent Government: The Rise of the Total State and Total War* (Spring Mills, Pa.: Libertarian Press, [1944] 1985), pp. 58–59: "The German and Russian systems of socialism have in common the fact that the government has full control of the means of production. . . . But there is a difference between the two systems—though it does not concern the essential features of socialism. The Russian pattern of socialism is purely bureaucratic, like the administration of the army or the postal system. . . .The German pattern differs from the Russian one in that it (seemingly and nominally) maintains private ownership of the means of production and keeps the appearance of ordinary prices, wages, and markets. There are, however, no longer entrepreneurs but only shop managers. . . .The government tells the shop managers what and how to produce, at what prices and from whom to buy, at what prices and to whom to sell. The government decrees to whom and under what

What these planners fail to realize is that, by and large, Russia can live in economic self-sufficiency. Those imports which the Russian authorities do not want to miss can be bought by the exportation of gold mined in Russia and of some other raw materials. The Soviets are not faced with the problems of manufacturing for the world market.

But the Germans must face these problems. The German pattern of socialist management was precisely adopted for the purpose of not impairing the vital nerve of Germany's economy, export of manufactures. It failed utterly. In 1932, the deepest point of the Depression, German exports were 5,700 million marks; in 1938 they were only 5,300 million marks. Taking the figures of 1930 as 100, the index of foreign trade in 1937 was 72 for Germany, but 97 for the United States and 101 for Great Britain. Even these figures understate the decline of Germany's foreign trade, for they are based on the artificial rate of the German mark and on the high prices at which Germany traded with the clearing countries.[15] Besides, we must take into account that Germany paid enormous export subsidies, amounting to 1,500 million marks in 1938.

Disregarding both sound theories and experience, Great Britain's rulers believe that the only way to solve the nation's postwar problems is full government control.[16] In the three years preceding the outbreak of the present war, Great Britain paid for only 58 percent of its imports by exporting merchandise. The rest was mainly paid by the net national income

---

terms the capitalist must entrust his funds and where and at what wages laborers must work. Market exchange is only a sham. All the prices, wages, and interest rates are fixed by the central authority. . . . The government, not the consumer, directs production. This is socialism in the outward guise of capitalism." See also Mises, *Planning for Freedom*, enlarged 4th ed. (Grove City, Pa.: Libertarian Press, [1952; 1980] 1996), pp. 3–5 & 23–25. —Ed.]

15 ["Clearing countries" were nations, mostly in the southeastern Balkan region of Europe with whom Nazi Germany had made "barter trade agreements," under which goods were imported and exported at nonmarket prices arranged by the respective governments; see Mises, *Human Action: A Treatise on Economics* (New Haven, Conn.: Yale University Press, 1949), pp. 796–99. This section on "Remarks About the Nazi Barter Agreements" is not included in later editions of *Human Action.* —Ed.]

16 [The British Labor Party came to power in July of 1945 and soon began nationalizing a series of large British industries and instituted economic planning. On the results of British nationalization and planning in the postwar period, see John Jewkes, *Ordeal by Planning* (London: Macmillan and Co., 1948); Ivor Thomas, *The Socialist Tragedy* (New York: Macmillan Co., 1951); and R. Kelf-Cohen, *Nationalization in Britain: The End of a Dogma* (London: Macmillan Ltd., 1958). —Ed.]

from shipping and from overseas investments. After the war, these two sources will bring much less than they used to bring before the war. If Great Britain is to preserve its prewar standard of imports of food and raw materials, it must increase the volume of its exports of merchandise by half or two-thirds.

Deluded by the fallacies of socialist doctrines, British public opinion considers this fact as a sufficient justification for the abandonment of the free enterprise system. No attempt was ever made to prove the thesis that a government-controlled industry would produce more cheaply or better than private entrepreneurs. No unbiased man would dare to assert that government agencies are better fitted than merchants to adjust production to the needs of consumers in various overseas countries, to overcome the handicap of trade barriers, and to meet successfully the competition of other exporting nations.

A reconstruction of the United Kingdom's badly battered industrial equipment can hardly be effected without the aid of American credits. It is unlikely that enterprises, subject to government control and at every turn obstructed by bureaucratic regimentation, will inspire more confidence in American investors and bankers than entrepreneurs who are free to go their own way.[17]

The truth is that what the British really have in mind is to balance foreign trade not by an expansion of exports but by a restriction of imports. This would be tantamount to a resumption and intensification of the unfortunate economic warfare that was the characteristic feature of the interwar period and one of the main causes of distress and political conflict. It would not only lower the standard of living of the British masses, it would also bring disaster to all other nations and frustrate all endeavors to safeguard durable peace.

The plans of the French government are no less contrary to purpose than those of the British. The French want to divide their industries into three groups. Each group will be subject to a different treatment. The first section, comprised of mining, public utilities, and some essential processing industries, is to be expropriated and directly operated by bureaucrats. The second section will seemingly remain in the hands of business, but

---

17 [On the pattern of British imports and exports at the end of the Second World War and the year following (until American and Canadian government credits were extended to enable the British government to increase imports), see Bertrand de Jouvenel, *Problems of Socialist England* (London: Batchworth Press, 1947), pp. 74–83.—Ed.]

will be completely controlled by the government, according to the Nazi methods. Only the third section, consisting of the enterprises manufacturing consumers' goods for export, is to be left free. Of course, the French realize very well that it would be simply idiotic to deliver the Paris *haute couture*,[18] the *parfumerie*, and the production of champagne and brandy to bureaucratic management. However, they are mistaken in the expectation that these and other famous French export industries could thrive within an environment of government-controlled business. The inefficiency of the controlled sections will impose a heavy burden upon the free section. The whole incidence of taxation will fall upon the export industries and suffocate them.[19]

All the smaller nations of Europe want in some way or other to copy the British and French plans. They all aim at foreign exchange control.[20] One must not forget the fact that the smaller a country, the greater, comparatively speaking, is its foreign trade. If a New York businessman sells something to a place three thousand miles away, or buys something from such a place, it can still be domestic trade. But if a man in Zurich or Copenhagen buys or sells something over a distance of two hundred miles, it always means foreign trade. In a small country, foreign exchange control practically subjects all enterprises to government control. And all these nations are firmly resolved to utilize foreign exchange control for the most rigid restriction of imports.

While Europe can flourish only under a system of international division of labor, the Europeans have espoused a hyperprotectionist policy hostile to any kind of imports. While exporting manufactures is only possible under a free enterprise system, Europe is opposed to any kind of profit-seeking business. They abhor as orthodox and reactionary that sys-

18 [*Haute couture* is a French expression for "high fashion." — Ed.]

19 [On the failure and partial reversal of socialist planning in France in the immediate postwar period, see Vera Lutz, "The French 'Miracle,'" in Arthur Seldon, ed., *Economic "Miracles": Studies in the Resurgence of the French, German, and Italian Economies Since the Second World War* (London: Institute of Economic Affairs, 1964), pp. 75–167. — Ed.]

20 [Foreign exchange controls restrict the free acquisition of domestic and foreign currency on the foreign exchange market. The government usually requires exporters to sell foreign currency earned for the domestic currency at a nonmarket rate of exchange, and rations access to foreign currencies by domestic importers. On the introduction and effects of foreign exchange controls in the interwar period in Germany, Austria, and Hungary, see Howard S. Ellis, *Exchange Control in Central Europe* (Westport, Conn.: Greenwood Press, [1941] 1971). — Ed.]

tem which in the past made Europe prosperous, and advocate enthusiastically the methods which failed everywhere they have been tried.

A few remarks more are needed in order to discuss some special plans regarding those countries whose leaders expect to enter into a close economic and political cooperation with Russia. Left-wing politicians of Poland, Czechoslovakia, and Austria hope that such a cooperation can open the Russian market for their industries. They would provide Russia with manufactures, and Russia would provide them with food and raw materials. Let us, for the sake of argument, assume that such plans could be realized. But at any rate it would be unrealistic to expect that the Soviets would be prepared to pay for the manufactures of their vassals' prices, which would secure for the wage-earners of these nations a standard of living higher than that of the Russian masses.[21] If the Russians were in a position to pay world market prices for imported manufactures, they could as well increase their buying in America or anywhere else. The only advantage which the Soviets could find in such a kind of bilateral exchange would consist in the cheapness of the products. The standard of living was very low indeed in the three above-mentioned countries when compared with Western European standards, to say nothing of American standards. But even in the years of the Great Depression, it was much higher than that of the Russian peasants and workers.

American common sense is quite correct in criticizing European disunity. It is simply craziness that the various European nations, many of them inferior in size, population figures, and economic power to the greater part of the American states, are anxious to fight one another by all devices of economic nationalism. But a European customs union would not solve Europe's economic problem if not supplemented by economic freedom. The economies of the various European countries do not complement each other. Europe as a whole depends upon the importation of food and raw materials from other parts of the world, and must consequently export manufactures.

It is a sad fact that Europe has lost the advantages that one hundred and fifty years of economic freedom have secured for it. A great part of the capital accumulated in previous years has been squandered. Saving and

21 [On the artificial terms of trade between the USSR and Eastern European countries in the postwar period, which were arranged to benefit the Soviet Union, see William Henry Chamberlin, *The European Cockpit* (New York: Macmillan Co., 1947), pp. 209–11. —Ed.]

capital accumulation must start anew. The scarcity of capital has necessarily lowered the marginal productivity of labor. For a period of transition, wage rates and standards of living must necessarily be lower than they were in the years preceding the wars. No government tampering with industrial relations and no labor union pressure and compulsion can alter this fact. On the contrary, the more government or union interference delays the accumulation of new capital, the more it protracts the period of transition and the return to prosperity. There is no other recipe than this: Produce more and better, and save more and more. Privations cannot be spared. The nations must suffer for the deficiencies of their policies. It would be wrong to blame the economists who establish this truth with seeming callousness. The economists have done all they could do when for more than eighty years they warned these nations about the consequences of their misguided policies.

There is but one way toward a steady rise in the general standard of living: the progressive accumulation of capital and the improvement of methods of production which this additional capital renders feasible. However, before the war the countries of continental Europe were committed to policies which not only checked the further accumulation of capital, but even resulted in the consumption and erosion of capital accumulated. The main vehicle of these policies was credit expansion. It is true that credit expansion at first creates an economic boom. But the artificial prosperity of the easy money orgy of a few years must finally lead to a slump and depression. Credit expansion is very popular with politicians who do not worry about tomorrow. But conscientious statesmen must not espouse short-run policies. Only long-run policies are sound.

Of course, there are pseudo-economists preaching the gospel of short-run policies. "In the long run we are all dead," says Lord Keynes.[22] But it

22 [John Maynard Keynes (1883–1946) was the most famous British economist of the twentieth century. He advocated active government intervention in the market to overcome unemployment through deficit spending and monetary expansion. His most influential book was *The General Theory of Employment, Interest, and Money* (1936). The phrase, "In the long run we are all dead," was used by Keynes in "A Tract on Monetary Reform," in D. E. Moggridge, ed., *The Collected Writings of John Maynard Keynes*, Vol. IV (London: Macmillan Ltd., [1923] 1971), p. 65, in reference to the quantity theory of money and the proposition that, in "the long run," changes in the money supply only influence the general level of prices. In *Omnipotent Government: The Rise of the Total State and Total War* (Spring Mills, Pa.: Libertarian Press, [1944] 1985), p. 263, Mises pointed out that, "Lord Keynes did not coin this phrase in order to recommend short-run policies, but in order to criticize some inadequate methods and statements in monetary theory.... However, the phrase best characterizes the economic policies recommended by Lord Keynes

all depends upon how long the short run will last. The classical formulation of the short-run principle was provided by the Marquise de Pompadour:[23] "*Après nous le déluge.*"[24] The lady was fortunate enough to die in the short run. But her successor, Madame Du Barry, outlived the short run and was beheaded in the long run.[25] Europe has now entered the stage in which it is experiencing the long-run consequences of its short-run policies. The shortsighted politicians bump their heads against the walls, the reality of which they stubbornly try to deny.

Europe's distress is also a calamity for all other parts of the world. It makes illusory the plans for America's postwar recovery to the extent that they are based on the expectation of a full revival of international trade. If Europe does not recover soon, it will not be able to buy sufficient quantities of American products. Even complete free trade in this country will not revive international trade if the European nations do not abandon their anti-import policies.

There is much talk about American credits for the reconstruction of Europe. But credits are sound only if the debtor makes the proper use of

and his school." This view of Keynes was shared by some of Mises's contemporaries. For example, Joseph A. Schumpeter wrote in a review of Keynes's *General Theory* in the *Journal of the American Statistical Association* (December 1936), p. 794: "Let him who accepts the message there expounded [in *The General Theory*] rewrite the history of the French *ancien régime* in some such terms as these: Louis XV was a most enlightened monarch. Feeling the necessity of stimulating expenditure he secured the services of such expert spenders as Madame de Pompadour and Madame du Barry. They went to work with unsurpassed efficiency. Full employment, a maximum of resulting output, and general well-being ought to have been the consequence. It is true that instead we find misery, shame, and that in the end of it all, a stream of blood. But that was a chance coincidence." And F. A. Hayek wrote in *The Pure Theory of Capital* (London: Macmillan Ltd., 1941), pp. 409–10: "A policy has been advocated [by Lord Keynes] which at any moment aims at the maximum short-run effect of monetary policy, completely disregarding the fact that what is best in the short run may be extremely detrimental in the long run.... I cannot help regarding the increasing concentration on short-run effects...not only as a serious and dangerous intellectual error, but as a betrayal of the main duty of the economist and a grave menace to our civilization.... Are we not even told that, 'since in the long run we are all dead,' policy should be guided entirely by short-run considerations? I fear that these believers in the principle of *après nous le déluge* may get what they have bargained for sooner than they wish." —Ed.]

23 [Jeanne Antoinette Poisson Le Normant d'Etioles, Marquise de Pompadour (1721–64) was a mistress of Louis XV of France. —Ed.]

24 [This is a French expression that means "After us, the flood." —Ed.]

25 [Jeanne Bécu, Comtesse Du Barry (1743–93) was another mistress of Louis XV of France. During the French Revolution she was arrested for treason and guillotined. —Ed.]

the money borrowed. Credits are neither charity nor lend-lease: They mean business. There must be a reasonable chance that the debtor will employ the amount credited for an improvement of his conditions, and accordingly will be able to pay interest and principal. Credits granted to foreign governments for the continuation of inappropriate economic policies harm both the creditor and the debtor. It would be very unfortunate indeed if American credits were accorded to governments which will waste them in the pursuit of illusory policies.

It is not true that a country needs foreign credits for the stabilization of its foreign exchange rate. If there is neither inflation nor credit expansion, such credits are superfluous. But if a country takes recourse to what is called today euphemistically an "expansionist policy," no credit can prevent a devaluation of its currency. Credits are needed for the acquisition of industrial and agricultural equipment that can raise the productivity of labor. But they are useless if employed for the continuation of deficit spending.

Yet, people are right in saying that postwar reconstruction in all parts of the world depends entirely upon America. But America must give something much more essential than credit; it must provide an ideology. It must revive the idea of economic freedom, private initiative, and individual enterprise. After the war, this nation will enjoy all over the world an unprecedented moral prestige. If America stands for economic freedom, no country will be in a position to withdraw from this influence. The great ideological conflict between totalitarianism and individualism will be decided in this country, and all other peoples will follow the example set by America.

America is indebted to Europe for many things. From Europe came its citizens, its civilization, and its religious and moral principles. But it will discharge this debt with compound interest if it gives Europe anew the political and economic ideas which in the past have produced in Europe and America the highest human civilization hitherto known. The freedom mankind needs most in our day is freedom from utopian superstitions. What ranks above all else for economic and political reconstruction is a radical change of ideologies. Economic prosperity is not so much a material problem; it is, first of all, an intellectual, spiritual, and moral problem.

CHAPTER IV

The Fundamental Principle
of a Pan-European Union[1]

I

Economic nationalism is a policy which aims at furthering the well-being of one's own nation or of some of its parts through inflicting harm upon foreigners by economic measures, for instance: trade and migration barriers, expropriation of foreign investments, repudiation of foreign debts, currency devaluation, and foreign exchange control. We do not have to deal with the question whether or not the ends sought by the policy of economic nationalism, namely improvements of the material well-being of their own fellow-citizens or of some groups of these fellow-citizens, can be really attained by the application of these methods. We have only to establish the fact that economic nationalism results in war if some nations believe that they are powerful enough to brush away, by military action, the measures of other countries which they consider as detrimental to their own interests.

The free traders want to make peace durable by the elimination of the root causes of conflict. If everybody is free to live and to work where he wants, if there are no barriers for the mobility of labor, capital, and commodities, and if the administration, the laws, and the courts do not discriminate between citizens and foreigners, the individual citizens are not

1 [This paper was delivered at a "Pan-European Conference" held at New York University June 4–5 & 18, 1943. The Pan-European Union movement was founded by Richard N. Coudenhove-Kalergi (1894–1972) as a private association advocating the political and economic integration of Europe as a solution to the dangers of war and social conflict on the continent. He popularized the idea in his books, *Pan-Europe* (New York: Alfred Knopf, 1926) and *Crusade for Pan-Europe: Autobiography of a Man and a Movement* (New York: G. P. Putnam & Sons, 1943).—Ed.]

interested in the question where the political frontiers are drawn and whether their own country is bigger or smaller. They cannot derive any profit from the conquest of a province. In such an ideal world of democracy and free trade, war does not pay.

The illusion of many pacifists is the belief that all that is required for the abolition of war is the building up of international offices and the establishment of an international court whose rulings should be enforced by an international police force.

There are plenty of people who believe in the doctrines of economic nationalism and therefore object to the abolition of trade and migration barriers. These men have to know that what they aim at must result in the perpetuation of disunity and conflict. If the armed guards of Atlantis have the right and the power to prevent the citizens of Ruritania from selling the products of their toil and trouble on the markets of Atlantis, no covenant will hinder the government of Ruritania from the appeal to arms, provided that it believes itself strong enough to conquer or defeat Atlantis. Under such conditions, war preparedness is the only means to safeguard peace. Arm and watch your borders day and night!

This war was not caused by Nazism alone. The lamentable failure of collective security was not less instrumental in bringing about the disaster than the criminal plans of the Nazis. The war would never have started if the democratic nations had in time forced the Nazis to abide by the disarmament clauses of the Treaty of Versailles[2] or if the Germans and their abettors had expected to encounter on the first day of hostilities a united and adequately armed front of all these nations which are today united in fighting them. But collective security was unrealizable among nations fighting one another unswervingly in the economic sphere.

II

There is no unanimity with regard to the definition of the terms federation, confederation, and federal union. However, all people agree that internal trade and migration barriers and discrimination among the citizens of the various member states are incompatible with the essence of a federal constitution. Domestic free trade and equality of citizenship rights are char-

2 [On the Treaty of Versailles, see Chapter I, "Postwar Reconstruction," footnote 38. —Ed.]

acteristic features of every federal union. The cases of the United States of America, of the British Dominions, Canada and Australia, of Switzerland, of the federal republics of Latin America, and of pre-Hitler Germany provide the proof of the correctness of this statement.

In our age of government interference with business, there are, within every federal union, forces aiming at the establishment of trade barriers between the member states and at discrimination against those citizens who belong to other member states. Even in the United States, many state and local laws have been enacted in recent years which tend to prevent goods and services from moving freely between the various states and communities of the country. However, the U. S. Constitution does not permit states to levy tariff duties on imports or exports or to discriminate against the ships, the commerce, and the citizens of other states. The states do not dare to violate the Constitution openly, but they time and again have exercised their rights in the fields of taxes, police, and corporate powers in violation or evasion of the Constitution.[3] The immense majority of the nation condemns such procedures, and it is very unlikely that they will succeed. But if the unbelievable were to happen and this system were to prevail, the U. S. would no longer be a federal union in the sense in which this term has been applied in this country since the ratification of the Constitution.

When the Pan-European movement was inaugurated, its program included the economic unification of Europe and equal rights for all citizens of all member states. It was this idea which made the concept of Pan-Europe popular both in Europe and in other continents. The citizens of the United States sympathize with the Pan-European tendencies because they are convinced that their realization means the abolition of trade and migration barriers within Europe.

It would be a misnomer to say that the Pan-European movement aims at the establishment of a European federation or federal union if it is not intended to abolish intra-European trade and migration barriers.

---

3 [On various attempts on the part of U. S. state governments during the 1930s to restrict or control the free trading of goods and services across state lines as a method to stimulate state-level output and employment, see James Harvey Rogers, *Capitalism in Crisis* (New Haven: Yale University Press, 1938), Chapter VII, "From States' Rights to State Autarchy," pp. 135–53; Raymond Leslie Buell, *Death by Tariff: Protectionism in State and Federal Legislation* (Chicago: University of Chicago Press, 1939); and Ralph Cassidy, "Trade Barriers Within the United States," *Harvard Business Review* (Winter 1940), pp. 231–47.—Ed.]

III

It is futile to shape a Pan-European Bill of Rights if this Bill does not give every European the right to live and to work within the whole territory of Pan-Europe. Most of the European constitutions grant to the citizens of their own nations all those other rights which a new Bill of Rights could bring them. What they cannot obtain from their own country and what only a European constitution can give them is the right of Pan-European citizenship.

It would be paradoxical indeed to organize a Pan-European system in which every Ruritanian is an outcast, a pariah, a metic as soon as he leaves his small country of Ruritania and wants to enter Atlantis or Thule. One cannot adopt the ideas of Monsieur Charles Maurras[4] and of Professor Carl Schmitt[5] as guiding principles for a free and united Europe.

The workers of Eastern and Southern Europe do not care a button for a Pan-European system which does not grant them the right of free mobility. The Ruritanian factory hands do not want again to face a situation that brings dismissal for them because some other European country has forbidden the importation of the products of the factory in which they work.

The citizens of the various European nations cannot derive any profit from the establishment of a European bureaucratic apparatus and of a special European covenant. Such institutions will not be more beneficial than the activities of the League of Nations and of the Permanent Court of In-

---

4 [Charles Maurras (1868–1952) was a well-known French political theorist who espoused what he called "integral nationalism," which emphasized the supremacy of the state over local and individual interests, and especially the interests of the nation-state in international relationships. During the German occupation of France in the Second World War, he was a vocal supporter of the Vichy French government, which collaborated with Germany. He was arrested by the Free French in 1944 and sentenced to life imprisonment. He was released for "health reasons" shortly before his death.—Ed.]

5 [Carl Schmitt (1888–1985) was the most famous constitutional theorist in pre-Hitler Germany and the leading jurist defending the Nazi system after 1933. He forcefully defended the Nazi race laws prohibiting intermarriage between "Aryans" and Jews. He ended a 1936 lecture by quoting Hitler, "In defending myself against the Jew...I am doing the work of the Lord." Schmitt also called Hitler's violent purges of 1934 against segments of the Nazi movement "the highest form of administrative justice." But in the late 1930s, he was accused by some Nazis of earlier "Jewish contacts," and his rise in Nazi power circles was halted.—Ed.]

ternational Justice, and not more successful than the Briand-Kellogg Pact.[6] The Ruritanians will never say: "We are Europeans," if they know that thirty-odd European governments are busy day and night discriminating against them.

A European federation means that the Ruritanian enjoys in Atlantis the same status that is granted to a Texan in Massachusetts.

IV

There are people who believe that it is utopian to aim at the immediate abolition of intra-European trade and migration barriers. They want to postpone the solution of this problem to some later date. For the time being they aim at an alleged federation that acquiesces in economic nationalism on the part of its member states.

Perhaps these skeptics are right. But then frankness would oblige them to admit that under present conditions the Pan-European program is unrealizable.

It is beyond doubt that it would simply be suicidal on the part of the European democracies to open their borders to the immigration of the subjects of the totalitarian nations. In the present state of the German and Italian mentality, these immigrants would be nothing else than vanguards of Nazi and fascist armies. But this is only one more proof of the fact that the European federation cannot include Germany and Italy. The compact bloc of about one hundred and twenty million Germans and Italians would be in a position to sabotage the working of the federation, whatever its constitution may be. But this is a different problem.

V

It is necessary to emphasize that we do not have to deal with the general aspects of the free trade problem. Our task is only to find out whether a European federation is compatible with trade and migration barriers between the member states. It is obvious that the answer has to be in the negative.

It is a poor method of evading the acknowledgment of this truth to rec-

---

6 [On the Kellogg-Briand Pact, see Chapter I, "Postwar Reconstruction," footnote 6. —Ed.]

ommend starting Pan-Europe with internal trade and migration barriers and postponing their abolition until more propitious times. We are not interested in the questions that future generations will have to solve. He who opposes free trade for our time is a protectionist and should admit it openly.

Schiller's Marquis of Posa says to King Philippe, "This century is not ripe for my ideal [of tolerance and freedom of thought]; I am a citizen of the centuries to come."[7] But Schiller did not profess this opinion with re-

---

7 [Friedrich von Schiller (1759–1805) was one of Germany's most famous poets, dramatists, and literary critics. The passage referred to is from Schiller's drama, "Don Carlos, Infante of Spain: A Dramatic Poem," [1787] in *Friedrich Schiller: Poet of Freedom* (New York: New Benjamin Franklin House, 1985), pp. 93–95:

Marquis of Posa, a Knight of Malta, speaking to Philippe II, King of Spain:

"I can not be the servant of a Prince.
I shall not cheat the buyer, Sire. — If you
Do think I merit an appointment, then
You only wish the deeds prescrib'd. You only
Desire my arm and courage in the field,
My head alone in council. Not my deeds,
But the applause, which they find at the throne,
Should be the purpose of my actions. But for me,
For me hath virtue its own worth. The bliss,
Which with my hands the Monarch would implant,
I would create myself, and 'twere my joy
And my own choice, what else but my duty.
And is that your opinion? Can you bear
Within your own creation strange creators?
Should I reduce myself to be the chisel,
When I could be the artist? I do love
Humanity and in a monarchy
I may love no one but myself.

That which your majesty would spread abroad
Through these hands — is that the bliss of man? —
Is that the bliss, that my pure love doth grant
To all mankind? — Before this happiness
Your majesty would tremble — No! A new
One's been created by Crown policy —
A bliss, which *it's* still rich enough to spread,
And in the heart of mankind new desires,
Which by this happiness are satisfied.
Upon its coins it lets the truth be struck,
The truth, which it can tolerate. All stamps
Which don't resemble this one are rejected.

gard to his own time, the eighteenth century; it referred to the sixteenth century, and the proof of its correctness was seen in the fact that in the sixteenth century only a few secluded armchair philosophers advocated freedom of thought. If Schiller had maintained this view with regard to his own age, too, we would not qualify him as a liberal but as a supporter of despotism.

Our task is to prevent a Third World War. This task requires immediate action. We cannot prevent the outbreak of a new war in 1960 by a free trade policy postponed to the year 1970 or 2000.

VI

It is a thankless job indeed to express such radical and "subversive" opinions, and to incur the hatred of all supporters of the old system which has amply proved its inexpediency. But it is not the duty of an economist to be fashionable and popular; he has to be right. Those timid souls who fear challenging spurious doctrines and superstitions because they have the support of influential circles will never improve conditions. Let them call us "orthodox"; it is better to be an intransigent orthodox than an opportunist time-server.

And yet, is that which profiteth the Crown—
Enough for me? May my fraternal love
Be lent to the encroachment of my brother?
Know I he's happy—ere he's free to think?
Do not select me, Sire, to circulate
That happiness which *you* have coin'd for us.
I must decline, to circulate these stamps.—
I can not be the servant of a Prince.

I'm dang'rous, for I've thought beyond myself.—
I am not one my King. My wishes here
Are mouldering. The rage so ludicrous
For innovation, which doth but increase
The weight of chains it can not fully break.
Will *my* blood ne'er inflame. The century
Is not yet ripe for my ideal. I live
A citizen of those, which are to come."—Ed.]

CHAPTER V

Aspects of American Foreign Trade Policy[1]

I   *Physical Conditions*

The natural conditions of production in the United States are more favorable than in any other country, with the sole exception of Russia. (But
Russia does not count at all on the world market of industrial products
and only little in the export of raw materials. Thanks to the anticapitalist policy of the Czars and to the inadequacy of communist methods of
production, it is one of the most backward countries.) In most branches
of production, the input of capital and labor required for the production of one unit of a product is lower in the United States than abroad.
Only foodstuffs and raw materials, such as rubber, wool, coffee, tea,
cocoa, and some metals are produced in other countries at lower physical costs.

II   *Capital Supply*

The United States is the richest country with regard to capital. This means
that the equipment of the country's productive apparatus (machinery and
so on) is greater per unit than abroad.

1 [This paper was delivered as a lecture at the New York University Faculty Club on March
15, 1943. — Ed.]

III *Effects of* Laissez-faire, Laissez-passer

In a world of perfect *laissez-faire, laissez-passer,* there prevails a tendency toward a concentration of capital and labor in those areas that offer the most favorable conditions for production. Capital and labor have the tendency to move to those places where the physical input required for the production of one unit is lowest. Capital and labor are not equally distributed among all the parts of a geographical area and have a tendency to move to the places offering the most favorable conditions for the various branches of production. The same forces that bring about this result within each country would, in a world of perfectly free trade, bring about a similar international distribution of capital and labor.

IV *Foreign Investment*

In the course of the nineteenth century, the capitalists got the conviction that they could safely invest their capital in foreign countries. They considered the risk involved in foreign investments as only slightly higher than that involved in domestic investments of the same class. Thus the capitalists of Western Europe provided the capital needed for a modern equipment of the apparatus of production of the then economically backward countries.

Experience with foreign investments has not been propitious. Except for investments made in the Anglo-Saxon countries and in some smaller European countries, the greater part of the exported capital was lost or will most probably be lost in the near future. Nowadays, almost all debtor countries are anxious to expropriate the foreign capitalist. Bonds are either openly repudiated or rendered valueless for the owner by means of inflation, currency devaluation, foreign exchange control, or confiscatory taxation. Foreign property is liable to discriminatory taxation or undisguised confiscation. The prejudice against foreign capital is so firmly and universally accepted by public opinion that the governments of the creditor nations sometimes encourage the debtor nations' policy of expropriating their own citizens' titles.[2]

In the postwar world, the United States will be more or less the only

---

2 [See Chapter II, "Postwar Economic Reconstruction of Europe," footnote 5.—Ed.]

country that could possibly export large amounts of capital. But the American capitalist will shun foreign loans and investments. Once bitten, twice shy.

Notwithstanding the tremendous capital consumption brought about by the war, by inflation, and by some cherished policies, on the one hand, and the urgent need for capital for the readjustment of American industries for peacetime production, on the other, the United States will be, after the war, the country comparatively best equipped with capital. America's technical preponderance will be much greater than in the past. Its superiority over all other countries—perhaps with the exception of Canada and Sweden—will be enormous. All other industrial countries will completely lack the means to keep pace with America.

V Discrepancies in Wage Rates

In a world of perfect mobility of labor, there prevails a tendency toward an equalization of the price of labor. Workers move from areas in which the productivity of labor—and, therefore, wages—are lower, to areas in which they are higher.

All countries—not only the United States—have erected immigration barriers preventing the competition of immigrant labor on the domestic labor market. Thus the gulf separating the comparatively overpopulated countries from the comparatively underpopulated countries cannot be bridged. The discrepancies in wage rates and standards of living are perpetuated.[3]

VI Foreign Trade and Costs of Production

International trade is possible only if the costs of production are lower in the exporting countries than in the importing countries.

There are people who say that import duties are required in order to render competition fair, to deprive foreign producers of the advantage which they derive from lower costs of production, and to equalize conditions for domestic and foreign production. The consistent application of

3 [See Chapter I, "Postwar Reconstruction," footnote 18.—Ed.]

this principle would necessarily lead to a total exclusion of imports and, consequently, to the perfect autarky (economic isolation) of each country.

Goods can be imported only if they are produced abroad at lower costs. Commodities can be imported from Thule into Atlantis only if either the national conditions of production are more favorable in Thule, or if Thule compensates unfavorable conditions of production by lower wage rates.

The predominantly industrial countries of Europe can neither feed nor clothe their population from domestic foodstuffs and raw materials. They have to pay for the imports of those items by the export of manufactures. Most of these manufactures are produced from imported raw materials. Although their physical costs of production are higher than for competing industries of other countries, they have to undersell on the world market. They can only compete by paying lower wages.

The conditions of some of these European countries—especially those of Great Britain—were in the past, to some extent, less unfavorable because they had foreign investments in the predominantly agricultural countries. Part of the foodstuffs and raw materials needed came into these European countries as payment of interest and as dividends, as it were. In the postwar era, Great Britain—with the greater part of its foreign assets gone either as a means for financing the war or by the default of the debtor nations—will not be much better off than the poor European countries were already in prewar days.

The United States, too, depends on some imports of food and raw materials. Some commodities that the Americans would not like to miss cannot be produced at all in this country, or only at unreasonably higher costs. America could withdraw from international trade only to the serious prejudice of its standard of living.

VII   *Protection for Whom?*

It would be idle to discuss American business conditions under the assumption that the immigration barriers were to be removed. A realistic investigation of postwar problems must take for granted that immigration will be kept at a very low level.

The restriction of immigration results in higher wages. The potential market wage rates, that is, wage rates as they would be established without any pressure and compulsion exercised on the part of the government or trade unions, will remain at a higher level than those of a hypothetical state of free immigration. (We will have to deal later with the effects of union policies.)

Under this assumption, we have to ask: "Protection for whom? Which section of the population is interested in American anti-import policies? What are their economic, social, and political consequences?"

VIII *Protection for Farmers*

It is obvious that American business is not interested in a policy of high prices for agricultural products.

In the absence of government measures designed to keep the prices of farm products at a higher level than those established on an unhampered market, prices would fall and domestic consumption of farm products would increase. But there is no doubt that many farmers would have to restrict their production or give up production completely. This would result in an inflow of hands [workers] into the market for industrial labor and in a tendency to lower potential wage rates in manufacturing.

It is not true that industry would suffer because the farmers would restrict their buying of manufactures. Counteracting any possible decline in the purchase of manufactured goods by farmers would be: (a) the increased purchasing of consumers who will be spending less for food; (b) the increased purchasing of former farmers and farmhands who will, under these changed conditions, be working in industry; (c) the increased purchasing on the part of the foreign importers of farm products, (for instance, Argentina).

The artificial increase of domestic farm commodity prices is virtually a subsidy paid on the part of the nonagricultural sector of the nation to the advantage of the agricultural sector. It is vain to describe it as a benefit to industry on the grounds that the farmers spend their additional income on buying manufactures. If a grocer makes a man a gift of ten dollars, the gift still remains an expense of the giver and a benefit for the receiver, even if the latter spends the whole amount in buying groceries in the benefactor's shop.

Agriculture was once the nation's most important export trade. Conditions have changed to the disadvantage of American farming because impoverished Europe must restrict its purchases and because other competitors have become stronger (for instance, Canada and Argentina in the

market for wheat). A readjustment of American farming to actual conditions is unavoidable. Government interference can delay it only for a time
and will prolong the hardships of the period of transition and adaptation.

IX   Operation of the Law of Comparative Costs

American processing industries would not need protection in a state of
laissez-faire, even if there were immigration barriers. They are — but for
some special branches, like Paris dressmaking or English cloth — paramount in the world. Natural conditions of production are extremely favorable in the United States: The supply of capital is more abundant than
anywhere else, the ingenuity of the entrepreneurs, the efficiency of the in-
ventors and designers, and the skill of the workers, are unsurpassed. The
technical equipment of American factories and the methods of business
management and marketing are unparalleled.

This does not mean that, in a world of perfect free trade, America
would not import anything and, consequently, not export anything. There
are foodstuffs and raw materials which cannot be produced at all at home
or only at much higher costs. There is tourism, which will expand the
more the living standard of the Americans improves.

But even if we abstract from the exports destined to pay for these outlays and from capital export, we have to realize that America would not develop all branches of industry in a uniform way. The Ricardian law of
comparative costs has demonstrated in an irrefutable way that it is advantageous for every country to concentrate its efforts upon the expansion of
those branches of production in which its superiority is highest and to import commodities in whose production its superiority is comparatively
lower, even though these, too, could be produced at home under more favorable conditions than abroad.[4]

Under free trade for products and capital and immigration barriers for

4 [The theory of comparative advantage was formulated in 1817 by the classical economist
David Ricardo (1772–1823) in "On the Principles of Political Economy and Taxation," in
Piero Sraffa, ed., *The Works and Correspondence of David Ricardo*, Vol. I (Cambridge:
Cambridge University Press, 1951), pp. 128–49; see also Ludwig von Mises, *Human Action:
A Treatise on Economics*, (Irvington-on-Hudson, N.Y.: Foundation for Economic Educa-
tion, 4th rev. ed., 1996), pp. 159–64; and Gottfried Haberler, *The Theory of International
Trade, with Its Applications to Commercial Policy* (London: William Hodge and Co., 1936),
pp. 125–208. — Ed.]

labor, there would prevail in America a tendency to prefer those branches of manufacturing in which wages form a smaller part of the total costs of production. The country would favor more the expansion of the heavy industries and less those branches which require comparatively more labor. The resulting imports would bring about neither bad business nor unemployment. They would be compensated by an increase in the export of goods which can be produced to the highest advantage in this country. They would raise the standard of living both in America and abroad.

Of course, an abrupt abandonment of protectionism would inflict many hardships upon those branches of American manufacturing which would shrink under free trade. It would be poor consolation for those affected that other branches of business will profit. But, let us not forget, that all branches of American industry are on the eve of a period in which they will have to readjust radically their methods of management and their equipment in order to meet the requirements of postwar markets. In such a period of transition it would be easier to execute the changes necessary for free trade business.

X   Unemployment

On the unhampered market, prices are set at the point at which the amount of the commodity which the buyers will take is equal to the amount which the sellers will sell. Everybody who is prepared to pay the market price can buy as much as he wants, and everybody who is prepared to take the market price can sell as much as he wants.

The same is true for the market price of labor, for wage rates. There is always some amount of voluntary unemployment because there are workers who do not want the jobs which are offered them and are waiting for better opportunities. But, on the unhampered market, unemployment is more or less a transitory phenomenon. There is no serious problem of unemployment, there is no mass unemployment prolonged year after year.[5]

But it is different if—either by government decree or by trade union pressure—wages are fixed at a higher rate than that which the unham-

---

5 [On the causes for unemployment in the market economy, see Mises, *Human Action*, pp. 587–634; also W. H. Hutt, *The Theory of Idle Resources* (Indianapolis: Liberty Fund, [1939] 1977).—Ed.]

pered market would have fixed. Then the demand for labor shrinks and permanent unemployment of a part of the potential labor force results.[6]

The concept of "full employment" is a demagogic slogan if it does not refer to a definite wage rate. There is but one means to obtain full employment: to abstain from the enforcement of minimum wage rates higher than the potential market rates. Mass unemployment is not, as the socialists would have us believe, a phenomenon inherent in capitalism. It is, on the contrary, the result of the endeavors to sabotage capitalism by government or trade union interference.

All the other methods suggested for the attainment of full employment are ineffectual.

Noninflationary government spending (i. e., not financed by additional credit expansion or by the issue of additional bank notes) absorbs capital or, if financed by income taxation, income which would have been invested or spent otherwise. It abolishes, on the one hand, as many jobs as it creates on the other.

Inflation, credit expansion, and currency devaluation are only successful if money wage rates lag behind the rise in commodity prices, i. e., if they result in a fall in real wage rates.

Labor service (*Arbeitsdienst*, the favorite means of totalitarian governments) compensates the viciously higher wages of the workers employed in private industry at union rates by viciously lower wages of the men employed in "emergency" public works.[7]

If it is made illegal for employers to discharge employees whom they cannot employ gainfully, the enterprises suffer losses and are forced to consume a part of their capital. The government succeeds in the short run, but, in the long run, a more drastic fall in wage rates becomes inescapable.

Such are the long-run consequences of manipulating wage rates by decree or by trade union compulsion. Let us turn to the short-run consequences.

6 [On the prolonged unemployment of the 1930s, see Ludwig von Mises, "The Causes of the Economic Crisis" (February 1931) in Percy L. Greaves, ed., *Von Mises, On the Manipulation of Money and Credit* (Dobbs Ferry, N.Y.: Free Market Books, 1978), pp. 173–203; see also Richard K. Vedder and Lowell E. Gallaway, *Out of Work: Unemployment and Government in Twentieth-Century America* (New York/London: Holmes and Meier, 1993); and Kent Matthews and Dan Benjamin, *U. S. and U. K. Unemployment Between the Wars: A Doleful Story* (London: Institute of Economics Affairs, 1992).—Ed.]

7 [On wages and standards of living under the Nazi economy in Germany, see Gustav Stolper, *The German Economy: 1870 to the Present* (London: Weidenfeld and Nicolson, 1967, pp. 150–52.—Ed.]

XI   *Trade Unionism under Free Trade*

Every attempt to raise wage rates above the point established on the unhampered labor market disarranges the conditions of competition. If there is free trade and the rise is limited to one country only, as is normally the case, foreign competitors whose costs have not changed find it easier to underbid the domestic producers. Under free trade, the undesired effects of minimum wage rate policies would appear immediately. The domestic entrepreneurs would be soon forced to restrict their production and consequently to dismiss workers. It would become obvious for trade union members that union methods are not an appropriate means to improve their standard of living.

It is different if foreign competition is barred by import duties. Then the entrepreneurs can raise prices without being menaced by foreign competition. The harmful consequences of the wage raise are either delayed for a short time or disguised in such a way that the laymen do not see them. If prices are raised to such a height that the wage earners' gains are absorbed by the consumers' losses, real wage rates remain unchanged and the undesirable consequences of union policy do not appear. But the whole nation suffers on account of the fall of the productivity of labor resulting from the partial withdrawal from the international division of labor.

The function of protectionism in an industrially efficient country is to mask the effects of unionism. Trade unions would never have acquired their present-day prestige if every wage rise attained by strikes and violence against strikebreakers had immediately and visibly resulted in the dismissal of a part of those employed.

XII   *Business and the Tariff*

It follows that American big business is not interested in the maintenance of protection. The greater the role played in any branch of business by material equipment in relation to the amount of labor employed, the greater will American superiority be in the postwar period. The German and the British metallurgical and chemical works will be seriously handicapped by the shortage of domestic capital and by the difficulty of providing foreign capital.

Conditions will be different only with those branches of American industries in which labor costs are the most important item in the total costs of production.

It is true that free trade will lower American prices by preventing their rise above the world market level. But on the other hand, it will lower wage rates, too.

As a whole, the nation would profit from free trade, provided only that the postwar readjustment of the country's industrial apparatus is effected with regard to free trade conditions.

If there is a section of the population whose "class interests" require protectionism, it is certainly not business, but rather employed trade union members (as distinguished from the unemployed) and farmers. They should be charged in the eyes of public opinion with the responsibility for a policy which necessarily leads to high prices for consumers' goods.

XIII *America and European Reconstruction*

The usual way of representing the problems of American postwar policy with regard to international relations is to speak of an alternative: isolation and national egoism on the one hand, and sacrificing national interests for the cause of foreign nations on the other. This way of viewing the matter is, however, not correct.

First of all, we have to realize that America can do very little for the reconstruction of broken-down Europe and for a return to sound, peaceful conditions. The problem of European reconstruction is primarily a problem of mentalities and ideologies—a moral issue—and not an economic and financial problem. What Europe needs most urgently is the substitution of a mentality of peaceful cooperation for their mutual hatreds and antagonisms. The prewar state of affairs was one in which every nation, even the smallest one, waged a permanent economic war against all other nations. Every nation was anxious to inflict as much evil as it could upon foreigners and domestic minorities, in the form of tariffs, the quota system, foreign exchange control, and so on.

In the greater part of Europe, every nation considered all its neighbors as deadly foes and was ready to profit from every occasion in order to rob them of a part of their territory. For instance, take the case of Poland which, in the twenty-one years of its national autonomy, seized by the use of arms territories belonging to three neighboring states, namely, Russia, Lithuania, and Czechoslovakia.[8] America could occupy the European continent

8 [In 1920–21, Poland fought a war with Soviet Russia, during which it occupied and annexed large territories predominantly populated by Ukrainians and Belorussians; in 1920,

and rule it according to the principles applied by Great Britain in India. But even this undemocratic policy, which nobody recommends, would not mean more than a temporary solution. Europe's rebirth must come from within; it cannot be enforced upon reluctant or indifferent peoples by a foreign army and by foreign administrators and educators.

It is vain to look for new institutions or for new constitutional devices. What is needed first is not a new covenant for the League of Nations or a European federation but a radical change of mentalities. Only an extermination of the spirit of violence, conquest, and oppression can save European civilization.

It is not true that America can aid Europe's reconstruction by granting large credits. In the years between the two world wars many billions of dollars flowed from America to Europe.[9] Some governments used these credits for the prolongation of a policy of wasteful spending, other governments — foremost among them the German Reich — for rearmament. Perhaps Europe would have been better off without any American credits. At any rate, they did not further Europe's prosperity. America lost its money, that is certain, too.

America has paid a high price indeed for its ignorance of European conditions. If the American bankers and investors had been better informed, they would not have lent any money to governments and government agencies which consider it as patriotic to repudiate foreign loans. They would not have provided the German Reich with a part of the funds required for rearmament. In the twenties, more financial isolation on the part of America would have served better the cause of peaceful reconstruction.

It is a pity that German books are not better known abroad. Already more than forty years ago the intellectual leaders of imperial Germany — the professors Gustav von Schmoller and Adolph Wagner — frankly declared that the main goal of German twentieth-century policies was the establishment of a great German dominion in South America, and that the "vain pretensions" of the Monroe Doctrine would not prevent them from accomplishing this task. The Nazis did not build up a new doctrine;

Poland occupied and seized a portion of eastern Lithuania; in 1938 (following the Munich agreement that dictated the partial dismemberment of Czecholovakia), Poland annexed a strip of Czech territory surrounding the city of Teschen. — Ed.]

9 [Between 1925 and 1930, the United States lent European nations $4.3 billion. Of that total, $1.65 billion went to Germany. — Ed.]

they only gave a new name to doctrines which were already paramount in Germany at the end of the nineteenth century.[10]

In view of the attitudes of Germany (and of Japan, too), political isolation of the Western hemisphere is unfeasible. Conflicts in Europe and Asia must sooner or later implicate America, too. The establishment of two big totalitarian empires, one on the other side of the Atlantic, the other on the other side of the Pacific, would threaten America's independence in a dreadful way. Japanese rule of Australia or German control of the French and Spanish coastlines would be intolerable for this country. America fights this war for its own future, not only for the sake of the other democracies. In this age of international division of labor and of air power, each country's destiny is linked with the fate of the rest of the world.

XIV Business and Socialism

In dealing with the question of what the genuine interests of business are, we have to distinguish between interests with regard to the fundamental problem of social organization and interests with regard to economic policies within the framework of a society based on private ownership of the means of production and private enterprise (capitalism or the market society).

The first problem is in our day mostly dealt with from the viewpoint of Marxist ideas. According to this doctrine, there prevails an irreconcilable conflict between the interests of the exploiting classes and those of the exploited. Only the exploiters (capitalists, entrepreneurs, and owners of large landed properties) are interested in the preservation of capitalism, which gives them the unfair privilege to withhold a part of the income that should duly be distributed to the workers. On the other hand, the class interests of the proletarians ask for the establishment of the socialist commonwealth, that is, for the substitution of public control of business for private enterprise.

If this doctrine were correct, the cause of capitalism would be hopeless. A minority could not succeed in imposing lastingly on the majority a system of social organization that serves only its own selfish interests at the expense of the majority.

It is not the task of these cursory statements to prove anew that the so-

10 [See Chapter I, "Postwar Reconstruction," pp. 9–10.—Ed.]

cialist doctrine is entirely wrong and that capitalism is the only system which can supply the masses with all the commodities required for a really human way of life. This is the task of economic theory, and it has been fulfilled.[11]

It is not true that the preservation of private enterprise—one should rather say, the return to private enterprise through the abandonment of the attempts to impose government control on business—serves only the selfish class interests of the "bourgeoisie." Everyone, without any exception, comes off much better under capitalism than under socialism.

When businessmen oppose measures designed to bring about socialism (central planning), they do not embark upon class struggle and they do not fight for selfish interests. They simply do their duty as citizens.

XV   Business under Protectionism

The unhampered market is a democracy in which every penny gives a right to vote.[12] Its operation forces the capitalists and the entrepreneurs to adjust their activities to the consumers' demand. The consumers decide through their buying and abstention from buying what should be produced and in what quality and quantity. A businessman who is slow in adjusting his production to the demands of the consumers suffers losses and will, if he does not change his methods, finally be outstripped by more efficient

11 [See Ludwig von Mises, *Socialism* (Indianapolis: Liberty Fund, [1951] 1981); *Liberalism in the Classical Tradition* (Irvington-on-Hudson, N.Y., and San Francisco, Calif.: Foundation for Economic Education and Cobden Press, [1927] 1985), pp. 70–75; *Human Action*, pp. 698–715; F. A. Hayek, *Individualism and Economic Order* (Chicago: University of Chicago Press, 1948), pp. 119–208; Trygve J. B. Hoff, *Economic Calculation in the Socialist Society* (Indianapolis: Liberty Fund, [1949] 1981); Murray N. Rothbard, "Ludwig von Mises and Economic Calculation under Socialism," (1976) in *The Logic of Action*, Vol. I (Lyme, N.H.: Edward Elgar, 1997), pp. 397–407; Don Lavoie, *Rivalry and Central Planning: The Socialist Calculation Debate Reconsidered* (New York: Cambridge University Press, 1985); and Richard M. Ebeling, "Economic Calculation under Socialism: Ludwig von Mises and His Predecessors," in Jeffrey M. Herbener, ed., *The Meaning of Ludwig von Mises* (Norwell, Mass.: Kluwer Academic Press, 1993), pp. 56–101.—Ed.]

12 [See Frank A. Fetter, *The Principles of Economics* (New York: Century Co., 1904), p. 394: "Every buyer then determines in some degree the direction of industry. The market is a democracy where every penny gives a right to vote."—Ed.]

men. Production for profit means consumers' sovereignty.[13] In the management of business, the entrepreneur is an intermediary only. The real bosses are the consumers whose wants the entrepreneurs are bound to satisfy as efficiently as the state of technological knowledge and the available factors of production will allow.

People are merciless as consumers. They do not care about the vested interests of capital or of labor. When technological progress offers them a new method of enjoyment, they turn to the novelty and abandon the old. They are eager to buy on the cheapest market. They are continuously driving business to their utmost effort.

The absence of any privilege for the less efficient producer is a characteristic feature of modern capitalism. In the Middle Ages, production was regulated by statute. The guilds had the right to bar access to trade to every nonmember, to force their members to cling to traditional old-fashioned methods of production, and to prevent selling at lower prices than those fixed by them in a monopolistic way. The abolition of this system paved the way for the unprecedented economic progress of the age of steam and electricity. It was America's great chance that the colonists did not bring with them from the old country any plans for restrictions on business.

A privilege protecting an entrepreneur or a group of entrepreneurs against the competition of people producing cheaper and better products furthers, at the expense of the rest of the people, the class interests of this branch of production, provided that the access to this branch is restricted. If everybody is free to enter this field of business, the privilege is of temporary value only; the inflow of additional entrepreneurs will bring down excessive earnings to normal levels.

A privilege serves the class interests of those privileged only if the other classes are not privileged at all or not to the same extent. If all are privileged to the same degree, everybody loses, as a consumer, what he has profited as a producer. But that is not all. Every member of the community is hurt by the restrictions imposed on improved and cheapened production.[14]

13 [On the concept of "consumers' sovereignty," see W. H. Hutt, *Economists and the Public* (London: Jonathan Cape, 1936), pp. 257–72; and Hutt, "The Concept of Consumers' Sovereignty," *Economic Journal* (March 1940), pp. 66–77; also Mises, *Human Action*, pp. 269–72.—Ed.]

14 [See Mises, "The Clash of Group Interests" [1945] in Richard M. Ebeling, ed., *Money, Method, and the Market Process: Essays by Ludwig von Mises* (Norwell, Mass.: Kluwer Academic Press, 1990), pp. 202–14.—Ed.]

It is a mistake to believe that the interests of all manufacturers, with regard to protectionism, are uniform.

No manufacturer can profit from a tariff which imposes import duties in an equal amount on all foreign goods. What he gains in selling his products is absorbed by the higher prices which he has to pay for his equipment, for the semimanufactured articles, and for the raw materials and by the higher prices of consumers' goods. It is true that some branches of production can expand while they would shrink under free trade. But, on the other hand, some branches which would expand under free trade, have to shrink. The result—a fall of imports and a corresponding fall of exports—does not favor anybody. On the contrary, the whole nation suffers because the average productivity of capital and labor declines, as commodities have to be produced in places which are less fit for these purposes.

If protection is granted to some branches of manufacturing only, the short-run interests of those who have already invested in this branch are favored. But in the long run, they will lose their advantage by the competition of new factories.

It is not true that it is an advantage for a nation to replace imports by domestic products. With the present state of technology, it would be possible for Great Britain or for Canada to prohibit the import of grapes and coffee and to grow them in hothouses. Everybody would qualify this as lunacy. But it differs only in degree, not in principle, from other protectionist schemes. Just as the cheapest way for the British to provide coffee and grapes for themselves is to produce cloth for export, so the cheapest way for Americans to get handmade embroideries is to export motorcars and fountain pens.

The popularity of protectionism is due to the error that imports can be reduced without a corresponding restriction of exports.

If we abstract from foreign investments, we have to realize that a rise of imports, of tourists' expenditures abroad, and of services received from foreign countries means that the nation's material well-being is improving and that the nation is rich enough to pay with exports for what it wants to buy abroad.

It is not true that imports create domestic unemployment or lower the domestic standard of living. As imports have to be paid by exports, they do not restrict the volume of domestic production. Free-trade channels production into those lines in which its net return is highest. A free-trade America would, for instance, import tablecloths from China and pay by exporting motorcars.

All this is valid, whatever the foreign trade policies of foreign countries are. America would profit from free trade even if all other nations cling to protection.[15] If, for instance, France erects trade barriers against American imports, it will reduce American purchases of French products, unless France does not import from countries to which American exports exceed American imports.

Thanks to the fact that America offers, on the average, the most favorable physical conditions of production and that it is richer in capital than the other countries, and thanks to the immigration barriers, potential market wage rates will be higher than in the rest of the world, perhaps with the exception of Australia and New Zealand. The only reason which could be brought forward in favor of protection is that protection disguises—but without removing it—the futility of all methods of raising by an alleged prolabor policy the standard of living of *all* wage-earners above the level that makes for full employment.

XVI *Trade Union Principle versus Market Price Principle*

America's main postwar problem will be the clash of the trade union principle and the market-price principle. A good deal of the nation's capital will be consumed by the war effort. It will be impossible to provide the bulk of the nation with all the commodities needed for the maintenance of the prewar standard of living before the re-equipment of factories with new machinery is accomplished. A serious lowering of real wage rates and of the standard of living for a period of transition is unavoidable. If boom wage rates are to be preserved, mass unemployment will result and the reconstruction of the domestic apparatus of production will be hindered.

Public opinion is under the spell of trade union ideology. Wage cuts are considered as out of the question, and unemployment is considered as the evidence of capitalism's failure. The slogan "freedom from want" fascinates the masses. Nobody tells them that capitalist America has succeeded better in fighting want than the totalitarian countries of Europe. Article 118 of the Constitution of the USSR gives all Russians the right to

---

15 [On the arguments of the classical economists for a policy of unilateral free trade, see Richard M. Ebeling, "The Global Economy and Classical Liberalism: Past, Present, and Future," in Richard M. Ebeling, ed., *The Future of American Business* (Hillsdale, Mich.: Hillsdale College Press, 1996), pp. 9–60.—Ed.]

receive employment "with compensation measured by the quantity and quality of their work." But the standard of living of the Russian worker is much lower than that of the workers of any European country, to say nothing of America.

It is of no use to indulge in illusions. If radical change of ideology does not occur, postwar America will turn toward socialism either of the German or of the Russian pattern.[16]

There is, it is true, a lot of dissatisfaction with the working of the bureaucratic institutions and with the management of trade unions. But people do not indict the system as such—only the men who handle it. They want to abolish the shortcomings of government control and bureaucracy by more government control and more bureaucracy.[17] A reappearance of unemployment, unavoidable if unions do not accept temporary wage cuts, will swell the ranks of radicalism.

Businessmen have an aversion to ideological discussions and to "isms." Thus they left the field of theoretical discussion to the self-styled progressives and surrendered mentally to anticapitalist doctrines. Our contemporaries call "progressive" every step toward more government interference, and "democratic" all policies restricting the jurisdiction of voters and parliamentary institutions and vesting more powers in bureaucrats; they disparage private business and make it the scapegoat for all evils. They call "social gains" the policies which resulted in mass unemployment.

Every experience is today interpreted from the point of view of an anticapitalist bias. The poverty of the Russian masses is either passed over in silence or explained as the consequence of the "capitalism" of czarism or of the animosity of Western capital. America's high standard of living is—in the light of these interpretations—a phenomenon which occurred in spite of capitalism. Armaments and war are the outcome of the machinations of the "merchants of death";[18] but at the same time, the same people blame American and British business and finance for its appeasement policy.

16 [On the similarities and differences between the Nazi and Soviet forms of planning, see Chapter III, "Europe's Economic Structure and the Problem of Postwar Reconstruction," footnote 13.—Ed.]

17 [See Ludwig von Mises, *Bureaucracy* (New Haven: Yale University Press, 1944).—Ed.]

18 [This refers to the book by H. C. Engelbracht, *Merchants of Death: A Study of the International Armament Industry* (New York: Dodd, Mead and Co., 1934), which argued that wars were instigated by armament manufacturers trying to stimulate business for their wares.—Ed.]

No political party can change the trend toward all-round government control and full socialism if such doctrines remain supreme. The fate of Western civilization depends on whether or not a radical ideological reversal occurs.

There is no such thing possible today as the political isolation of a nation. America's peaceful life is no longer sheltered behind a wall of waves since the airplane has become the foremost weapon of aggressors. Economic isolation would only hurt the economic well-being of the nation. But ideological isolation, that is, the abandonment of the Russian and Prussian doctrines of state omnipotence, would serve best America's own interests and at the same time set an example to the rest of the world.

XVII *Concord and Conflict of Group Interests*

Within the unhampered market society there is no conflict between the interests of the various branches of business and trade or between the interests of various individuals. That some people can make profits by supplying their fellow citizens with better and cheaper commodities does not harm the consumer; it benefits him.

But things are different if privileges are granted to people who cannot stand competition on the unhampered market. Then the particular interests of these privileged come into conflict with the interests of the rest of the nation. The political scene degenerates into a race for privileges. Every group is anxious to secure more privileges than any other group. Political parties become pressure groups fighting for class privileges.

Some groups may profit from such policies of protection. There is no doubt that the owners of submarginal farmland and silver mines as well as some labor autocrats are favored by them. The immense majority of the nation only suffers losses as the total amount of goods available for consumption shrinks.

It is unlikely that some groups of business could, in the long run, succeed in endeavors to be included into the small class really profiting from privileges. The anticapitalist bias of public opinion will ask for a confiscation of business profits originating from protective tariffs. Protection for manufacturing owes its popularity only to the belief that it is a means to reduce unemployment. Nothing is more unpopular nowadays than business profits. People are intent on confiscating them by taxation or on making them disappear by price control.[19]

It will not be an easy task to defeat these tendencies. But it will be impossible if the radicals are able to provide their claims with an appearance of justification by pointing out that a few enterprises owe their profitability to the working of tariffs.

The main justification of private enterprise is that it serves best the well-being of the nation. But public opinion will be reluctant to acknowledge this fact if it realizes that business, too, is asking for government interference in order to keep prices high.

---

19 [The American economy was placed under a comprehensive system of price controls during the Second World War; see Colin D. Campbell, ed., *Wage-Price Controls in World War II, United States and Germany* (Washington, D.C.: American Enterprise Institute, 1971); and F. A. Harper, "The Crisis of the Free Market," [1945] in *The Writings of F. A. Harper*, Vol. I (Menlo Park, Calif.: Institute for Humane Studies, 1978), pp. 19–129. —Ed.]

CHAPTER VI

A Noninflationary Proposal for Postwar Monetary Reconstruction[1]

I *The Gold Standard*

A ❧ THE GOLD STANDARD AS AN INTERNATIONAL STANDARD

The nineteenth century very successfully set up the gold standard as a monetary international standard. At the beginning of our century, almost all commercially important nations had adopted either the gold standard or the gold-exchange standard as their national standard. Both of these monetary systems tied a particular country's national currency unit to a definite quantity of gold, fixed by a duly promulgated act of that country's legislature. A divergence of the purchasing power of the national currency unit from the purchasing power of its legally fixed gold-parity was effectively prevented. Fluctuations in foreign exchange rates could only arise within definite and very narrow limits; they could not overstep the gold points.[2] These very small fluctuations exclusively concerned the professional dealers in gold and foreign exchange. For all other practical purposes, exchange rates between the currencies of the countries that had adopted either the gold standard or the gold-exchange standard were perfectly stabilized. International trade and commerce, international credit transactions and investments, transportation, and traveling were not hampered by any monetary frictions.

This satisfactory state of affairs was not the outcome of any interna-

1 [This monograph was written by Mises in 1944. — Ed.]

2 [The "gold points" represented the upper and lower limits of fluctuations of a country's foreign exchange value under the gold standard, beyond which it would be profitable to either export gold out of or import gold into that country. — Ed.]

tional treaties, agreements, or conventions, or of the operations of an internationally established institution or bank. It was an achievement of the various national governments acting of their own accord and aiming at nothing else but the most convenient arrangement of their own nation's economic matters. Governments were eager to stabilize foreign exchange rates because they considered such stability as beneficial for their own people's economic well-being. A sound money policy was not designed as a policy for the benefit of foreign interests, but as a policy highly beneficial for a country's own welfare.

There were, it is true, in the course of the nineteenth century various attempts toward the establishment of an international monetary or even of a world monetary union. Some of these plans were actually put into effect.[3] The most conspicuous case was the Latin Monetary Union inaugurated in 1865. Its episodic existence was not of great avail. It did not render any considerable service to the cause of monetary stability. Eventually, the First World War gave it the finishing blow.[4]

The reasons for this failure are obvious. The maintenance of monetary stability requires an adequate conduct of domestic economic policies; misguided domestic economic policies bring about conditions that must result in a depreciation of a country's currency and in a rise of its foreign exchange rates. Such was the case of France in 1871 and of France and Belgium in 1914, not to mention Greece and Italy.[5] A monetary union is futile if it does not give to a governing board of such a union full control of each

3 [See Henry B. Russell, *International Monetary Conferences: Their Purposes, Character, and Results* (New York: Harper and Brothers, 1898).—Ed.]

4 [The Latin Monetary Union was created by convention between France, Belgium, Switzerland, and Italy on December 23, 1865. Its purpose was to stabilize the exchange value between gold and silver coins used in their respective economies, following the fall in the market value of gold resulting from the increase in gold supplies in the 1850s and 1860s. The union was terminated formally on December 31, 1926, due to national inflationary policies and their consequences during and following the First World War.—Ed.]

5 [During the Franco-Prussian War (1870–71) the French government suspended specie for outstanding notes of the Bank of France beginning on August 12, 1870. It did not resume specie payments until January 1, 1878. During the First World War, France again resorted to inflationary financing to cover a large portion of its war-related expenditures. It suspended specie payments for notes in 1914 and did not return to a stabilized currency until 1927. During the First World War, Belgium was occupied by Germany, resulting in a suspension of normal financial and monetary dealings.—Ed.]

member state's monetary and banking system and if it does not restrict the national sovereignty of its members with regard to other important foreign exchange matters.

B ᴥ THE REQUISITES OF MONETARY STABILITY

The maintenance of the gold standard is possible only if a nation strictly abstains from all endeavors to inflate its currency system, either by the issue of additional paper money or by bank credit expansion. Nothing else is needed. But if, on the contrary, a nation takes recourse to inflation and credit expansion, no scheme, however sophisticated, can prevent a fall in that currency's purchasing power and a general rise in that country's prices, wage rates, and foreign exchange rates.

It is an inveterate mercantilist superstition that an "unfavorable" balance of trade or an "unfavorable" balance of payments can endanger the maintenance of stable rates of foreign exchange.[6] An excess of imports of merchandise over exports is immaterial if it is counterbalanced by other items of the balance of payments. An unfavorable balance of payments, that is, an outflow of gold and foreign exchange results in a restriction on the domestic money market that makes commodity prices drop and rates of interest rise. The fall of domestic commodity prices brings about a restriction of imports and an increase of exports. The rise of interest rates attracts short-term funds from abroad. The deficit of the balance of payments is self-liquidating.

The mercantilist fable owes its present-day prestige mostly to the anti-reparation propaganda of the German nationalists.[7] The payment of repa-

6 [Mercantilism was a system of national economic policy practiced by the leading countries of Western Europe in the sixteenth, seventeenth, and eighteenth centuries. Its leading idea is that unregulated international trade can work to the detriment of a nation, especially if it results in a net outflow of gold, silver, or other precious metals due to an "unfavorable" balance of trade. See Eli Heckscher, *Mercantilism*, 2 vols. (New York: Macmillan Co., 1935).—Ed.]

7 [As part of the Treaty of Versailles ending the First World War between the Allied Powers and Germany, reparations payments were imposed upon Germany as compensation for damages suffered during the conflict. German nationalists and National Socialists argued in the 1920s and early 1930s that heavy financial reparations were forced upon Germany as a means of keeping the country economically and militarily weak and benefiting France and Great Britain.—Ed.]

rations, asserted the German nationalists and their foreign supporters, would necessarily devalue the German currency system. Historical experience does not provide us with an elucidation of the problem, for, as far as the Germans really paid, they did so out of funds borrowed abroad. Yet the case is too important to be passed over in silence.

If the German government had collected (in German Reichsmarks) the amount needed for the reparation payments—about 2.5 percent to 3.5 percent of the German national income—by taxing its citizens, every taxpayer would have been forced to reduce correspondingly his consumption of either German or imported products. In the first case, the prices of domestic products would have dropped, and this would have created a tendency to increase exports and thereby the amount of foreign exchange available. In the second case, an amount of foreign exchange that otherwise would have been used for the purchase of imported goods would have become available. Thus collecting at home the amount of Reichsmarks required for the payment would have automatically provided the quantity of foreign exchange needed for the execution of the *transfer*. An excess of exports over imports was not a prerequisite for the payment of reparations. The fact that a nation makes such payments has the tendency to create such an excess of exports. The *transfer* problem is a spurious problem.[8]

Many people find fault with the gold standard because the maintenance of stable foreign exchange rates is incompatible with an easy money policy and credit expansion. They contend that, but for the gold standard, domestic credit expansion could lower the rate of interest and thus make business more prosperous. The gold standard, they say, does not serve the interests of the many, but of the moneylenders. They violently ask for a policy which, without regard for the maintenance of foreign exchange stability, aims at a continuous credit expansion and at the establishment of permanent boom conditions.

It is true that in a country that does not care about the stability of foreign exchange rates, credit can be easily expanded and rates of interest temporarily lowered. However, the boom thus created cannot last. It must

8 [In the late 1920s, there was a heated debate between the British economist, John Maynard Keynes, on the one hand, and a number of other continental economists, including Bertil Ohlin (Sweden), Jacques Rueff (France), and Gottfried Haberler and Fritz Machlup (Austria), on the other, over the ability of Germany to pay reparations out of its domestic production and currency proceeds from international trade. Keynes basically claimed that Germany did not have the ability to pay; the other economists countered that Germany did. —Ed.]

sooner or later result in a slump and depression with all their disastrous consequences. It is impossible to substitute for nonexistent capital goods the purely fictitious funds of a credit expansion. The rate of interest is a market phenomenon just like commodity prices and wage rates. It cannot be lowered, with unchanged conditions in the supply of capital goods, by the government printing office or by the manipulation of banks. It is not true that the rate of interest is, but for the short initial stage of a credit expansion, lower in the countries with unstable foreign exchange rates. On the contrary, the expectation of further progress in the increase of the quantity of the circulating medium tends to raise the rate of interest. It includes, under these conditions, an anticipation of the loss that the creditor will suffer from the further fall of purchasing power and of the corresponding gain of the debtor.

Credit expansion and inflation tend toward an upward movement of domestic prices and wage rates. If all commodity prices and wage rates were to rise at the same time and to the same extent, even violent changes in the purchasing power of the monetary unit would be economically neutral and would not affect the income and the wealth of the citizens. But this condition can never occur. The rise of prices and wage rates that inflation causes occurs at different times and to different degrees for various kinds of commodities and of labor. Some classes of prices and wages rise more quickly and to a steeper level than others. This unevenness is the main source of the social consequences of inflation.[9]

While inflation is underway, some people enjoy the benefit of higher prices on the goods and services they sell, while the prices on goods and services they buy have not yet risen at all or have not risen to the same extent. These people profit from their fortunate circumstance. Inflation

---

9 [The idea of the "unevenness" or "non-neutral" effects on changes in prices following an increase (or decrease) in the money supply has been a central theme in the Austrian School theory of money, especially in the writings of Ludwig von Mises. See Mises, *The Theory of Money and Credit* (Indianapolis: Liberty Fund, 3rd rev. ed., [1924; 1953] 1981), pp. 160–68 and 225–46; "Monetary Stabilization and Cyclical Policy" (1928) in Percy L. Greaves, ed., *Von Mises, On the Manipulation of Money and Credit* (Dobbs Ferry, N.Y.: Free Market Books, 1978), pp. 78–103; "The Non-Neutrality of Money" [1938] in Richard M. Ebeling, ed., *Money, Method, and the Market Process: Essays by Ludwig von Mises* (Norwell, Mass.: Kluwer Academic Press), pp. 68–77; *Human Action: A Treatise on Economics*, 4th rev. ed. (Irvington-on-Hudson, N.Y.: Foundation for Economic Education, 1996), pp. 398–432. See also F. A. Hayek, *Prices and Production*, 2nd ed. (New York: Augustus M. Kelley, 1967), pp. 1–31 & 129–31.—Ed.]

seems to them "good business" or a "boom," but their gains are always derived from the losses of other sections of the population. The losers are those in the unhappy position of selling commodities and services whose prices have not yet risen at all or not to the same degree as the prices for the things they buy for their own consumption.

Besides, inflation injures the interests of the creditors and benefits the debtors. The higher prices rise, the lower the purchasing power of the principal and of interest payments falls. The dollar that was loaned out could provide more goods and services than the dollar that is repaid.

The unevenness of the price changes brought about by inflation explains why inflation puts a check upon imports and encourages exports. For technical reasons, inflation affects the prices of foreign exchange at an early stage of the price-changing process, at any rate long before all commodity prices and wage rates have been adjusted to the new state of monetary affairs. This means that in the course of the depreciation, foreigners are in the profit-making position while, on the other hand, the domestic residents are in the losing position. Foreigners can buy more of the domestic products of the country that has inflated its currency and have to pay for their purchases by selling a smaller amount of their own products. The inflation-producing country, it is true, exports more, but it receives less for its exports. Inflation forces upon that nation a restriction of consumption. Only people completely blinded by mercantilist fallacies can view such an outcome as advantageous.

There will always be in every country pressure groups eager to harvest a windfall profit from inflation. The selfish class interest of the debtors and of those who hope to be in the profit-making position with regard to the changes of commodity prices and wage rates can be benefited by inflation. But for the immense majority, inflation always works havoc.

In earlier days, the debtors were mostly the poor and the creditors the rich. But in a capitalist society, things are entirely different. It is an atavistic prejudice to assume that a policy tending to favor the debtors at the expense of the creditors is, in our time, a policy to benefit the poor and disadvantage the rich. On the contrary, under present conditions the creditors are mainly to be found among people of moderate income and wealth. Every person who has a savings account with a bank, who owns bonds, who is entitled to a pension or social security allowance, or who has paid for an insurance policy is a creditor. On the other hand, the owners of mortgaged farms and real estate, the owners of common stock of corporations that have issued bonds and debentures or borrowed from the banks, the stock exchange speculators, and the big-scale dealers in commodities are debtors. The immense majority are creditors, while only a minority are debtors.

Inflation was one of the main sources of economic distress from which almost all nations have suffered in the last decades.[10] But these inflations were not the unavoidable outcome of an inductive state of economic and social affairs; they were the result of conscious policies on the part of governments. The instability of foreign exchange rates was not an act of God. It was the consequence of purposeful political action.

C The Two Most Popular Arguments in Favor of Inflation

All pro-inflation arguments are very old. They have been long since exploded by economics. But they are very difficult to oppose and very popular with some people.

Today statesmen and politicians prefer two methods of justifying inflation: the government-spending doctrine and the war doctrine. Both are utterly fallacious.

If a government procures the means needed for an increase of public expenditure by taxation or by borrowing from the funds saved and accumulated by the citizens, it does not add anything to the total amount of expenditure in the country and it does not create new opportunities or jobs. What the government spends is entirely taken from the pockets of the individual citizens and corporations. The spending and investing capacity of the public is curtailed to the same extent to which the spending ability of the government expands.

It has been asserted that government spending is necessary because our economic system has reached that stage of maturity and saturation. The entrepreneurs, it is said, no longer have any use for the savings of the public. Thus idle funds accumulate in the banks while unemployment spreads.[11]

10 [The decades in question were the 1920s, 1930s, and 1940s.—Ed.]

11 [In the 1930s, there emerged a "stagnation thesis," which argued that the U. S. economy had reached a point of economic maturity resulting in a disappearance of technological and industrial innovations. As a consequence, the economy would stagnate. Employment and investment opportunities would become increasingly dependent upon an activist government utilizing monetary and especially fiscal stimulus through deficit spending. The most prominent proponent of the stagnation thesis during this time was

It is true that the opportunity for American savings to go into private enterprise is at the present moment restricted, although it is no less true that the extent of this restriction and the amount of "idle" dollars have been exaggerated in a rather grotesque way. However, this restriction is not due to the evolution of capitalism and free enterprise. It is the result of government policies aiming at the destruction of private enterprise. When the profits of successful business management are confiscated by taxation, only less favorable opportunities are left to the adventurous entrepreneur. In embarking upon a new enterprise, the capitalist faces the risk of loss, but he cannot expect an adequate net profit that could be considered as a sufficient reward for the risks he runs. Where there is no hope of profit left, there cannot be any question of entrepreneurial activity. An honest and conscientious businessman does not borrow other people's money if he cannot expect that the profitability of the project planned will enable him to pay back the interest and principal. The restriction of profits through taxation results in a restriction of business. There is no such thing as capitalism without profits. In feigning a fight against an alleged "strike of capital," governments and politicians are fighting an evil that they themselves have purposely created.

A government may finance its budget deficit by inflation. (This means, in the Anglo-Saxon countries, especially in the U. S., mainly borrowing from the commercial banks; in the continental countries of Europe, it means mainly the issue of additional paper money and of irredeemable legal-tender bank notes.) Then the government puts itself and some groups in the profiteering position and the majority of the population in the losing position. No new material means of production, no new capital goods are added to the wealth and income of the nation. Here, too, the government's additional spending power is entirely derived from the income or capital of its citizens. The nation's material potentialities are not improved a bit.

The same is true in the case of war.

If a nation is under the sad necessity of being forced to resist aggression and to fight a war for the preservation of its liberty and civilization, it must not only sacrifice the lives and the health of its best sons. The conduct of war requires an enormous expenditure. The citizens must curtail their current consumption. They must, moreover, use up a part of the capital ac-

---

Alvin Hansen (1887–1975); see his work *Fiscal Policy and Business Cycles* (New York: W. W. Norton and Co., 1941). For a critical study of the stagnation thesis, see George Terborgh, *The Bogey of Economic Maturity* (Chicago: Machinery and Allied Products Institute, 1945).—Ed.]

cumulated in previous years. In time of war, a huge government expenditure is unavoidable and entirely justified from any point of view.

What a belligerent government needs to fight a war are various products and raw materials at the nation's disposal. At any rate, the citizens have to carry the whole burden temporarily, even if they hope that they will be indemnified after a victory by reparations to be paid by the defeated aggressors. The government must tax the citizens or borrow from the public (not from the commercial banks). The citizens must restrict their consumption and their investments or even hand over to the government a part of their capital.

It is simply not true that the conduct of war forces a government to take recourse to inflation. The amount of material goods available for the provision of the armed forces cannot be increased by inflation. It can only be increased by curtailing the citizen's consumption, by suspending the replacement of equipment used in the processes of production (disinvestment), and by improving and intensifying the methods of production. The volume of production can only be increased by working more, harder, and better. Inflation is not a means to provide more and better weapons. It is only a method of withdrawing the funds needed for the increased government expenditure from the citizens' pockets. As such, it is the alternative both to taxation and to borrowing money from the public.

Whether there is peace or war, inflation as a method of financing government expenditure is always the outcome of a deliberate policy. We do not have to deal with the problem of determining which method of war financing is best. We have only to emphasize that in time of war, too, inflation is neither necessary nor unavoidable. There are, of course, politicians who consider inflation as the lesser evil when compared with a total financing of war expenditures by taxes and loans from the public. These men underrate the danger of domestic unrest brought about by inflation and still more by the futile attempts of the government to fight its unavoidable consequences—the rise of prices and wage rates—through price controls. [12]

D ❧ THE METAL GOLD

The emergence of the gold standard was a historical phenomenon. As such, it cannot be entirely elucidated by factors commonly styled as rational. If things had taken another course, another commodity—for instance, silver—might have been universally accepted as the common medium of

---

12 [On wartime financing of government expenditures and inflation, see also Mises, *Nation, State, and Economy* (New York: New York University Press, [1919] 1983), pp. 151–71.—Ed.]

exchange. Yet, the preeminence assigned to gold is a fact that can be altered, if at all, only at the cost of very troublesome effort.

Such a venture, however, would be quite useless and would mean nothing but a waste of time and labor. There is, as far as we can see today, nothing that would serve the purpose of a common medium of exchange better than does gold. There was nothing wrong with the gold standard. Its merits, not its shortcomings, induced politicians to sabotage it. Of course, the gold standard is not perfect. No human institution is. But it worked quite satisfactorily in the past. It will not prove less satisfactory in the future, provided that people will let it work.

From the viewpoint of domestic economic conditions, the superiority of the gold standard lies in the circumstance that it keeps the monetary unit's purchasing power free from the influence of political parties and pressure groups. The drawback of any system of fiat money is exactly this, that such a standard is liable to arbitrary manipulation on the part of various and changing political party ideologies and policies. Under fiat money, there will always be selfish groups aiming at the attainment of an advantage either through deflation or inflation. Party bias will disorganize the economic structure of the society through monetary experiments. Monetary history, to put it mildly, does not disprove such statements.

If it were possible to discover an uncontested and, indeed, incontestable principle that could be used as an iron rule for the manipulation of purchasing power, it would be possible to eliminate, at least to some extent, the arbitrary character inherent in fiat money manipulation. But this is quite illusory. There are many and various systems for the calculation of index numbers. Each of them has some merits and some defects. There is no method available that could command general recognition. No one method is accepted as the only correct and adequate solution of the problem. And each method yields a different result. Thus an index number system cannot provide a solid and undisputed basis for currency manipulation. It cannot eliminate various arbitrary judgments in its construction and thus silence the voice of numerous greedy pressure groups. In advocating the application of an index number system whose results happen at the moment to provide a quasi-scientific justification of their group interest, every political party will be in a position to allege the favorable doctrines of some economists and statisticians, while their adversaries will quote dissenting opinions of no less renowned experts.[13] There is no means

13 [On the limits and arbitrary elements in the construction of index numbers, see Chapter VII, "The Main Issues in Present-Day Monetary Controversies," in this volume; and

to free a tabular standard from the inherent possibility of purely arbitrary and party-ridden manipulation.[14]

Nothing can be easier than drafting blueprints for some new monetary system. It is the favorite sport of people obsessed by fantasies and the lust for spurious reforms only for the sake of reforming. But the trouble is that all these suggested systems will never be able to meet with the approval of the enemies of the gold standard, provided that they are not methods for the establishment of permanently progressing inflation. The opposition to the gold standard is motivated by the craving for inflation profiteering. What the inflationists aim at is not high prices and wages as such, but a state of affairs in which the prices of the commodities and services they sell rise more quickly than the prices of the commodities and services they buy. With regard to the price of food, it is of no concern to a man whether he earns ten dollars under a food price of ten dollars or twenty dollars under a food price of twenty dollars. What he desires is a situation in which the rise in food prices lags behind the rise in his earnings. When the inflationary movement comes to a standstill and food prices catch up with the rise in his income, he loses the advantage gained and asks for a new inflation. But inflation cannot go on permanently. An endlessly progressing inflation must necessarily end in the complete breakdown of the currency system with all its unfortunate social implications. America's Continental currency in 1781,[15] the French *mandats territoriaux* in 1796,[16]

Mises, *The Theory of Money and Credit*, pp. 219–22; "Monetary Stabilization and Cyclical Policy," pp. 83–89; *Human Action*, pp. 219–23. —Ed.]

14 [A "tabular standard" was popularized by Yale University economist Irving Fisher (1867–1947). It required the elimination of a dollar, which represented a fixed weight of gold. Rather, the gold content of a dollar would be adjusted to reflect a constant purchasing power over goods and services, as calculated by a price index. —Ed.]

15 [Continental currency was comprised of the notes issued by the Continental Congress during the American Revolution to finance the expenses of the war against Great Britain. Their issuance resulted in a high inflation throughout the thirteen colonies. After the Revolution, they were partially redeemed, but at far below face value; see J. Laurence Laughlin, *A New Exposition of Money, Credit and Prices*, Vol. II (Chicago: University of Chicago Press, 1931), pp. 147–67. —Ed.]

16 [During the French Revolution, the revolutionary government issued *assignats*, a form of paper money that generated a high inflation, resulting in the imposition of price and wage controls. In 1795, they were exchangeable for *mandats territoriaux* at the rate of thirty to one. The *mandats* were scrip representing claims to land titles. The *mandats* were soon increased in such quantities that another inflationary process was set in motion. In 1797, the engraving plates for printing *mandats* were destroyed; see Andrew Dickson White, *Fiat Money Inflation in France* (Washington, D.C.: Cato Institute, [1913] 1980); Edwin W.

and the German mark in 1923[17] provide the most conspicuous historical examples.[18]

The return to the gold standard does not at all mean that the devalued currencies should, by means of a deflation, be brought back to the gold parity that they had before the inflation started. It would be needless to enter into a discussion of the considerations that induced Great Britain after the Napoleonic Wars and then again after the First World War to reestablish the prewar and preinflation gold parity of the sterling. Austria (in 1811, 1816, and 1892) and Russia (in 1839 and 1896) chose another method: They tried to stabilize the actual metal parity of their depreciated currencies.[19] After many unsuccessful deflationary experiments, this stabilization method was later adopted by almost all nations. There cannot be any question of this country's returning to the gold parity of the dollar abandoned in 1933.[20] For the United States, a return to the gold standard means the stabilization of the dollar's effective gold value at the time of the reform.

Kemmerer, *Money: The Principles of Money and Their Exemplification in Outstanding Chapters of Monetary History* (New York: Macmillan Co., 1935), pp. 173–97; and Richard M. Ebeling, "Inflation and Controls in Revolutionary France: The Political Economy of the French Revolution," in Stephen Tonsor, ed., *Reflections on the French Revolution* (Washington, D.C., and Hillsdale, Mich.: Regnery Gateway and Hillsdale College Press, 1990), pp. 138–56. — Ed.]

17 [During the First World War, the German government utilized the printing press to finance a large proportion of its war expenditures. But the inflation continued after the war, finally culminating in a hyperinflation that resulted in a complete collapse of the German mark in November of 1923. The two classic studies of the "Great German Inflation" are Frank D. Graham, *Exchange, Prices, and Production in Hyperinflation: Germany, 1920–1923* (New York: Russell and Russell, [1930] 1967) and Constantino Bresciani-Turroni, *The Economics of Inflation: A Study of Currency Depreciation in Postwar Germany, 1914–1923* (New York: Augustus M. Kelley, [1937] 1968). — Ed.]

18 Let us observe incidentally that the fall of a currency system has nothing at all to do with the question of whether a nation is victorious or defeated. The dictum of Karl Helfferich, German secretary of the treasury in the First World War — "The currency of the victor is always the best" — was silly propaganda talk. The American armies were victorious in 1781 and so were the French armies in 1796. [Karl Helfferich (1872–1924) was a prominent German financier, economist, and politician; he was German secretary of the treasury from January 1915 to May 1916. — Ed.]

19 [The Austro-Hungarian empire adopted the gold standard on August 2, 1892; the Russian empire adopted the gold standard on August 10, 1896. — Ed.]

20 [Under the Gold Reserve Law of 1934, the statutory price of an ounce of gold was raised from $20.67 to $35. — Ed.]

Present-day American conditions are, as everyone admits, contrary to the stated political purposes that brought them into existence. It is nonsensical to amass huge quantities of gold in order to bury them. But this state of affairs is not the outcome of the gold standard. It is, on the contrary, the effect of a deliberate anti-gold policy. If the law had not made it a criminal offense for individuals to own gold bullion and coins, the gold would not lie idle and useless in subterranean vaults.[21] It would be in the hands of the citizens and would thus fulfill a very important task: to put a check upon inflation.

If all nations were to agree upon an international currency consisting of international paper money issued by a world bank or of national paper money unconditionally redeemable in deposits with a world bank, it would be necessary to provide for future increases in the amount of this international paper money or of these deposits. If such an expansion of the quantity of the circulating medium were to be prevented for all time, the increasing demand for money, arising from economic progress and the intensification of trade and commerce, would result in a permanent tendency toward falling prices. The system would have a deflationary effect.

But if, on the other hand, a periodical increase of the amount of international paper money or of the deposits with the world bank were to take place, an insoluble problem would arise: How should the additional amount be distributed among various nations? Every group of nations would advocate a mode of repartition that would give them the greatest possible share.

The British plan for the establishment of an international clearing union wants to determine by quota the measure of each member state's right to enjoy the credit facilities provided by assignment through the union. The initial quotas, it suggests, might be fixed by reference to the sum of each country's exports and imports on the average of a period in the past.[22] Now, such a mode of distribution would be rather unfair to the

21 [As part of the New Deal legislative initiatives, by a resolution of Congress on June 5, 1933, gold clauses in all government and private contractual obligations were voided and all Americans were required to turn in their privately held gold for Federal Reserve Notes under penalty of confiscation and imprisonment.—Ed.]

22 [An "International Clearing Union" was proposed by Great Britain on April 8, 1943; the proposal had been prepared primarily by John Maynard Keynes (1883–1946) and was widely known as the "Keynes Plan." The day before, on April 7, 1943, the U. S. Treasury issued a proposal for "An International Stabilization Fund," which was prepared by Harry D. White (1892–1948), assistant secretary of the treasury. It was referred to as the "White Plan." The two plans had in common ideas for (1) an international agency to supervise

United States. This country's foreign trade forms a comparatively smaller part of its total trade than is the case with other countries. If an American buys a commodity from a place two thousand miles away, it is mostly still domestic trade. But if a Swiss or a Dane buys from a place two hundred miles away, it necessarily always means foreign trade. It would be difficult to find a mode of distribution more prejudicial to America.

Each nation will be eager to advocate a mode of distribution that will give it the greatest possible share in the manna of additional fiat money. The industrially backward nations of the East will, for instance, probably favor equal distribution per head of the population, a mode that would be manifestly unfair to the industrially advanced nations. Whatever system may be adopted, all nations would be dissatisfied and will complain of unfair treatment. Serious conflicts will ensue, and the whole scheme will disintegrate very soon.

It has been asserted that the gold standard can no longer work because nations and individuals are no longer prepared to comply with "the rules of the game." However, the gold standard is not a game, but a social institution. Its working does not depend on the readiness of any people to observe some arbitrary rules. It is controlled by the operation of inextricable economic law.

The critics of the gold standard try to give emphasis to their objections by citing the fact that, in the interwar period, a rise in the rate of discount failed to stop the external drain, that is, the outflow of specie and the transfer of deposits into foreign countries. But this phenomenon, too, was caused by the governments' anti-gold and pro-inflation policies. If a man expects that he will lose 40 percent of his deposit by an impending devaluation, he will try to transfer his deposit into another country and will not change his mind merely because the bank rate in the country planning a devaluation rises 1 or 2 percent. Such a rise in the rate of discount is obviously not a compensation for a ten, twenty, or even forty times greater

the level of foreign exchange rates of national currencies, (2) regulatory powers by this international agency to prevent disruptions to international economic equilibrium, (3) provision by this agency for multilateral clearings of participating countries' accounts, and (4) power by this agency to increase the world supply of financial liquidity for facilitation of international payments. The establishment of the International Monetary Fund after the Bretton Woods Agreements in July of 1944 was an outgrowth of these plans. For an explanation and comparison of the Keynes and White plans, see Jacob Viner, "Two Plans for International Monetary Stabilization," *The Yale Review* (September 1943), pp. 77–107; and Peter F. Drucker, "The Currency Plans," *The Fortnightly* (August 1943), pp. 73–83.—Ed.]

loss. Of course, the gold standard cannot work if the governments are anxious to sabotage its operation.

It may seem strange that men should cling to a monetary system under which the formation of purchasing power is influenced by the changing and, to some extent, accidental conditions of gold mining. But the only alternative to this system is fiat money with all its sinister implications, since it is impossible to discover an objective rule for the guidance of a planned monetary manipulation.

The British plan pretends that it aims "at the substitution of an expanding, in place of a contracting, pressure on world trade." What it really aims at is inflation, even hyperinflation. The new-fangled term "expansionist" is but a poor substitute for the good old term "inflationist."

It is not true that the rigid gold standard really amounts to a continuous contraction or decline in prices. Notwithstanding the enormous increase in the supply of commodities, the general trend of prices was, under the gold standard, in an upward direction. The unfortunate attempts, repeated again and again, to create artificial booms through the method of credit expansion, interrupted this slow but steady tendency toward rising prices with periods of violent upward movements in prices. During the depression phase that inevitably followed the artificial boom, a period of falling prices usually occurred. But this did not interfere with the general trend toward rising prices and a steady fall in gold's purchasing power.[23]

E   The Silver Problem

Since time immemorial, the service of a common medium of exchange was rendered competitively by two precious metals, gold and silver. With the progress of industrialization and the intensification of both the domestic and international division of labor, the inconveniences arising from this monetary dualism became unbearable. The unification of the money function in one medium of exchange became imperative.

It was not in the plans of the governments to substitute monometallism

---

23 [On why a steady year-by-year rise in the purchasing power of money (or fall in prices in general) due to increases in production, output, and intensified division of labor need not carry any negative economic effects, see Mises, *Human Action*, pp. 468–71; see also Allen G. B. Fisher, "The Significance of Stable Prices in a Progressive Economy," *Economic Record* (March 1935), pp. 49–64, and "Does an Increase in Volume of Production Call for a Corresponding Increase in Volume of Money?" *American Economic Review* (June 1935), pp. 197–211; and George Selgin, *Less than Zero: The Case for a Falling Price Level in a Growing Economy* (London: Institute of Economic Affairs, 1997).—Ed.]

for the parallel coexistence of two standards, gold and silver. The mode of unification at which the governments aimed was bimetallism, that is, a state of affairs in which both precious metals would be connected in a uniform system. They tried to impose upon the public a legal rate for the mutual exchange of gold and silver. In so doing, they were free from any bias in favor of either of the two metals. They tried to stabilize the exchange ratio prevailing on the market at the time of their legislative interference.[24] But it is beyond the power of any government to stabilize the price of any commodity. Prices are fixed by the public on the market. Within a market economy, governments cannot control prices. (And within a socialist system, on the other hand, there are no prices at all; these are, of course, the totalitarian governments.) As soon as the market ratio of exchange between the two metals deviated from the legal ratio, the limitations of government action become manifest.[25] The operation of Gresham's Law converted the officially established double standard into a monometallism in which the metal that the market—that is, the citizens—valued less than at the legally decreed ratio became the only de facto standard.[26]

The issue of gold versus silver was determined by the course of British events. Great Britain was economically far ahead of the rest of the world during the period that decided the outcome of the rivalry between the two metals. Its industrial achievements and its wealth bestowed an enormous prestige upon its institutions. The gold standard was surrounded with a brilliant halo because it was the British standard. The adoption of gold monometallism by Great Britain set the example that was later, step by step, imitated by all other commercially important nations. The fact that Great Britain's monetary policy, aimed at the establishment of a double standard, had assigned to silver an exchange value that was above the market ratio prevailing in the critical period of the late seventeenth and early eighteenth centuries resulted in the establishment of the gold standard first in the British Isles and later, with the exception of China, in the rest of the world.

24 [On the history and effects of bimetallism, see J. Laurence Laughlin, *The History of Bimetallism in the United States* (New York: D. Appleton and Co., 1896); and, Francis A. Walker, *International Bimetallism* (New York: Henry Holt and Co., 1896).—Ed.]

25 [See Mises, *The Theory of Money and Credit*, pp. 89–91.—Ed.]

26 ["Gresham's Law" was named for Sir Thomas Gresham (1517–79), financier and advisor to Queen Elizabeth I. In a proclamation dated September 27, 1560, Gresham warned that since the government had fixed the exchange rate between gold and silver at a level different from the market rate, the more undervalued coins were sure to be exported. In other words, the bad (overvalued) money would drive out the good (undervalued) money. —Ed.]

The demonetization of silver brought about a serious fall in its price. It thus hurt the interests of the silver producers. They fought the gold standard and advocated either the silver standard or bimetallism because they desired a higher price for silver. In these endeavors, they were supported by groups which sought the same end because of pro-inflation considerations. The American presidential election in 1896 decided the campaign in favor of gold.[27]

Today, the problem of silver is no longer a monetary problem. It is a problem of silver mining as a special branch of economic activity. As far as the United States is concerned, it is partly a domestic economic problem, like that of wheat or cotton, and partly a problem of the relations between the U. S. and Mexico.

A return to the silver standard or to a double standard is simply out of the question. But the future of silver mining is not at all desperate. It is not unlikely that after the war an increased nonmonetary demand for silver will remedy the conditions of the mines, even if the silver-buying policy of America were to be discontinued.[28]

II   *The Monetary Chaos*

A ❧ MONEY IN THE AGE OF GOVERNMENT INTERFERENCE WITH BUSINESS AND ECONOMIC NATIONALISM

The gold standard was the standard of an age that, by and large, favored free enterprise, the international division of labor, and peaceful cooperation among nations. Its maintenance was considered undesirable in an epoch of economic warfare and shooting war.

In the years between the two world wars, monetary policy had been

27 [During the 1896 presidential contest between candidates William McKinley and William Jennings Bryan, the great debate was over the issue of whether America required a gold standard or a bimetal standard that would allow for the free minting of silver. Silver advocate Bryan made a famous speech in which he declared that the American people should not be crucified on "a cross of gold."—Ed.]

28 [After the Silver Purchase Act of 1934 was enacted, the U. S. government began purchasing silver at 50 cents per ounce and then issuing silver certificates on the additional silver reserves as though silver was worth $1.29 per ounce. This was essentially a method of achieving monetary expansion. Silver purchases almost ended by 1942. In July of 1946, the Treasury's purchase price for silver was raised to a little more than 90 cents per ounce. After 1955, the Treasury sold silver to keep silver prices from rising. By November of 1961, it suspended silver sales.—Ed.]

transformed into a weapon used in both domestic class war and in international conflict. The governments were eager to use it against domestic groups and against foreign countries. The result was chaos.

When a nation embarked upon a policy of inflation in the nineteenth century, public opinion for the most part condemned the resulting currency depreciation as an undesired event, indeed often even as an economic catastrophe. The deviation from the legally established gold parity was considered an evil, and the foremost aim of governments was to return as soon as possible to monetary stability. A rise of foreign exchange rates was viewed as proof of an unsatisfactory management of public affairs.

Beginning in the early 1930s, quite different opinions and attitudes were adopted. Nations began to consider currency devaluation as a blessing. The ascendancy of economic nationalism altered their attitude with regard to rising foreign exchange rates; they were no longer deemed an evil but an asset.

This allegedly new monetary policy aimed at an expansion of exports and at a restriction of imports. It has been pointed out in the previous section that this effect amounted to placing foreigners in the profit-making position and the domestic population in the losing position. Moreover, the apparent advantage thus gained is only a temporary one and is bound to disappear if the devaluation is not repeated after some lapse of time. A country eager to readjust its foreign trade relations by such methods cannot rest content with a single devaluation; the measure has to be applied again and again. For example, Czechoslovakia devalued its currency in February of 1934 and then again in October of 1936. France devalued the franc in September of 1936 about 30 percent. But it did not stabilize the price of foreign exchange and instead went on with its domestic inflation. Correspondingly, the British pound rose from one hundred and five francs in the days after the devaluation in September of 1936 to one hundred and seventy-nine francs in May of 1938. Yet some experts of the French treasury considered even this too moderate a devaluation and advocated a pound price of two hundred or even two hundred and fifty francs.

The devaluation policy necessarily must turn into a race among various nations. Each is anxious to outdo the others. It is the very nature of an inflationary policy that it tends toward an accelerated pace. The further it goes, the greater become the political difficulties of stopping its progress.

In spite of all warnings on the part of economists and of repeated experience with credit expansion, the commercially leading nations embarked in the 1920s on a credit expansion of unprecedented dimensions.

The inextricable breakdown came in 1929. It was in itself not a new phenomenon. The previous booms had always ended in the same way. But in this age of government interference with business and pressure group supremacy, strong resistance against the necessary adjustment of commodity prices, wage rates, and interest rates prevented a relative rapid return to normalcy and sound market conditions. Yielding to the demands of pressure groups, the government substituted "quantitative import controls" for the comparatively mild protectionism of earlier days. They embarked, moreover, upon a policy of restricting output. They either compelled the producers to cut production or subsidized them for not using their full productive capacity. A corollary of these measures designed to bring about government-made scarcity and to keep prices high was the endeavor of the labor unions to prevent a drop in wage rates or even to raise them. The result was lasting unemployment of a great part of the potential labor supply.[29]

The prices and wage rates of the boom period cannot be maintained when the boom comes to an end. Their fall is a necessary condition of recovery. But public opinion violently asked for government interference for the purpose of preventing this readjustment. Thus the governments were forced to go ahead with inflation. They devalued their currency systems and embarked upon more credit expansion.

It has been asserted that the devaluations were necessary because prices and wage rates had become rigid. To remedy this state of affairs, people said, parities had to be made flexible. This was a euphemistic mode for expressing the longing for more inflation. They spoke of "flexibility," but what they had in mind was always only downward foreign exchange flexibility. Nobody contended that his own country's currency was undervalued with regard to foreign currencies; nobody advocated an upward readjustment of his own country's foreign-exchange parity. No government ventured to raise the value of its currency in relation to foreign currencies; it was always devaluation alone that was targeted.

Prices and, still more, wage rates, it is true, had become rigid. But this was not due to any other reason than expectations of impending govern-

29 [For Mises's analysis of the causes of the Great Depression and its severity, see his monograph, "The Causes of the Economic Crisis," in *On the Manipulation of Money and Credit"* (February 1931), pp. 173–203; see also Lionel Robbins, *The Great Depression* (New York: Macmillan Co., 1934); and Murray N. Rothbard, *America's Great Depression* (Princeton, N.J.: D. Van Nostrand, 1963).—Ed.]

ment interference. A businessman or a farmer will not accept lower prices if he has well-founded expectations that the government will interfere very soon in order to keep prices high. A trade union leader will not agree to wage cuts if he knows that the government backs his resistance to downward adjustments in money wages.

The term "full employment" is a demagogic slogan if it does not refer to any definite height of wage rates. If the union rates exceed the market rates, unemployment becomes unavoidable for many. The governments and the unions can create as much unemployment as they want. With minimum wage rates higher than the potential market rates, mass unemployment will never disappear.

There was full employment both in Soviet Russia and in Nazi Germany. Where there is compulsory labor service, there cannot be unemployment. There is no unemployment in a penitentiary. If the workers of the West had been ready to agree to wage rates which, although lower than those of the boom years, would still have secured them a standard of living very much higher than that of the German workers—not to speak of the Russian workers—there would not have been any unemployment. It was insincere demagogy to refer to German or Russian conditions as an example for the Western democracies.

The policies adopted by the democracies were self-contradictory. On the one hand, they were eager to bring about a rise of commodity prices by restricting domestic output and by barring access to imported goods. On the other hand, they tried to make wage rates rise. The politicians promised in one breath to the producers "reasonable," that is, high, prices and to the consumers a low cost of living. One government agency complained of the malnutrition of the masses, while another agency of the same government subsidized farmers in order to restrict output. Such inconsistencies and contradictions are, of course, the characteristic mark of every pro-inflationary policy.

B ❧ The Fallacies of Price Control

Governments make inflation. But at the same time, they pretend to fight against its inextricable consequences.

A government inflates its currency because it wants to use the additional spending power for a curtailment of civilian consumption and for an increase of public spending. A belligerent government, for instance, wants to withdraw various commodities from the public, since it badly needs them for the conduct of war. The citizens, therefore, must correspondingly consume less.

But the inflation, that is, the additional paper money and bank deposits, brings about an increase in the national income (in terms of the inflated currency). The citizens have more money to spend, while the supply of goods available for civilian consumption drops. There are fewer goods to buy, but the citizens have more money to buy them. A serious rise of prices is unavoidable.

A rise of prices could be prevented only by financing the war exclusively by taxes and loans from the public without any inflation. If the government does not like a rise of prices and wage rates, it would have to abstain from inflation.

Price controls are futile. If, for instance, the price of one commodity is fixed at a level lower than the potential market rate corresponding to inflation conditions, many producers, in order to avoid losses, will stop producing this commodity. The marginal producers will go out of this particular branch of business. They will use the factors of production—both material and human, that is, labor—for the production of other goods not affected by government price ceilings. This outcome is contrary to the intention of the government. It has fixed the price of the commodity in question because it considers it as a vital necessity. It did not want to reduce its supply. The only method of preventing a fall in its supply would be to repeal the maximum price decree. But the government does not like this alternative, either. Thus it goes further and fixes the prices of the factors of production needed for the production of the commodity in question. But then the same problem appears with regard to the supply of these factors of production. The government has to proceed still further and fix the prices of the factors of production needed for the production of those factors of production that are needed for the production of the commodity whose price fixing started the whole process. It is forced not to leave out of its price-ceiling controls any goods, whether consumer or producer goods, and any kind of labor and services. It has to determine for what kinds of production every factor of production has to be used, since the market, now paralyzed by government price controls, no longer provides to entrepreneurs a guide for rational production decisions. The government has to force every entrepreneur and every worker to continue production and to work in accordance with its orders. It has to tell every businessman what to produce and how; what materials to buy and from where and at what prices; whom to employ and at what wage rates; to whom to sell and at what prices. If any gap were to be left in this all-round fixing of prices and wage rates, and if any were not clearly instructed to work in accordance with the government's orders in this all-round command system, then entrepreneurial activity—and capital and labor—would flow into those branches of business that remained free. The government's plans would be partially frustrated since the intention is precisely to increase or to maintain the production of those goods whose prices it has fixed.

But if such a system of all-round price and production control by the government is finally reached, the country's social and economic structure has been entirely changed. If all prices and wage rates are fixed, if the capitalists are no longer free to determine the way in which they may use their capital, if—as a result of all-round government price-fixing—the height of profits and of interest rates is virtually determined by the authorities, socialist all-round planning has been substituted for capitalism and free enterprise. Prices, wage rates, and interest rates are no longer what they were under a market system. They are now mere quantitative terms set by government decree within the framework of a socialist society. Money is no longer money, that is, a medium of exchange, but is a counter. There are no more entrepreneurs, but only shop managers bound to obey unconditionally the orders issued by the authorities. Everyone's standard of living is fixed by the government; everyone is a civil servant, a clerk in the great machine. This is socialism of the German type, *Deutscher Sozialismus*, as practiced by the Nazis. The *Fuehrer* alone operates the whole system; his will alone decides and directs every subject's activity and fixes his standard of living.[30]

Many British and American statesmen and politicians are fascinated by the alleged success of the German system of price controls. You have only to be so brutal and ruthless as the Nazis are, they say, and you will succeed in controlling prices. What these people, eager to fight the Nazis by adopting their methods, do not see is that the Nazis did not enforce their system of price controls within a market society; instead, they have established a full socialist system, a totalitarian commonwealth.

30 [On the nature and actual working of the Nazi form of the planned economy, see Guenter Reimann, *The Vampire Economy: Doing Business under Fascism* (New York: Vanguard Press, 1939); and Walter Eucken, "On the Theory of the Centrally Administered Economy: An Analysis of the German Experiment," *Economica*, Part I (May 1948), pp. 79–100, and Part II (August 1948), pp. 173–93. Also, Richard Pipes, *Property and Freedom* (New York: Alfred A. Knopf, 1999), pp. 218–25.—Ed.]

It is necessary to realize that price controls are contrary to purpose if they are limited to some commodities only. The state of affairs that the controls then bring about is, from the viewpoint of the price fixing authority and the public, more unsatisfactory than the previous state that it intended to alter. The government did not want at all to restrict the supply of the commodities in question. It wanted to make it easier for the consumers to get them, not more difficult. But if the government does not draw from this failure the conclusion that it has to abandon all attempts to control prices, it must go further and further until it substitutes socialist all-round planning for the market economy. Within a market economy, there is no such thing as a satisfactory working system of price controls.

Production can either be directed by the prices fixed on the market by the buying or by the abstention from buying on the part of the public. Or it can be directed by the government's control board of production management. There is no third solution available. There is no third social system feasible that would be neither market economy nor socialism. Government control of only some prices must result in a state of affairs that—without any exception—everyone considers absurd and contrary to purpose. Its inextricable result is chaos and general social unrest.[31]

C ❧ FOREIGN EXCHANGE CONTROL

Foreign exchange control is the corollary of domestic control of prices and wage rates. The government fixes the price of foreign exchange at a lower rate than the market. It makes it a criminal offense to buy or to sell foreign exchange at a higher price.

Such a measure would result in preventing all deals in foreign exchange. People who already own foreign exchange or acquire it in the course of their transactions will try to keep it in order to avoid losses. There will be no supply of foreign exchange on the market, while the quantity demanded for it will expand precisely because its price has been reduced

---

31 [For Mises's detailed criticisms of various forms of government intervention in the market economy, including price controls, see *Critique of Interventionism* (Irvington-on-Hudson, N.Y.: Foundation for Economic Education, [1929] 1996); *Liberalism in the Classical Tradition* (Irvington-on-Hudson, N.Y. and San Francisco, Calif.: Foundation for Economic Education and Cobden Press, [1927] 1985), pp. 60–104; *Interventionism: An Economic Analysis* (Irvington-on-Hudson, N.Y.: Foundation for Economic Education, [1940] 1998); *Human Action*, pp. 716–79; *Planning for Freedom* (South Holland, Ill.: Libertarian Press, revised 4th ed., 1980).—Ed.]

by the government. Almost all economic transactions with foreign countries will at once come to a standstill, provided that the government is strong enough to prevent the emergence of a black market.

Therefore, the government is driven to go further. It must nationalize all dealings in foreign exchange. It expropriates all owners of foreign exchange and gold. Every resident is forced to "sell" his holdings to a government agency at the official rate. Thus this agency becomes the only dealer in foreign exchange. But even this measure fails to remedy the evil. It does not increase at all the amount of foreign exchange available. It only hands it over to the government agency. The effects of the maximum price decree remain—namely, a restriction of exports and of the supply of foreign exchange.

The government wishes to save face and, therefore, without changing the wording of the decree, maintains an "ostrich policy." It pretends that its enforcement agency exactly complies with the decree. But if the agency were really to sell foreign exchange at the official rate, its activity would amount to subsidizing a group of privileged import dealers, while the bulk of business would not get any foreign exchange at all. On the other hand, its indemnifying the expropriated owners of foreign exchange at the official rate only would mean taxing, and thereby impeding, export trade. As all this would be undesirable, even idiotic, the government itself turns toward various makeshifts and tricks for the illusion of its own decree. The genius of the experts has been to invent various fanciful terms for these methods. But whether they speak of export premiums, subsidies, taxation of windfall profits, or anything else, the essence of all these methods is the same: The government actually buys and sells foreign exchange not at the official rate, but at the market rate. To the extent that a privileged person, notwithstanding, gets foreign exchange at the official rate, this is a deliberate gift to "friends" of the government at the expense of the treasury.[32]

It has been advanced in favor of foreign exchange control that the prices on the domestic market did not change proportionately with the rise of foreign exchange rates. Thus businessmen engaged in foreign trade

---

32 [On the establishment and workings of exchange controls in Germany, Austria, and Hungary in the period between the two world wars, see Howard S. Ellis, *Exchange Control in Central Europe* (Cambridge, Mass.: Harvard University Press, 1941); see also Oskar Morgenstern, "The Removal of Exchange Control: The Example of Austria," *International Conciliation*, No. 333 (October 1937), pp. 678–89.—Ed.]

make windfall profits whose confiscation seems to be fair and does not hamper trade. It has been pointed out above that commodity prices lag for some time behind the rise of foreign exchange rates. But three things have to be observed. First, this does not refer to goods whose domestic supply depends totally or mainly on imports from abroad. Second, the fact that the prices of all imported goods must rise very quickly and that export trade becomes temporarily more profitable creates a tendency toward a restriction of imports and an expansion of exports, that is, toward an increased supply of and a lower demand for foreign exchange. It is contrary to purpose that the government counteracts a tendency that, from its own point of view, appears beneficial. Third, with the absence of foreign exchange control, the windfall profits of export trade would very soon disappear under the pressure of competition.

At any rate, foreign exchange control is tantamount to the full nationalization of foreign trade. For the United States, this would not mean very much, as the amount of its foreign trade is a comparatively small part of its total trade. But for almost all other countries, nationalization of foreign trade results in dictatorial powers for the government. Where every branch of business depends, to some extent at least, on the buying of imported goods or on the exporting of a smaller or greater part of its output, the government is in a position to control all economic activity. He who does not comply with any whim of the authorities can be ruined either by the refusal to allot him foreign exchange or to grant him what the government considers as an export premium, that is, the difference between the market price and the official rate of foreign exchange. Besides, the government has the power to interfere in all the details of every enterprise's internal affairs; to prohibit the importation of all undesirable books, periodicals, and newspapers; and to prevent everybody from traveling abroad; from educating his children in foreign schools; and from consulting foreign doctors. Foreign exchange control was the main vehicle of European dictatorships. When Hitler came to power in 1933, in order to impose his dictatorship upon the whole German nation he had nothing to do but to enforce the foreign exchange control established by one of his predecessors, Mr. Bruening, in 1931.[33]

33 [Heinrich Bruening (1885–1970) was a Christian trade union leader and German Center Party politician. He was appointed Chancellor of Germany in March of 1930 by Ger-

D ❧ Foreign Exchange Equalization

There is but one means to keep a local and national currency permanently at par with gold and foreign exchange: unconditional redemption. The central bank has to buy at the parity rate any amount of gold and foreign exchange offered against domestic bank notes and deposit currency; on the other hand, it has to sell, without discrimination, any amount of gold and foreign exchange asked for by people ready to pay the parity price in domestic bank notes, coins, or deposit currency. Such was the policy of central banks under the gold standards. It worked very satisfactorily and secured stability of foreign exchange rates.

Pegging a certain rate of foreign exchange is tantamount to redemption.

A foreign exchange equalization account, too, can only succeed in its operations as far as it clings to the same methods.[34]

The reasons why European governments have preferred foreign exchange equalization accounts to the operation of central banks are obvious.

Central bank legislation was an achievement of democratic governments that would not dare to challenge, openly at least in the conduct of financial policies, the public opinion of the democratic countries. The operations of central banks were, therefore, adjusted to economic freedom. For that reason, they were considered as unsatisfactory in this age of rising totalitarianism. The main characteristics of a foreign exchange equalization account, as distinguished from central bank policy, are:

1 *The authorities keep the transactions of the account secret.* The law has obliged the central banks to publicize their actual status at short intervals (as a rule, every week). But the status of the foreign exchange equal-

---

man President Paul von Hindenberg. He resigned in May of 1932 and later immigrated to the United States.—Ed.]

34 [A "foreign exchange equalization fund" was meant to serve as a "buffer" supply of gold or foreign assets, which would enable a government to resist variations in its currency's foreign exchange rate (a) by buying all of its own currency offered for sale on the foreign exchange market at the established rate of exchange, if there were speculative selling of its currency, and (b) by selling its own currency in any amount demanded on the foreign exchange market at the established rate of exchange, if there were speculative buying of the currency. The funds set aside for this purpose were considered at best sufficient to fight off short-term fluctuations in the country's exchange rate.—Ed.]

ization accounts is only known to the initiated. Officialdom renders a report to the public only after a lapse of time when the figures are of interest to historians alone and of no avail at all for the businessman.

2 *This secrecy makes it possible to discriminate against people not favored or even opposed by the authorities.* In many continental countries of Europe, it resulted in scandalous corruption. Others used the power to discriminate for the oppression of minorities.

3 *The parity is no longer fixed by a law duly promulgated by parliament and therefore known to every citizen.* Its determination depends upon the arbitrariness of bureaucrats. From time to time, the newspapers reported, "The Ruritanian currency is weak." A more correct description would have been to say, "The Ruritanian authorities have decided to raise the price of foreign exchange slightly."

A foreign exchange equalization account is not a magic wand for remedying the evils of inflation. It cannot apply any means other than those available to "orthodox" central banks. And it must, like the central banks, fail in the endeavor to keep foreign exchange rates at par if there is domestic inflation and credit expansion.

E ❧ THE PROBLEM OF URGENT IMPORTS

Many people believe that an urgent demand for foreign goods can render the balance of payments unfavorable and thereby result in a rise of foreign exchange rates, even if there is no domestic inflation. They think that the government can, by means of foreign exchange controls, prevent the importation of unnecessary luxury goods and, thus, both increase the amount of foreign exchange available for the importation of vital necessities and stop the upward movement of foreign exchange rates.

This doctrine is utterly fallacious.

Foreign trade is an exchange of commodities and services, just as is domestic trade. No government interference is needed to prevent the residents of New York from "exporting" all their money to the agricultural districts of the country, although their demand for food is more urgent (in the sense in which the supporters of this doctrine use to apply the term) than the demand of the farmers for the commodities with which the New Yorkers supply them. Every resident of New York who wants to buy food "imported" from the countryside has to pay for it and, therefore, to earn the money needed for its purchase. The population of New York can buy only as much as they can pay for. If the money they pay to the farmers were not to flow back through the buying of New York products and amenities on the part of the farmers, they would be forced to restrict their consumption.

No government interference is needed to prevent any individual citizen from the evils of an unfavorable balance of his own payments. If he is foolish enough to spend all his money on luxury goods, he will have to forego vital necessities. In extreme cases, it may prove expedient to place a man not fit to manage his own affairs properly under the care of a guardian. This guardian's duty, to be sure, will not be to restore a disturbed balance of payments, but to force the man to use his money in a more reasonable way. But the government—at least in democracies—is not the guardian of the citizens.

It is exactly the same with a nation's foreign trade. The country that does not get credit has to pay cash for the whole of its purchases. If it lacks this money, that is, this foreign exchange, it must restrict its imports.

Let us assume that a country is without a domestic production of bread and motorcars. The entire population consumes bread, and a few wealthy men drive cars. The government wants to increase the poorer citizens' consumption of bread. It forbids the importation of motorcars and other luxury goods, expecting that more foreign exchange then will be available for the importation of bread. But this is an error. What really follows is that the rich spend the money they used to spend for cars for the expansion of their consumption of other domestic products. This additional demand raises the prices for these products and prevents their exportation. The government's interference does not give the poor more money for the purchase of bread. It only results in a change in the consumption of the rich and a curtailment both of imports and exports. If the government really wanted to increase the poorer citizens' consumption of bread, it would have to tax the rich in such a way that they could no longer afford to buy and drive cars. Then the government must distribute the collected (domestic) money to the poor, thus enabling them to spend more money for bread. The grain dealers will buy the foreign exchange no longer asked for by the motorcar trade and will import more foreign cereals. We do not need to inquire whether such a policy would be wise and whether it would, in the long run, prove disastrous. But it can, in the short run, achieve the ends desired by the government, while the prohibition of the importation of luxury goods must fail, even in the short run.

After the war, many countries will badly need imports from abroad. However, they will not be in a position to procure more foreign goods than they can pay for, either out of their own funds or out of funds borrowed abroad. (We are not referring to the relief work of charitable agencies; it is obvious that such gifts do not disturb the equilibrium of the balance of payments.)

The contrary opinion is due to the mistaken assumption that people import from abroad without regard to the prices they must pay for foreign goods and the amount of money that is available to them to purchase those goods; only later, when payment is due, do they supposedly discover that they lack the money needed to cover their purchases. It is unnecessary to explode such myths. However, they were almost universally regarded as true in the last several decades and they provided a spurious justification for an unswerving hostility to imports. They were a cog in the doctrinal structure that brought about economic nationalism and the trend toward national autarky.

Except for charitable gifts on the part of the United States, there is only one means available to make it possible for the victims of the Nazis to purchase an excess of imports over their current exports: foreign credit. Monetary manipulations are of no avail.

F 〜 THE "HOT MONEY" PROBLEM

One of the characteristic features of the gold standard, as experienced first in Great Britain and then later in almost all other countries, was that it was a one-reserve system. The country's reserve of gold and foreign exchange was almost entirely concentrated in the central bank.[35] The other banks and the bankers no longer kept any considerable funds of gold and foreign exchange in their institutions. They relied upon the central banks' reserves entirely. This made them dependent on the central banks. The supremacy of the central bank encouraged the government's inflationary experiments.

More serious shortcomings of the one-reserve system emerged with the appearance of the unfortunate circumstances of the last decades. Many capitalists became anxious to protect their capital against their own government's policies of confiscatory taxation, open expropriation, and devaluation. They entrusted their funds as demand deposits to commercial banks and bankers of countries whose currency conditions at the moment

35 The establishment of separate foreign exchange equalization accounts did not alter this state of affairs. For all practical purposes, the central banks' reserve and the foreign exchange equalization account form a homogeneous unit.

seemed to be worthy of more confidence. As soon as doubts concerning the stability of this country's currency appeared, they hurried to withdraw their balances and to transfer them to another country in which the risk of an impending depreciation seemed less likely.

The banks and the bankers of the countries visited temporarily by such "hot money" did not handle this situation adequately. They did not bother about the responsibility arising from the acceptance of such demand deposits. They used the funds entrusted to them for expanding their loans and did not weigh the consequences. The only cautious method of dealing with this hot money would have been to keep a reserve of gold and of foreign exchange large enough to pay back the entire amount in case of a sudden withdrawal. Of course, this would have forced the banks to charge the customers a commission for keeping their funds safe.

Let us look at the situation of the Swiss banks on the day in September of 1936 when France devalued the franc. The depositors of hot money became frightened. They feared that the Swiss might follow the French example. It was to be expected that they all would try to transfer their funds immediately to London or New York or even to Paris, which for the coming weeks seemed to offer a smaller risk of currency devaluation. But the Swiss commercial banks were not in a position to pay back these call-deposits without the aid of the Swiss National Bank. They had lent these deposits to businesses—in large part, to businesses in countries that, through foreign exchange controls, had blocked the use of their balances in foreign exchange transactions. The only way out would have been to borrow from the Swiss National Bank. Then they would have maintained their own solvency. But the depositors paid out would have immediately asked the National Bank for the redemption in gold or foreign exchange of the bank notes received. If the National Bank were not to comply with this request, it would thereby have actually abandoned the gold standard and devalued the Swiss franc. If, on the other hand, the bank had redeemed the notes, it would have lost the greater part of its gold reserve. A panic would have resulted. The Swiss themselves would have tried to procure as much gold and foreign exchange as possible. The entire monetary system of the country would have collapsed.

The only alternative for the Swiss National Bank would have been for it not to have assisted the other banks at all, but this would have been equivalent to the insolvency of the country's most important credit institutions.

The Swiss government had only one means to prevent an economic catastrophe: to follow suit forthwith and to devalue the Swiss franc. The matter did not brook delay.

By and large, after the Second World War, Great Britain will face similar conditions. London was the world's banking center before the First World War. It has long since lost this function. But foreigners and citizens of the [British] Dominions still kept, on the eve of the present war, considerable short-term balances in British banks. Besides, there are the large deposits due to the central banks in the "sterling area."[36] They all are frozen by foreign exchange restrictions. But it is likely that they will be withdrawn as soon as these restrictions are dropped. The menace of this hot money is one of the main problems of Great Britain's postwar monetary policy.

The essential aim of the British proposals for an International Clearing Union (the so-called "Keynes Plan") is to relieve Great Britain of the burden of these hot-money debts. They are to be taken over by the international bank. There they should create new credits in *bancor* (or, according to the American plan, in *unitas*). Thus the starting operation of the new international bank would have to be an inflationary experiment of huge dimensions for the benefit of the British banks. Frozen credit could, by a stroke of the pen, be converted into ready money. Debts, which the British debtors cannot pay in accordance with the terms of the contract, would by a miraculous operation become British assets.

Great Britain's embarrassment is similar to the dilemma that Switzerland had to face in 1936. It is, at any rate, a British problem and has to be treated as such. We can easily understand why the British are opposed to a solution that would impair their country's currency system. If the Bank of England were to increase its issue of bank notes to the extent needed for the reestablishment of the liquidity of the commercial banks, it would bring about a tremendous inflation and, consequently, a serious fall in the sterling's purchasing power and a violent rise of foreign exchange rates.

The only alternative to this procedure is to deal with the matter as one deals with other cases of temporary insolvency. A realistic appreciation of the case cannot help recognizing that the British banks and bankers concerned are in a position in which they cannot meet their commitments in

36 [The "sterling area" referred to those countries that were members of the British Commonwealth and the dependent colonial empire of Great Britain, as well as a number of other nations (such as Denmark, Greece, and Turkey) that continued to peg the value of their respective currencies to the British pound following Britain's abandonment of the gold standard in September of 1931 and that maintained a portion of their central bank reserves in British sterling on deposit in London with the Bank of England.—Ed.]

accordance with the terms of the underlying contracts. They must invite their creditors for a consideration of the problem. They must openly confess their inability to fulfill their obligations. They must offer their creditors an immediate payment of such an amount as they can afford to the best of their ability and must ask for the permission to postpone the payment of the rest for a reasonable time. The creditors must willy-nilly accept a standstill agreement if they are convinced that their debtors are ready to make all endeavors toward payment. After all, for the creditor of an insolvent debtor no other choice is left than to accept as much as the debtor can pay.

The unfortunate effects of the monetary mismanagement of the past must be liquidated entirely without any burden on the new order to be created after the war. No sophisticated scheme will work satisfactorily if encumbered with the sad inheritance of the blunders of policies whose inadequacy is universally admitted.

III   *The Establishment of Sound Currency Conditions*

A ~ THE NEED FOR NATIONAL ACTION

The unfortunate state of international relations, which finally resulted in the tremendous catastrophe of the present war, was the outcome of bad domestic policies on the part of almost all nations. Within a world of economic nationalism, there cannot be any question of lasting peace. If the various nations do not radically change their domestic policies, no treaties and no international offices and tribunals will succeed in preventing armed conflicts.

The need for closer international cooperation to check some nations' lust for conquest and hegemony is imperative. However, some people back such projects only because they hope that an international organization will relieve them from the necessity of adequately rearranging their own domestic affairs.

This is especially the case in the field of monetary reconstruction. No international agreement and no international bank is required for the stabilization of foreign exchange rates. If every nation abandons all inflationary measures, stability of foreign exchange rates will result automatically. If, on the other hand, the various nations cling to inflation, no international settlement will secure monetary stability.

It is indeed comforting that doctrinarians, statesmen, and politicians who only a few years ago violently advocated unstable foreign exchange rates and fanatically backed inflationary policies have now recognized at least some of their fallacies and are anxious to return to the stability of foreign exchange rates. Such magnanimous avowal of errors committed in the past is extremely rare. It is the mark of personal sincerity and honesty. It merits the highest admiration.

Yet, not enough attention is paid to the fact that sound monetary policy must begin at home.

B ❧ THE POSITION OF THE UNITED STATES

The main financial and economic burden of the war rests on the people of this country. Without Lend-Lease, the other Allied nations would have long since been forced to stop fighting and resisting the aggressors. Besides, the United States has built up the biggest army, the strongest navy, and the most formidable air force. The gallantry of the American armed forces is on the point of defeating the Germans and will finally crush Japan.

Notwithstanding this unprecedented effort, this country will emerge from the war as the world's paramount nation. Its economic, financial, political, and military power will supersede that of any other nation. Its moral and intellectual prestige will be unparalleled. All other nations will look with awe at America and will expect American aid for their own postwar reconstruction.

Such an eminent position involves a great responsibility. Not only moral and altruistic considerations, but no less its own material interests will compel the United States to care about other nations' well-being. In this age of international division of labor, in which every point of the earth's surface can be reached from New York in less time than was needed one hundred and twenty years ago to travel from New York to Chicago, no nation can flourish and live in safety if the rest of the world suffers from chaotic conditions.

However, even the most altruistic attitude on the part of this country will prove useless if the other nations do not try to manage their own affairs in the most efficient way. The greatest sacrifices made by America will be futile if the beneficiaries do not abandon policies essentially detrimental to their own vital welfare. American aid would do more harm than good if, for instance, credits granted by America were to be used by the borrowers for the continuation of bad policies and for the postponement of urgent reforms.

The greatest and most valuable service that this country can render to the rest of mankind would consist of the best possible management of its own domestic affairs for the attainment of domestic prosperity. Then the example set by America will be imitated by the other nations.

This is true with regard to monetary and financial reconstruction, too. After the war, America will have to choose between the continuation of its present inflationary policy and the return to monetary stability. If it decides in favor of inflation, no action on the part of any other nation or on the part of any group of nations will be of any effect. Stability of foreign exchange rates could then only be attained if the other nations were ready to keep pace in their domestic inflation with that of America.

But if, on the other hand, America turns toward a policy of monetary stability, that is, practically to the gold standard, all those nations that are anxious to get American credits will follow suit. Stability of exchange rates will ensue automatically.

C ❧ A New Gold Standard in America

1. The core of American currency reform lies in balancing the national budget entirely by means of taxes and of loans granted by the public. Since under present conditions the commercial banks are expanding credit practically openly for the sake of financing the Treasury, this would virtually stop the further progress of inflation.

It would be highly desirable if this decisive measure could be achieved as soon as possible. There is danger in delay. The longer inflation goes on, the more detrimental become its inextricable evils, and the more difficult it is to stop it spontaneously. But realistic reflection has to admit that notwithstanding the most serious endeavors of the administration and of Congress, political conditions may hinder the balancing of the budget for the duration of the war.

The abandonment of inflation brings about economic frictions that have been styled by economists as the "stabilization crisis."[37] The effects of

---

37 [The phrase "the stabilization crisis" came into use during the period that followed the "Great German Inflation" in November of 1923. It referred to a period of postinflation readjustment during which capital and labor had to be reallocated as a cure for the misdirection of resources during the inflationary episode. With the discovery that some capital had been consumed during the inflation, investment horizons had to be shorted and redirected. See Constantino Bresciani-Turroni, *The Economics of Inflation: A Study of Currency Depreciation in Postwar Germany*, pp. 359–97. —Ed.]

the capital consumption caused by inflation become visible and unavoidable.[38] The illusions created by the affluence of fiat money vanish. Payday dawns. A painful process of recovery and readjustment starts.

Yet these disastrous consequences are unavoidable. They can only be aggravated by postponing the reform. No inflation can go on forever. It must result in the total devaluation of the currency system if it is not stopped in time. There cannot be any doubt that American common sense will choose the second alternative and will not follow the example set by Germany in 1923.[39]

As soon as Congress will have succeeded in balancing the budget, the demagogues will complain of alleged deflation and will violently ask for "reflation," that is, a continuation of inflation. It will be the task of the press to explain to the nation the futility of such objections and proposals.

2. The second step of the reform has to consist of the adoption of a rigid 100 percent reserve plan. Every further increase of bank deposits subject to check and of any kind of bank notes, paper money, and money certificates has to be prohibited unconditionally, if the total additional amount of such money and money substitutes is not entirely backed by an *ad hoc* deposit of gold with one of the Federal Reserve banks. Such *ad hoc* deposits have to remain blocked permanently; a release is only permitted if a corresponding reduction in the amount of bank notes or deposits takes place.

For the interval preceding the promulgation of the dollar's new gold parity, the heights of the *ad hoc* gold deposit required for every additional dollar should be fixed in accordance with the market price (in terms of dollars) plus a margin of ten percent. With the promulgation of the dollar's new gold parity, a readjustment of the amount of the *ad hoc* deposits should take place, and any forthcoming excess could be released.

38 [On the process of capital consumption due to economic miscalculations during an inflation, see Mises, *Nation, State and Economy*, pp. 160–63 and *The Theory of Money and Credit*, pp. 234–37; Fritz Machlup, "The Consumption of Capital in Austria," *The Review of Economic Statistics* (January 15, 1935), p. 13. As Machlup notes, "The discussion of capital consumption and economic decline was provoked by the course of events observed in Austria during the war, the postwar inflation, and during the years of social reform.... Professor Ludwig von Mises was the first, so far as I know, to point to the phenomenon of the consumption of capital."—Ed.]

39 [For Mises's 1923 analysis of the process and effects of the Great German Inflation and the methods for ending it, see "Stabilization of the Monetary Unit—From the Viewpoint of Theory," in *On the Manipulation of Money and Credit*, pp. 1–49.—Ed.]

It would be superfluous to apply the same rigidity to the issue of additional fractional coins by the government. The danger that such tokens could serve as a vehicle of inflation can easily be removed by the obligation of the treasury to exchange any amount of them exceeding one dollar against bank notes or—later—against gold coins.

3. The third step, to be made simultaneously with the second, has to consist of the repeal of all laws and decrees that prevent the establishment of a free market for gold and foreign exchange. Every individual and every corporation should regain the right to own, to buy, and to sell *ad libitum* gold and foreign exchange.

At the same time, all restrictions on the export of gold and foreign exchange and the payment to foreigners should be removed. This must not interfere with blocking the accounts of enemy aliens and of governments at war with the United States. Besides, the balances due to countries that have blocked—either by foreign exchange control or by other methods— the balances of Americans, should remain blocked, too. This problem must be settled by special agreements.

4. After some higgling and oscillating, the market will show a somewhat stable gold price. Then the time will be ripe for the fourth and final step: the adoption of the new gold parity of the dollar. The parity has to be fixed at such a level that no sensible changes on the American markets turn up. The dollar should be neither overvalued nor undervalued. Its actual gold parity should be stabilized.

Technically, the maintenance of the new gold parity must be achieved by the same methods of buying and selling gold that were used in previous years for the maintenance of the then legal parity.

D   The Domestic Economic Consequences of the Gold Standard

The adoption of a rigid 100 percent reserve scheme for any future increase of bank notes and deposits subject to check would not prevent further expansion in the quantity of money. It will only make the gold standard effective, as the expansion of the currency will entirely depend on the newly mined gold. It will not stabilize prices. No method can stabilize prices in a nonstationary state of society. Price changes are the characteristic mark of every progressive society. The attempts toward price level stabilization are utterly hostile to any improvement of economic conditions. They tend to perpetuate existing conditions while all our hopes must be founded on further improvement.

What the 100 percent reserve scheme, as defined above, aims at is the prevention of credit expansion. Credit expansion does not remedy any evil. It does not really add anything to the supply of goods. Its only lasting effect is to bring about capital malinvestment. The artificial boom must end in a slump. He who wants to prevent the depression has to prevent the boom. The boom is neither good business nor prosperity; it is the illusion of both. What is needed is the elimination of the business cycle. Not stability of prices, but stability of the trend of business is desirable.

The progress of capital accumulation supplies the means for the improvement of methods of production. The higher the productivity of labor, and thereby wage rates, is in a country, the greater is the amount of capital per head. But capital consists mainly of capital goods, that is, material factors of production; money is only an exiguous part of capital. Credit expansion creates only additional money substitutes, not, to be sure, material agents of production. It makes prices rise, but it does not strengthen productive capacity. To repeat, it leads to malinvestment, which is a waste of capital goods.[40]

It was the aim of the British Bank Act of 1844 to prevent credit expansion by tying the issue of additional bank notes to a 100 percent reserve.[41] The plan failed because it did not impose the same limitations upon bank deposits subject to check. Its only effect was that deposits be-

40 ["Money substitutes," in Mises's terminology, refers to claims to a commodity money (such as gold) in the form of bank notes or checks that are readily and generally accepted in transactions and that are believed to be redeemable on demand at the banking institution that has issued them. Mises distinguished between money substitutes that are backed 100 percent by commodity-money reserves at the issuing institution ("money certificates") and those money substitutes issued by a bank that are less than fully backed ("fiduciary media"). Loans extended on the basis of 100 percent reserve backing were referred to as "commodity credit," and those loans extended on the basis of less than 100 percent reserve backing were called "circulation credit." See Mises, *The Theory of Money and Credit*, pp. 63–76, 155–56, and 293–404; and *Human Action*, pp. 432–44. — Ed.]

41 [The British Bank Act was passed in July of 1844. It divided the Bank of England into two parts, a note issue department and a banking department. The note issue department was restricted in the amount of bank notes it could issue on the basis of government debt (a maximum of fourteen million pounds); and notes issued beyond this had to be fully backed on the basis of additional deposits of gold coin or gold and silver bullion. — Ed.]

came the main vehicle of credit expansion.[42] If future credit expansion is to be avoided, it is necessary to apply the one hundred percent reserve principle also to bank deposits, which are now—at least in the Anglo-Saxon countries—the chief means of bank loan expansion.

It is illusory to expect that any method other than the one hundred percent reserve plan could possibly work under postwar conditions. The pro-inflation policy of the last decades and the fallacious teachings of some doctrinarians have produced a mentality that would make people abuse any gap left in the frame of anti-inflation legislation. If any kind of credit expansion is not radically banned, it will be impossible for the administration and for Congress to withstand the attacks of pressure groups asking for inflation. Balancing the budget is one of the most tedious tasks of statesmanship. A parliament is always in an embarrassing situation when the public asks at the same time for lower taxes and for an increase of expenditures. If the loophole of credit expansion is left, it will certainly be used and misused again. In the gloomy days of reconstruction, when the whole world will be suffering from the consequences of the war, an inflationary policy will be extremely tempting. Only the acceptance of a rigid principle will prevent an unprecedented credit expansion and its unavoidable outcome, a slump more terrible than that of 1929.

E ❧ Monetary Reconstruction in the Rest of the World

With the establishment of a rigid domestic gold standard, the United States will have achieved all it can for the world's monetary reconstruction. The rest must be left to national action on the part of each country.

It would be a serious mistake if the United States were to apply—whether alone or in joint action with other nations—any kind of pressure in order to induce any nation to accept the gold standard or tie up its national currency with the dollar or with any other foreign currency. Such a move would be easily misunderstood. The nations in question would believe that, in establishing a sound currency, they were granting a favor to the United States. They would complain about illusory sacrifices. They would indict the gold standard as a system detrimental to their own welfare, one serving only the selfish interests of America. They would fancy

---

42 [On the inadequacy of the British Banking Act of 1844, see Mises, "Monetary Stabilization and Cyclical Policy," pp. 144–45, and *Human Action*, pp. 571–75.—Ed.]

that they are entitled to claim an indemnification on the part of America for alleged disadvantages.

This country, it is true, has a selfish interest in the well-being of all other nations. But it would be a grotesque misrepresentation of the state-of-affairs to assert that America's concern about any other nation's well-being is greater than that of the other nations in question, themselves. No nation, in rearranging its own currency system, renders a favor to the United States. If it best serves its own interests, it takes care of its own economic affairs. Such a policy may be beneficial to all other countries and to the United States, too, but it is, for all that, primarily a policy for the sake of national interests. It does not give them the right to ask for a reward from this country.

Almost all other nations have, even more than America, only the choice between a rigid gold standard and hyperinflation with all its consequences. If they were to choose the second alternative, they will very soon collapse and jeopardize their social structure and their political independence. Common sense and patriotism will force them to adopt the gold standard of their own accord.

Foreign intervention would be futile. It is impossible to compel a sovereign nation to cling to a policy of stable foreign exchange rates. If the national government is refractory, it will always know how to smuggle in inflation and will plead its innocence by referring to *force majeure*. A policy of stable foreign exchange rates must be the outcome of a nation's insight into the disadvantages of fluctuating exchanges.

It will be very hard indeed for many nations to properly balance their budgets. But it will be an iron necessity, as a balanced budget is a prerequisite to the abandonment of inflation and the return to stable foreign exchange rates. And only nations that have succeeded in these attempts will get foreign credit and investments.

The international capital and loan market has been knocked to pieces by the policies of those countries that most urgently need the aid of foreign capital. These countries' governments have not only evaded fulfillment of contracts and agreements into which they had voluntarily entered, but also, by means of foreign exchange controls, they have prevented citizens who are ready to pay from meeting their obligations. If the methods adopted by most of the European countries in the 1930s were to prevail, it can hardly be expected that any reasonable capitalist would buy foreign bonds or shares. Experience has taught the capitalists to be more cautious. They will not lend in the future if they are not fully assured of the creditors' ability and willingness to abide by the terms of the contract. For the investor, after all, foreign investments mean business.

It is contrary to purpose to lend money to a government that does not balance its budget and that does not abstain from any action jeopardizing the stability of foreign exchange rates. Such a debtor will use the money borrowed only for the postponement of unavoidable financial reform. It will either spend it for deficit financing or for futile attempts to peg the national currency. The regular procedure applied in these spurious pegging operations was this: The government inflated its currency by issuing additional quantities of legal tender notes. Then, after a while, it used a portion of the funds it borrowed from abroad on the foreign exchange market in order to buy back a fraction of the amount of additional legal tender that it had issued a short time before. Such measures did not end the inflation. They only slowed its pace a little. When the funds acquired through foreign borrowing were exhausted, the government was in a more precarious position than before it received the loan.

Lending to foreign governments and municipalities is only sound if the debtor intends to use the funds in a way that will improve the people's material well-being and, thereby, the taxpayers' ability to bear the burden of payment of interest and principal.

Lending to domestic business and farming is safe if it can be expected that the debtor will be able and willing to pay interest and principal. Buying domestic shares is reasonable if the prospects for the corporation's profitability are satisfactory. But in lending to foreign businesses and farming enterprises, or in undertaking direct investment abroad, the capitalist may also have to pay a price in regard to the country's financial and monetary policy. If the nation does not balance its budget properly and if it clings to inflation, the creditor must fear that foreign-exchange control will deprive him of his money even if the debtors are ready to comply with the terms of the contract and the enterprises yield a profit.

Foreign capital will be available, after the war, only to nations that unswervingly keep to a policy of balanced budgets and stable foreign exchange rates. This fact will induce all nations anxious to attract capital from abroad to adopt America's monetary policy. No pressure on the part of the American government will be required.

The government of the United States should not put obstacles in the way of reasonable foreign borrowing on the American capital and money market. An embargo upon capital export would be detrimental to the marketing of American farm products and the products of the American producers' goods industry. However, artificial encouragement of capital export would be faulty. Such an attitude, too, would be open to malicious misinterpretation. Let us remember that the Nazis complained that America forced loans upon Germany in order to enslave the Germans!

F An International Bank

Both the Keynes and the White plans provide for the establishment of an international bank. The British plan by Keynes refers to it as an "International Clearing Union"; the American plan by White calls it a "United and Associated Nations Stabilization Fund."[43]

It has been pointed out above that an international bank cannot render any service at all for the cause of foreign-exchange stabilization. The requirements of foreign-exchange stability are exclusively domestic: a budget balanced without recourse to inflation and credit expansion and, moreover, the abandonment of other attempts to expand credit. If a nation does not comply with these requirements, no operation of an international bank will prevent a drop in the value of its currency unit.

If a nation believes that its moral duty or its national interest oblige it to contribute to another nation's public expenditure, it must subsidize it openly and must not disguise the aid granted as a loan. Such was Great Britain's procedure when—in the eighteenth and in the early nineteenth centuries—it subsidized its continental allies.[44] Such is America's "Lend-Lease" policy in the present wartime emergency. This country—whose citizens have been for more than a century universally reviled as worshippers of the golden calf, as ruthless dollar-makers and narrow-minded callous egoists—not only bears the main burden of the material war effort, it has also made all preparations for a relief action of unprecedented dimensions. It is ready to feed the hungry and needy victims of the Nazis after their liberation on a much larger scale than it did during and after the First World War.

But business and money are different things. Charity work does not require the establishment of a bank. Neither does foreign investment and lending abroad.

Under present conditions, this country is practically the only one that

43 [See footnote 22.—Ed.]

44 [Mises is referring to the period in which Great Britain was at war with revolutionary and Napoleonic France.—Ed.]

can export capital. The American capitalists do not need the cooperation of foreign governments when they consider granting loans to foreign countries out of their own funds.

In the past, the London money market acted, by and large, as the world's clearinghouse. Later, New York entered the field. With Great Britain's financial prestige gone, the New York money market will, in the future, centralize the clearing function.

It is not unlikely that a further intensification of international business transactions will prove it expedient to give to the international clearing of transactions a more definite organization in the future. Today, there is no need for such reform, but, at any rate, a clearinghouse is not a bank. It does not grant credits.

What the British plan inadequately calls a "Clearing Union" would be, in fact, a bank with the power to expand credit. The very establishment of either of the two suggested new institutions would consist of a huge addition to the then-existing amount of bank deposits subject to check. According to the British plan, each member state shall have assigned a *quota* that will determine its right to enjoy the credit facilities of the union. Where do these quite arbitrarily determined credit facilities come from? The answer is obvious: They are fiat money, begotten by the magic of international planning. What the people need is a greater supply of goods, but the sorcerers want to give them more fictitious money.

The utterly inflationary tendencies of both plans are still more manifest in the provision that the proposed bank is to give its credit at a discount rate of 1 percent. At such a rate, the demand for additional credits would be practically unlimited.

It is needless to discuss whether the schemes suggested could possibly succeed in stabilizing foreign exchange rates among the member states. Let us, for the sake of argument, answer this question in the affirmative. But it is beyond doubt that the operation of this union or fund would result in a world inflation on an unprecedented scale.[45]

45 [On the institutional mechanisms that emerged out of the wartime proposals, see Michael A. Heilperin, *International Monetary Reconstruction: The Bretton Woods Agreements* (Washington, D.C.: American Enterprise Association, 1945); for criticisms of the British and American plans and the Bretton Woods Agreements, along lines similar to Mises's criticisms in this section, see Benjamin M. Anderson, "International Currency: Gold versus *Bancor* or *Unitas*," *Vital Speeches of the Day* (April 1, 1944), pp. 375–80, and *Economics and the Public Welfare* (Princeton, N.J.: D. Van Nostrand Co., 1946), pp. 573–94; and Henry Hazlitt, *From Bretton Woods to World Inflation* (Chicago: Regnery Gateway, 1984).—Ed.]

Under the gold standard, the most efficacious obstacle to boundless inflation was the lack of cooperation among the central banks of various countries. Even when all central banks simultaneously embarked upon credit expansion, there was no unanimity among them with regard to the extent and the pace of expansion. Each bank was under the necessity of restraining its own lust for expansion as it could never be sure whether the other central banks would keep pace. A central bank that is not relieved of the obligation to pay cash for its notes and deposits has to consider the relation between its liabilities and its reserve. It must avoid a drain on its resources. Even a central bank to whom the questionable privilege of suspending cash payment had been granted was impeded by the lack of cooperation. If it expanded credit at a higher ratio than those of other countries, it brought about a rise in foreign exchange rates.

No such brakes will inconvenience the activities of a world bank as proposed by both plans. It will be in a position to go on with inflation.

G The Reconstruction of the International Capital Market

Each nation is today prepared to lay blame for the disintegration of the international division of labor on the other nations. The truth is that the neomercantilist ideology has got hold of all peoples. In the last decades all nations, without exception, clung to a policy of economic nationalism. If this policy is not radically abandoned, there is no hope for a recovery of world trade. If the nations do not learn that the advantage derived from foreign trade lies entirely in importing goods that can be produced at home, if at all, only at a higher cost, and that exporting has no other aim than to pay for merchandise imported, they will not stop fighting imports. But as the restriction of imports must proportionally reduce exports, too, the world is quickly moving toward a state of each nation's economic self-sufficiency.

It is not true that an anti-import policy on the part of other nations or even of all other nations makes it impossible for an individual nation to adopt a more liberal policy. Let us, for the sake of argument, consider the most extreme case. A state of affairs in which one nation alone keeps to unrestricted free trade, while all other nations try to reduce imports by the application of various import-restricting methods, will not render the free trade nation's balance of payments or balance of trade unfavorable. If the free trade nation can no longer export those quantities of merchandise that it used to export before the other nations embarked upon protectionism, its imports will drop proportionally. If the rest of the world turns toward full autarky, then international trade would cease altogether; then, also, the only free trade country left would automatically become self-sufficient, whether it likes this outcome or not.

The fact that the predominantly industrial nations of Europe were eager to restrict their imports of foreign cereals, cattle, and meat did not force the predominantly agricultural countries to obstruct the import of merchandise. Neither did the adoption of protection for domestic industrial production on the part of the predominantly agricultural countries force the predominantly industrial countries to turn toward protection for domestic agriculture. The two moves were independent of each other, although they sprang from the same mentality. If the predominantly industrial countries bar access to foreign food, they thereby not only encourage the expansion of domestic food production but also their action results, at the same time, in an expansion of processing industries in the predominantly agricultural areas. Even if the predominantly agricultural countries cling to free trade, and even if natural conditions for the processing industries are extremely unfavorable with them, this effect could not be avoided. Both groups, of course, will suffer: the first group on account of the rise in food prices, the second group on account of the rise in the price of manufactures.[46]

We do not have to ask who is to blame more. Instead, the question is who hurts his own vital interests most, or, put another way, for whom is the revival of international trade most urgently needed?

It is obvious that the United States is comparatively in the most favorable position. This country is in a class by itself; it is neither predominantly industrial nor predominantly agricultural. It produces an excess of foodstuffs and raw materials and manufactured goods. It could, if absolutely necessary, live in economic self-sufficiency without great harm to its well-being. It is true that America, too, could profit much from an increase in the volume of its foreign trade, but foreign trade is not vital for America. It is so rich in natural resources and accumulated capital that it suffers less than other nations from the trend toward autarky.

It is different with the predominantly industrial countries of Western and Central Europe. Their supplies of natural resources are relatively poor,

46 [On the nature and effects of agricultural countries attempting to force industrialization through protectionism and industrial countries attempting to force agriculturalization through protectionism, see Wilhelm Röpke, *International Economic Disintegration* (Philadelphia: Porcupine Press, [1942] 1978), pp. 111–90.—Ed.]

and they are overpopulated. They can neither feed nor clothe their citizens properly out of their domestic resources. They must import foodstuffs and raw materials and pay for them by exporting manufactures. For them, foreign trade is vital. Their people would literally starve in an autarkic world. Yet they are fanatically committed to the methods of economic nationalism.

In a third class are the predominantly agricultural countries of Southern and Eastern Europe and some Latin American countries. Their processing industries are comparatively backward. They believe that they can improve their conditions by barring access to foreign manufactures. They are eager to create, artificially in a hothouse, as it were, domestic industries, producing at a cost much higher than those of other countries. They load the agricultural section of the population with the burden. They make the cost of agricultural production rise and thus impede export trade. The result is a very low standard of living. There is for them but little hope if they cannot maintain or expand their agricultural export and make the prices of manufactures drop.

Finally, there are the countries that nature has endowed with some valuable resources. They rely on the indispensability of their essential products and believe that they are in a much better position than the countries of the two aforementioned groups. They abuse their advantage by output restrictions and monopolistic price raising. Thus they push the consumer nations toward the production of substitutes. They will, in the long run, hardly come off better than the nations of the third group.

The pernicious consequences of these suicidal policies on the part of the countries of the second, third, and fourth groups were, in the critical years between the two world wars, to some extent delayed by the fact that the creditor countries, foremost among them the United States, did not stop granting credits and expanding foreign investment. The debtor countries received many billions of dollars, although their hostility to foreign capital displayed itself daily in new actions.

It has been asserted that this country, in the pursuit of a protectionist policy, did not adjust its conduct to the requirements of its creditor position. In barring access to foreign goods, it made it difficult for the debtors to pay interest and principal. This is true. But it is no less true that the American capitalists were slow in recognizing that economic nationalism had conspicuously increased the risk inherent in lending and investing abroad. They did not realize that many debtor countries considered imported capital as a gift or as a tribute due to them and were resolved never to comply with their obligations. If they had better understood this new mentality of the debtors, they would have discontinued exporting capital sooner. The international capital market would have disintegrated long since.

The fact is obvious: America still puts its stake into the gear of international transactions at a time at which the receiving countries were already withholding their stake. The receivers were benefited by getting what they badly needed. America was supplying, but it received only a fraction of what it had a fair claim to expect. America exported, the others imported —without pay.

Now, if the American capitalists were to withdraw altogether from the international capital market, the conditions of the United States would not deteriorate, but rather improve when compared with conditions in the preceding decades. A quantity of goods that would have been exported gratuitously, as it were, would become available either for domestic investment or for domestic consumption. Of course, a readjustment of domestic production would be necessary, as the country would not buy the same products that were previously exported. Some branches of industry and farming would suffer. But the country as a whole would be better off—or at least, it would not be worse off.

The debtor countries, on the other hand, would be heavily affected. They would have to forego the advantages derived from the excess of American imports.

Under such conditions, it is manifestly clear which countries urgently need a reconstruction of world trade and international capital transactions. America can look to the future with less apprehension than any other nation. America would, of course, sustain damage from a disintegration of world trade, but such a disintegration (which would mean the shrinking of international trade and the cessation of international capital transactions) would surely be a deadly blow to many other nations.

This realistic appreciation of conditions is not a plea for American indifference and inactivity with regard to postwar reconstruction of international trade, commerce, credit, and investment. America's economy would profit greatly from reconstruction. But in the beginning, all that America can and should contribute toward this end is to rearrange its own domestic affairs. The abandonment of inflation and the adoption of a monetary system that would prevent future inflation would not only benefit America, it would at the same time offer to all other nations the opportunity to settle their own problems.

Almost all nations are fully aware of the fact that they sorely need American aid. They cannot attain prosperity without importing goods from America. As they cannot pay cash, they want credits. Thus they must arrange their own affairs in a way that can inspire confidence in the prospective creditors. They must balance their budgets, abandon all inflationary measures, and stabilize foreign exchange rates. They must renounce, once and for all, all attempts to expropriate foreign creditors and investors. There can no longer be any question of discriminatory taxation, foreign exchange control, confiscation, and similar methods.

This is the only means to reestablish the international capital market. And without a reestablishment of the international capital market, there will be no revival of international trade.

APPENDIX

[The original outline for some of the ideas developed in this essay was prepared by Ludwig von Mises while he was still Professor of International Economic Relations at the Graduate Institute of International Studies in Geneva, Switzerland. In September of 1939, another member of the Institute's academic staff, the historian Guglielmo Ferrero, suggested to Director William E. Rappard a project for a series of periodic publications to be written by the Institute's scholars. The theme would be the "Problems of Europe." Each scholar would be asked to make a contribution analyzing the causes for Europe's present social, political, and economic problems, as well as proposals for reform and change for Europe's future. Dr. Rappard then shared this suggestion with the scholars and asked them to comment.

[On December 14, 1939, Mises submitted the following outline (see below) on what would have been his contribution to the publication project.[47] Unfortunately, the full text was not completed before he left Geneva for the United States in July of 1940. However, Mises did write an essay called "Monetary Reconstruction" in 1952, which was included as a new "Part Four" in the 1953 edition of *The Theory of Money and Credit*.[48] It differs in structure and content from the 1939 outline and from the essay on "A Noninflationary Proposal for Postwar Monetary Reconstruction," that is included in this volume. —Ed.]

47 [*Institut Universitaire de Hautes Études Internationales Geneve, Quarantieme Anniversaire 1927–1967* (*Graduate Institute of International Studies, Geneva, Fortieth Anniversary, 1927–1967*), p. 58. —Ed.]

48 [Mises, *The Theory of Money and Credit*, pp. 453–500. —Ed.]

Project of Ludwig von Mises
Graduate Institute of International Studies
Geneva, December 14, 1939

Monetary Reconstruction

I   Monetary Internationalism in the Past
   (1) The Gold Standard and the Gold Exchange Standard
   (2) International Monetary Unions, Their History, Their Working, and
       Their Failure
   (3) Cooperation of Central Banks
   (4) The Breakdown of the Gold Standard
   (5) Clearing Agreements

II A Critical Examination of Different Plans:
   (1) Return to the Orthodox Gold Standard
   (2) A Gold Standard with Flexible Parities
   (3) Cooperation of Foreign Exchange Equalization Accounts
   (4) International Bank Notes
   (5) An International Center for Trade Cycle Policy

III Limitations of National Sovereignty in Monetary Matters
   (1) Limitations in Accordance with the League of Nations
   (2) Limitations by the Terms of International Loans
   (3) Limitations by a Federal Union

IV Monetary Internationalism without Compulsion

CHAPTER VII

The Main Issues in Present-Day Monetary Controversies[1]

Introductory Remarks

This is not a systematic presentation of the problems of money and credit. Neither is it a complete exposition of the theories and doctrines dealt with. The aim of this paper is merely to enumerate certain topics that should not be neglected in a discussion of money and credit.

I   The Purchasing Power Controversy

A ❧ Is Money "Neutral"?

The older economists believed that—other things being equal—changes in the supply or demand of money make all commodity prices and wage rates simultaneously rise or fall in exact proportion to these changes. The price "level" changes, but the relations among the prices of individual commodities and services remain the same. Those mathematical economists whose theorizing culminates in the formulation of an equation of exchange still maintain this thesis.[2]

---

1 [The present essay was prepared in March of 1944 as a working paper for the Economic Principles Commission of the National Manufacturers Association. It served as background and preparation for *The American Enterprise System, Its Nature, Evolution, and Future*, 2 vols. (New York: McGraw-Hill, 1946), which was published as "the consensus of judgment among the Commission members," of which Mises was one.—Ed.]

2 [The American economist most closely identified with the formalization and use of the equation of exchange and who, in general, argued that changes in the money supply tended to generate proportional rises in the general level of prices was Irving Fisher (1867–1947).

Modern economic analysis rejects this assumption. The changes in the supply or demand of money do not affect all individuals at the same time and to the same extent. In the case of inflation, for instance, the additional quantity of money does not find its way at first into the pockets of all individuals, nor does every individual of those benefited first with the increase in the quantity of money get the same amount; and not every individual reacts to the same additional quantity in the same way. Consequently, the prices of various commodities and services rise neither at the same time nor to the same extent. The nonsimultaneous appearance and unevenness of the price changes brought about by increases in the quantity of money results in a shift of income and wealth from some groups of the population to other groups. Monetary fluctuations are not neutral, even apart from their repercussions on all contracts stipulating some form of deferred payments. Monetary changes are a source of economic and social change.[3]

B ❧ ARE CHANGES IN THE PURCHASING POWER OF MONEY MEASURABLE?

Even if we were prepared to leave out consideration of the nonsimultaneous appearance and unevenness of the price changes brought about by changes in the supply of or demand for money, we must realize that the index-number method does not provide a faithful criterion for the measurement of changes in the purchasing power of the monetary unit. Economic conditions are not rigid; they are—also apart from any changes occurring in monetary matters—continuously changing. New commodities appear, old commodities disappear. The quality of the various commodities is subject to change. Tastes, wants, and desires are changing and with them the valuation of the various goods offered on the market. A motorcar of 1920 and a motorcar of 1940 are entirely different things. Twenty-five years ago, where were vitamins, refrigerators, and talking pictures? How different is the role played today in the average American household by canned food, rayon, and radio sets? How much do clothes and shoes

---

See his *The Purchasing Power of Money* (New York: Macmillan Co., 2nd ed., 1920), p. 157: "There is no possible escape from the conclusion that a change in the quantity of money (M) must normally cause a proportional change in the price level."—Ed.]

3 [See Chapter VI, "A Noninflationary Proposal for Postwar Monetary Reconstruction," footnote 7, for references to Mises's writings on the non-neutrality of money.—Ed.]

change from one year to the next? Even standard foods like milk, butter, meat, and vegetables have in the last decades improved in quality to such an extent that it is impermissible to take them as equivalent with those marketed in the past. A method which tacitly assumes that nothing else had changed in the economic system than the available quantity of money is utterly illusory. The chairman of our committee has provided us with the results of an investigation undertaken in his corporation.[4] According to this information, only a fraction of the products manufactured today are of the same kind as the goods manufactured a few years ago. This is a typical case, more or less representative for all American processing industries.

Besides, mathematics provides us with various methods for the computation of averages from a given set of figures. Each of these methods has, with regard to the problem in question, some merits and some defects. Each of them yields different results. As it is impossible to declare one of these methods as the only adequate one and to discard all the others as manifestly unsuitable, it is obvious that the index-number approach does not provide an indisputable and uncontested solution that could command general acceptance.

C ❧ Is It Possible to Adjust Monetary Manipulation to a Nonarbitrary Standard?

The advocates of a manipulated currency pretend to aim at the stability of the monetary unit's purchasing power. They fail, however, to realize that in a changing economic world, the concept of a stable purchasing power is devoid of any real meaning.

There are three main objections to be raised against the proposals for a manipulated currency.

1. The various methods suggested for a measurement of changes in the monetary unit's purchasing power are arbitrary. Their results are contested by all those whose material interests would be hurt if they were to be used as a basis of monetary manipulation. In advocating the application of a certain index-number system, the results of which happen at the moment to provide a quasi-scientific justification of their particular interests,

4 [The chairman of the Economic Principles Commission of the National Association of Manufacturers (NAM) was Robert R. Wason, president of Manning, Maxwell, and Moore, Inc. He served as commission chairman from 1943 to 1945 and as president of NAM in 1946.—Ed.]

every pressure group and political party will always be in a position to cite the doctrine of some economists and statisticians. On the other hand, their adversaries will quote dissenting opinions of no less renowned experts. There is no means to free a *tabular standard* from the faults of purely arbitrary and party-ridden bias.[5]

2. It is impossible to know beforehand to what extent and at what date a definite amount of inflation or deflation (an increase or a reduction in the quantity of money and credit) will increase or reduce the prices of various commodities and services.

3. Apart from other deficiencies, the proposals for stabilization are faulty because they are based on the idea of money's neutrality. They all suggest methods to undo changes in the purchasing power of money that have already had their effects. If there has been an inflation, they wish to deflate to the same extent and vice versa. They do not realize that by this procedure, they do not undo the social consequences of monetary changes (that is, the shift of income and wealth from some groups to others), but simply add to them the social consequences of a new change. If a man has been hurt by being run over by an automobile, it is no remedy to let the car go back over him in the opposite direction.

D ❧ The Case Against Flexible Foreign Exchange Parities

If the purchasing power of an individual country's domestic currency changes, while the other countries' currencies do not change at all or not to the same extent, foreign trade is affected. As a rule, foreign exchange rates are adjusted at an early stage of the inflationary or deflationary process to the new state of the domestic money supply, even while the prices of some commodities and services still lag behind and are not fully adjusted for a time. As long as the inflationary or deflationary changes have not exhausted all their effects on the structure of prices, the comparatively low or high state of some prices results—in the case of inflation—in encour-

5 [The "tabular standard" was advocated and popularized by Irving Fisher; see his *Stabilizing the Dollar* (New York: Macmillan Co., 1920). Rather than the dollar representing a fixed weight of gold, the gold content of the dollar would be periodically changed to maintain a dollar of constant purchasing power, as measured and calculated by a price index. —Ed.]

aging exports and discouraging imports. From the viewpoint of mercantilist fallacies, a fall of the domestic monetary unit's purchasing power is, therefore, considered as a very fortunate occurrence.[6]

What really happens is this: The country exports more than it did before, and it gets, as compensation for these increased exports, a smaller amount of foreign products. Exports are, as it were, subsidized and imports penalized to the burden of the natives. The inflation is, by and large, tantamount to a tax imposed upon the domestic consumers in order to cheapen the consumption of domestic products by foreigners.

Nowadays, currency devaluation is mostly advocated as a remedy against the rigidity of wage rates. People are afraid of fighting openly the inappropriate policies of labor unions. They resort to an indirect attack. They hope that currency devaluation will, notwithstanding the rise of domestic commodity prices, not raise money wage rates and thus reduce real wage rates. Lord Keynes believes that "a gradual and automatic lowering of real wages as a result of rising prices" would not be "strongly resisted" by labor.[7] He does not see that wage rates are rigid only on the downside, not on the upside, too.

E ❧ The Case for the Gold Standard

The gold standard is not perfect. No human institution is.

The main argument in favor of the gold standard is that it renders the formation of the monetary unit's purchasing power independent of arbitrary action on the part of governments, political parties, and pressure groups. It places a check upon inflationary policies, and is the only standard which can possibly become an international, a world standard.

---

6 [According to the mercantilist ideas of the seventeenth and eighteenth centuries, international trade was beneficial only when the home country experienced a "positive" balance of trade, that is, when exports exceeded imports. A "negative" balance of trade—that is, when imports exceeded exports—was considered harmful. Thus anything that in general stimulated exports and limited imports was considered a desirable international trade policy from the mercantilist perspective.—Ed.]

7 [John Maynard Keynes, "The General Theory of Employment, Interest, and Money," in D. E. Moggridge, ed., *The Collected Works of John Maynard Keynes*, Vol. VII (New York: Macmillan Co., [1936] 1973), p. 264.—Ed.]

II   The Credit Controversy[8]

A ❧ THE BANKING PRINCIPLE

Some economists of the "Banking School" ventured to deny flatly that changes in the quantity of money available can affect prices and interest rates. They introduced into their reasoning the idea of monetary "hoards" as a *deus ex machina*. The amount of money kept in these mythical hoards changes in such a way as to neutralize automatically changes in the quantity of money. A surplus of money is swallowed by these hoards; a deficiency of money is made good by a restriction of the amount hoarded. This fable has long since been abandoned.

The bulk of the older Banking School economists and all contemporary representatives of this school do not deny that an increase in the quantity of money (metallic money, government paper money, irredeemable bank notes, and deposit currency) must—other things being equal—result in a general rise of prices. The core of their teachings is: Short-term credits granted by commercial banks in the form of bank notes or deposits created for this purpose do not affect prices and interest rates, provided they do not exceed "the needs of trade." Such loans provide the debtor with the funds required for the production and the marketing of goods. They are self-liquidating. If the purchased raw materials are made up and

8 [In the 1820s through the 1860s, there was a heated and highly sophisticated debate among two groups of British monetary theorists known as the "Currency School" and the "Banking School." The Currency School argued that (a) the note currency should vary precisely with the changes in the specie currency on deposit in the banking system; (b) the note currency should be fully convertible into specie; (c) the rate of interest was a significant influence on the volume of notes in circulation; and (d) the foreign exchange rate was a good guide for controlling the amount of paper currency in circulation. The Banking School argued that (a) the "needs of business" should regulate the quantity of bank notes issued, and the banks could not "force" notes into circulation in excess of the needs of business; (b) the Currency School was correct that bank notes should be fully convertible into specie; but (c) any drain of specie on the banking system might be counteracted by a decrease in the "hoards" of money held by people, and that any increase in specie or notes put into circulation might have no influence on spending and prices, because it might be absorbed into people's monetary "hoards." On the controversy between the Currency and Banking Schools, see Jacob Viner, *Studies in the Theory of International Trade* (New York: Augustus M. Kelley, [1937] 1965), pp. 218–89; Charles Rist, *History of Monetary and Credit Theory, from John Law to the Present* (New York: Augustus M. Kelley, [1940] 1966), 202–38; Lloyd Mints, *A History of Banking Theory, in Great Britain and the United States* (Chicago: University of Chicago Press, 1945), 74–114.—Ed.]

sold, or if the buyer of products settles his balance, the loan is paid off, and the bank notes or deposits disappear again. An actual need has brought them into existence. With the cessation of this need, they go off the stage. The amount of credit of this type which the market can absorb is determined by the volume of production and business activity. It is beyond the power of the banks to alter this volume. No credit expansion is to be feared if the banks strictly abide by the rule to limit their lending to satisfy the demand of producers or merchants for short-term credit.

The reasoning of the Banking School misses the essential problem. It is obvious that no credit expansion takes place if the banks keep the total amount of their lending at the same level. But if a new bank enters the field or if an existing bank embarks upon the granting of additional credit above the amount of its previous credits, credit expansion results.

It is not true that the volume of credit that the banks are in a position to grant, if strictly abiding by the aforementioned rules, is independent of the bank's policy. The market is always in a position to absorb a surplus of credit supply. An increase in the supply of credit brings about a tendency toward a lowering of the rate of interest. With the lower rate of interest, many projects appear attractive that did not appear so with a higher rate. The lowering of the rate of interest encourages the expansion of precisely those business activities that—according to the banking doctrine—are viewed as proper instances for the granting of bank credit. Thus the credit expansion automatically increases the "needs of trade." It stimulates business activities because it cheapens the exchange of future purchasing power for present purchasing power. While the supply of capital goods remained unaltered, there is now a greater demand for them on the part of business. Prices must, consequently, rise. A boom starts.

B ❧ THE CURRENCY PRINCIPLE

The "Currency School" intended to provide an explanation of the recurrence of economic crises. Its proponents first observed that the root cause of the depression is the preceding boom and substituted for the study of crises the study of the trade cycle.

Their reasoning ran this way: If the British banks expanded credit while conditions in the other countries remained unchanged, British prices would begin to rise, and those on the world market would lag behind them. Consequently, there would be an excess of British imports over exports. As the surplus of imported goods could not be paid for by shipping bank notes, the importers would have to export gold. Hence, gold would be withdrawn from the banks; their reserves would dwindle. This "external drain" would force upon the banks a restriction of their lending activities. The artificial boom would come to an end and give way to a depression.

The main fault of the Currency School was that it dealt with bank notes only and did not realize that deposits subject to check are only technically different from bank notes, while their economic significance is equal to that of bank notes. This failure vitiated the British Bank Act of 1844.[9] But it is easy to rectify this error by a simple extension of the theory.

C ❧ Austrian Theory of the Trade Cycle

Currency theory did not consider the problem of the consequences of credit expansion within an isolated country or of a synchronous credit expansion in all countries. It did not enter into a discussion of the way in which the market and the whole apparatus of production and distribution react to credit expansion. This task was accomplished by Austrian theory.[10]

The rate of interest established on a market not hampered by credit expansion, says Austrian theory, separates those business projects that can be carried out under the existing state of the supply of capital goods and con-

9 [The British Bank Act was passed in July of 1844. It divided the Bank of England into two parts, a Note Issue Department and a Banking Department. The Issue Department was restricted in the amount of bank notes it could issue on the basis of government debt (a maximum of fourteen million pounds); and notes issued beyond this had to be fully covered on the basis of additional deposits of gold coin or gold or silver bullion.—Ed.]

10 [The Austrian theory of the trade cycle was first developed by Mises in *The Theory of Money and Credit* (Indianapolis: Liberty Fund, [1924] 1981), pp. 377–404; refined in his monograph "Monetary Stabilization and Cyclical Policy" (1928) in Percy L. Greaves, ed., *Von Mises on the Manipulation of Money and Credit* (Dobbs Ferry, N.Y.: Free Market Books, 1978), pp. 111–71; briefly summarized in "The Austrian Theory of the Trade Cycle," (1936) in Richard M. Ebeling, ed., *The Austrian Theory of the Trade Cycle and Other Essays* (Auburn, Ala.: Ludwig von Mises Institute, 1996), pp. 25–35; and reformulated in a wider context in *Human Action, A Treatise on Economics*, 4th rev. ed. (Irvington-on-Hudson, N.Y.: Foundation for Economic Education, 1996), pp. 538–86 & 780–803; see also Richard M. Ebeling, "Ludwig von Mises and the Gold Standard," in Llewellyn H. Rockwell, Jr., ed., *The Gold Standard: An Austrian Perspective* (Lexington, Mass.: Lexington Books, 1985), pp. 35–59, which also contains footnote references to most of the Austrian School literature on money and the trade cycle from the period between the two world wars.—Ed.]

sumers' preferences from those that cannot. With the lowering of the rate of interest brought about by credit expansion, the entrepreneurs embark upon projects for the realization of which the available amount of factors of production does not suffice.[11] They are deceived by the appearance of a nonexistent richness in the supply of material factors of production. They behave like a master builder who has overestimated the amount of building material available, has used up too much for the foundations and cannot complete his plan on account of a lack of material. Some of the new projects will never be finished; others, when finished, will be useless for lack of the plants producing the required complementary producers' goods; others will not yield an adequate return on the capital invested.

It is true, the banks (or the governments) are in a position to prolong the boom for some time by injecting progressively increasing quantities of bank notes and deposits into the market. But the artificially created prosperity cannot last forever. Sooner or later it must come to an end. There are only two alternatives:

1. The banks do not stop and go on expanding credit at a progressively accelerated pace. But the spell of inflation breaks once the public has the conviction that the banks and the authorities are resolved not to stop. If no limit of the inflation and, consequently, of the general rise of prices can be foreseen, a general *Flucht in die Sachwerte*[12] starts. Everybody becomes aware of the fact that to hold cash and deposit balances with the banks involves loss, and that he does better to buy and store goods. Everybody is anxious to get rid of money and to exchange it for some other commodities, no matter how much he must pay for them. Prices are running away, and the purchasing power of the monetary unit drops to zero. The national currency system cracks up.

11 It is necessary to keep in mind that interest rates, in the course of a credit expansion, are—with the exception of the very beginning of the process—not always low when compared with the level which business used to consider as normal. But they are always low when measured by the standard that they would have to reach in a period of progressive inflation and its corollary, a general rise of prices, since they would have to include at such a time a compensation for the depreciation of the money unit going on in the period of the loan. [The theory of an inflationary "premium" or a deflationary "discount" attached to the rate of interest, based on debtor-creditor expectations of changes in the purchasing power of the monetary unit during the period of a loan, was first developed by Irving Fisher in *Appreciation and Interest* (New York: Augustus M. Kelley, [1896] 1965) and *The Rate of Interest* (New York: Macmillan Co., 1907); see also Mises, *The Theory of Money and Credit*, pp. 225–34 and *Human Action*, pp. 541–45.—Ed.]

12 ["Flight into Real Value," that is, nonmonetary forms of wealth.—Ed.]

2. As a rule, the banks do not let things go so far. They stop sooner by restricting credit. Then the day of reckoning dawns. The illusions disappear, people begin again to see reality as it is. The blunders committed in the boom become visible.

In every case, the slump is unavoidable. There is no means to make permanent a boom created by credit expansion and inflation.

The slump does not destroy values, but merely illusions. It does not make people poorer, it merely makes them aware of the impoverishment brought about by the malinvestment of the boom. It is not the depression that is an evil, but the preceding boom. The depression is the process of adjustment of economic conditions to the real market state-of-affairs. The fall in prices and wage rates is the preliminary step toward recovery and future real prosperity. He who wants to prevent the recurrence of economic crises must prevent the resumption of credit expansion.

In short, credit expansion is doomed to failure at any rate. There is no means to substitute fictitious capital created by monetary and credit manipulation for nonexisting capital goods. The only method to increase a nation's wealth and income is to save and to accumulate more real capital goods.

The rate of interest is a market phenomenon. In the long run, its height does not depend on the supply of money and credit. It is determined by the difference in the valuation of present goods and future goods.[13] An increase in the supply of money and credit only temporarily lowers the rate of interest. In bringing about malinvestments, it finally results in a reduction in the amount of capital goods available. The economy has to pay heavily for the orgy of the artificial boom.

D ❧ The Socialists' Rejection of Austrian Theory

In the eyes of the socialists, there is no such thing as a scarcity of material factors of production. Mankind could enjoy a life in plenty. Scarcity is merely an outcome of the capitalist mode of production and distribution.

---

13 [On the Austrian theory of "time preference" or "time valuation" as the basis for market rates of interest, see Mises, *Human Action*, pp. 479–537; Murray N. Rothbard, *Man, Economy, and State: A Treatise on Economic Principles*, Vol. I (Los Angeles, Calif.: Nash Publishing, 1970), pp. 313–86, and "Time Preference," in Richard M. Ebeling, ed., *Austrian Economics: A Reader* (Hillsdale, Mich.: Hillsdale College Press, 1991), pp. 414–22; Israel M. Kirzner, *Essays on Capital and Interest: An Austrian Perspective* (Brookfield, Vt.: Edward Elgar, 1996); Hans F. Sennholz, "The Böhm-Bawerkian Foundation of the Interest Theory," in Hardy Bouillon, ed., *Libertarians and Liberalism: Essays in Honour of Gerard Radnitzky* (Brookfield, Vt.: Ashgate Publishing Co., 1996), pp. 123–47.—Ed.]

Economic crises are an evil inherent in capitalism. They have nothing at all to do with the endeavors to expand credit and to lower the rate of interest by bank manipulation.

The consistent supporters of these tenets blithely assert that interest is a purely monetary phenomenon that could not exist in a barter economy. (Such were, for instance, the ideas of Silvio Gesell, the minister of finance of the short-lived communist Soviet regime in Munich;[14] Lord Keynes is full of praise for Gesell and calls him an "unduly neglected prophet.")[15] Others are less outspoken and cling to a more cautious language. But a faulty doctrine does not gain anything from the fact that its advocates lack the courage to profess frankly all the conclusions which must be drawn logically from the principles they have espoused.

Whoever does not share the opinion that the rate of interest is only a monetary phenomenon is under the necessity to demonstrate the mechanism by which that level of the rate of interest, which corresponds to the whole structure of market conditions, reestablishes itself when temporarily disarranged by an easy money policy. The only solution of this problem provided up to now is that of the Austrian theory.

All those economists who want to explain the trade cycle as being caused by factors other than credit expansion must admit that no boom could arise if the amount of money and credit available were not increased. This implies that they cannot help admitting the fundamental thesis of Austrian theory.[16]

E ❧ SALVATION THROUGH CREDIT MANIPULATION

Consistent supporters of the doctrine that the rate of interest is a monetary phenomenon only and that there is no harm in the endeavors to abolish it by credit manipulation cannot help approving plans to establish the millennium by a reform of the monetary and banking system. The best known

---

14 [Silvio Gesell (1862–1930) was a German "monetary crank" who proposed imposing a 5.4 percent annual tax on the holding of cash. The idea was to stimulate the use of money in transactions, rather than its being held as idle "hoards." Gesell argued that money taken out of hoards and used for investment purposes would so increase the supply of capital that the rate of interest could be pushed down to zero.—Ed.]

15 [Keynes, *The General Theory of Employment, Interest and Money*, p. 353.—Ed.]

16 [For Mises's criticisms of "nonmonetary explanations of the trade cycle," see *Human Action*, pp. 580–86; also, see F. A. Hayek, *Monetary Theory and the Trade Cycle* (New York: Augustus M. Kelley, [1933] 1966).—Ed.]

of the older projects of this type was that of the French socialist Proudhon, the man who coined the phrase "Property is theft."[17]

Such ideas are very popular with many successful businessmen. The Belgian Ernest Solvay advocated "social comptabilism,"[18] a system hardly distinguished from that of Proudhon. More than twenty years ago, Thomas A. Edison and Henry Ford suggested that the construction of roads be financed by the issue of additional paper money in order to avoid the payment of interest to the banks or the public.

The present-day variety of this old superstition is embodied in the doctrine of unbalanced budgets and government spending. As far as the government procures the means required for spending by taxing the citizens and by borrowing from the public, its spending curtails individuals' capacity to invest to the same extent that it increases that of the government. As far as the government borrows from the commercial banks or issues additional paper money, it embarks upon credit expansion and inflation.

In the early stages of every instance of credit expansion and inflation, there is always optimism. People do not want to pay attention to the warning voices of economists. They stubbornly insist that their present situation has nothing in common with the boom periods of the past, and that the theorists are wrong in predicting the breakdown of the "prosperity." But when the crisis comes, people become desperate; then they impeach not the faulty monetary and credit policies but the capitalist system as such.

III   The Foreign Exchange Controversy

A ❧ Purchasing Power Parity Theory

The exchange ratio between two different kinds of money tends to correspond to the exchange ratio between each of them and commodities and services. It is usual to call this ratio the static or natural ratio. If this exchange ratio between two kinds of money is disturbed, people will start

17 [Pierre-Joseph Proudhon (1809–65) was a French economist and philosopher who opposed private property as "theft" and advocated socialism and anarchism. He believed that interest could be eliminated as a source of income by ending money's connection to gold and issuing "claims" to the goods produced by labor.—Ed.]

18 [Ernest Solvay (1838–1922) was a Belgian industrial chemist, known for commercially developing an ammonia-soda process for producing sodium-carbonate widely used in the manufacture of glass and soap. In 1900, he published *Notes on Productionism and Comptabilism*, in which he advocated a system of production and a bookkeeping economy without the use of money.—Ed.]

operations—buying and selling—in order to profit from existing discrepancies. These transactions tend to reestablish the natural ratio.

It does not make any difference whether the two kinds of money are used in the same country simultaneously (as was the case under the old parallel gold and silver standard) or whether each country uses one of them only. The natural rate of foreign exchange is determined by the purchasing power of each of the two kinds of money.

If a payment has to be effected in a distant place, the transaction is burdened with the cost of shipping the money. These costs are avoided if claims and debts of various people in the two places can be cleared. If complete settlement of all payments due can be achieved in this way, no actual shipping of money is required. If an unsettled surplus turns up, it must be settled by transfers from place to place.[19]

The balance of payments does not determine the exchange ratio. It only determines how much of the cost of shipping money can be saved. If the two places or countries in question use the same precious metal as the standard, the balance of payments determines the fluctuations of the rate-of-exchange *within the rigid limits set by the cost of shipping money* (gold points or shipping points).[20]

B Balance of Payment Theory

Balance of payment theory asserts that foreign exchange rates are determined by the balance of payments.

This doctrine fails to realize that the amount of foreign trade depends on the structure of prices. If Atlantis imports from Thule a commodity A, for the unit of which two ducats must be paid in Atlantis, the commodity must be sold in Thule at the equivalent of two ducats in its local currency, that is, ten florins. If, without any inflation in Thule, the price of the ducat goes up to three florins, the importation of A must drop or stop altogether because at the price of fifteen florins, the demand for A in Thule shrinks

19 [On the purchasing power parity theory of foreign exchange rates, see Mises, *The Theory of Money and Credit*, pp. 195–213 and *Human Action*, pp. 452–58; the theory was also developed in a different formulation by Gustav Cassel, *Money and Foreign Exchange After 1914* (New York: Arno Press, [1922] 1972). See also Joseph T. Salerno, "International Monetary Theory," in Peter J. Boettke, ed., *The Elgar Companion to Austrian Economics* (Brookfield, Vt.: Edward Elgar, 1994), pp. 249–57.—Ed.]

20 [The "gold points" represented the upper and lower limits of fluctuations of a country's foreign exchange rate under the gold standard, beyond which it would be profitable to either export gold out of or import gold into that country.—Ed.]

or disappears altogether. A rise of foreign exchange rates that does not correspond to a rise of domestic prices (a fall of the purchasing power of the domestic currency) thus has the tendency to render the country's balance of payment "favorable."

But, object the supporters of balance of payment theory, things are certainly different if A is a vital necessity for the citizens of Thule. Then, they must import A, no matter how much its price goes up. This, too, is a fallacy. If the individual citizens of Thule spend more florins for the purchase of A, they must, if there is no domestic inflation, restrict their buying of other commodities, either domestic or imported. In the first case, the prices of these domestic commodities drop, and they become available for export. In the second case, the amount of foreign exchange that would have been absorbed by the importation of other goods becomes available for the purchase of A.

If there is domestic inflation in Thule, then—and only then—a rise of the price of A (in florins) will not hinder the importation of A, as soon as the price of A (in Thule) is affected by the general rise of prices.

C ❧ The Requirements of Foreign Exchange Stability

There is but one means to keep a nation's domestic currency at par with gold and the sound currency of other countries: to abstain from credit expansion and inflation.

CHAPTER VIII

A Draft of Guidelines for the Reconstruction of Austria[1]

I   *The Current Situation*

A ❧❧❧

Anyone seriously contemplating the reconstruction of an Austrian political system must first of all face the fact that the new Austria cannot in any respect revert to and carry on the policies of the old Austria.

The economic policies of the last fifty years, but especially those of the last twenty years, were policies of capital exhaustion and were bound to lead to a collapse. The National Socialists merely put the finishing touches on what the Austrians themselves had begun. There is no word strong enough to characterize the wrongheadedness of this wasteful management of resources.[2]

It in no way justifies or puts a gloss on this mismanagement of the economy to point out that many other, in fact, all other states have followed similar principles. Some of these other states are wealthier and thus have been able to keep on longer, because they have had more reserves.

---

1 [This confidential monograph was prepared at the request of Otto von Hapsburg, former archduke of Austria, and was dated May 1940; see Margit von Mises, *My Years with Ludwig von Mises*, 2nd enlarged ed. (Cedar Falls, Iowa: Center for Futures Education, 1984), pp. 68–69.—Ed.]

2 [On Austrian economic policies and conditions in the period between the two world wars, see K. W. Rothschild, *Austria's Economic Development Between the Two Wars* (London: Frederick Muller, 1947); and Gottfried Haberler, "Austria's Economic Development after the Two World Wars," in Sven W. Arndt, ed., *The Political Economy of Austria* (Washington, D.C.: American Enterprise Institute, 1982), pp. 61–75.—Ed.]

Others, again, were more restrained in using up resources and have been able to keep on longer because they conserved. The end result, however, will be the same everywhere: impoverishment. It is no consolation for us that others are bad off as well. The fact that at the end of the war all of Europe will be on the verge of destitution will not make our own situation any easier but, on the contrary, more difficult. There will be no one who can come to our assistance. We will have to work our way out of our misery ourselves.

B ❧❧❧

As a mountainous country with poor soil and few natural resources, Austria must rely on industrial activity to feed a population of six and a half million people. As an agrarian nation, Austria could at best eke out enough food for a population of one to two million. Austria must become an industrial nation to survive, or at least to survive as we would all wish.

To be an industrial country requires being predominantly an importer of raw materials and food and an exporter of industrial products. The mainstays of such an organism are the entrepreneurs of the export industry, who have the know-how to produce sufficiently high-quality and cheap industrial goods to sell on the world market. The industrial and commercial genius of these entrepreneurs creates work and livelihood for all the other citizens. The country lives on them; they are the pillars of the state edifice.

Old Austria produced about one thousand men of this kind. Their number was relatively large in terms of the country's total output, because the Austrian export industry was not so much a large-scale as a medium-scale industry, centered in Vienna and its vicinity. Compared to competing industries in other countries, it was poorly equipped with capital, and it had to contend with large natural obstacles. Austrian production sites are very disadvantageously located from the standpoint of transportation technology. Both the shipping in of coal and raw materials and the shipping out of finished goods are more expensive for Austrian industry than for the better-located industries elsewhere. Austrian industry also suffered from the government's barely concealed hostility. Incomparably higher taxes were imposed on it than on its foreign competitors. It was forced by trade unions to pay wages that it could not afford. The whole country was fighting against these thousand men, on whose vitality everyone was dependent.

These one thousand men are gone today, and so is Austrian industry. Austria will have to build up its export industry from scratch.

At least two-thirds of these one thousand men were Jews. They were deprived of their enterprises; many of them were slain or slowly tortured to death in concentration camps. The rest of them were expelled from the country.[3] They are scattered all over the world and trying to start afresh. They will not want to come back, because they are unable to abandon their new enterprises, in which they have invested the modest means that they salvaged or accumulated anew, or to leave their jobs in enterprises owned by others. They have brought along their best collaborators to their adopted countries; they are producing there—under more favorable natural and political conditions than Austria can offer them—items that used to constitute Austria's special strength and will be a serious competition for any future Austrian industry. To give one example, the numerous Viennese purchasing agents for American department stores had to terminate their activity in March 1938. The items that they used to buy in Vienna are now being produced in the United States or France, partially by Austrian emigrants.

The so-called Aryanization of firms was based on the Marxist idea that capital (machinery and raw material) and the labor input of workers were the only vital ingredients of an enterprise, whereas the entrepreneur was an "exploiter." An enterprise without entrepreneurial spirit and creativity, however, is nothing more than a pile of rubbish and old iron. Today the Aryanized firms, one and all, contribute nothing to exports. They are either working for the military or they have been liquidated. Commercial ties abroad, built up by more than one hundred years of unrelenting effort, have been destroyed. The core of skilled workers has been dispersed and

3 [At the time of the annexation of Austria by Nazi Germany in March of 1938, there were approximately 250,000 Jews in Austria. By May of 1939, that number had decreased to about 121,000, mostly through emigration. By December of 1941, the number had declined to 57,000, through forced deportation of Austrian Jews by the Nazi authorities to Eastern-occupied areas and concentration camps. According to one authority, only 216 Jews survived the war in hiding in Austria. In 1946, one year after the end of the Second World War, the Jewish population in Austria was about five thousand, due to the return of survivors from the death camps. On the terrorizing, property-confiscation, expulsion, exiling, and mass murder of the Austrian Jews by the Nazis beginning in 1938, see Bruce F. Pauley, *From Prejudice to Persecution: A History of Austrian Anti-Semitism* (Chapel Hill, N.C.: University of North Carolina Press, 1992).—Ed.]

displaced from its traditional skills. A worker who used to produce ladies' purses will never return to his former profession after having spent several years shoveling dirt at the "Westwall."[4]

The two or three hundred non-Jewish industrialists in the export business have fared better than the Jewish industrialists. They were neither murdered, tortured, nor despoiled like the Jews; some of them even participated actively in the Jews' despoliation. Yet they too could not conduct their enterprises in the old way because of foreign-exchange controls and the wartime command economy. They have all turned into producers of military supplies or *ersatz* items.[5]

When the new Austria becomes a state again, it will have a rural population of about one or two million people who will just barely raise the food they need for their own subsistence and four more million people who will be at a loss as to what to do with themselves. Austria will be left with rundown factory buildings and worn-out machines unsuited for the export tasks of the future.

Austrian industrial enterprises, expecting to produce for the domestic market, will face the same problems. It must be stressed that the Austrian population is dependent on the success of the export industry for its supply of all conceivable kinds of manufactured goods. If Austrians want to consume commodities containing raw material and semifinished goods of foreign origin, they must first earn the money required for the payment of these foreign raw materials and semifinished products by selling Austrian products to other countries.

A country with Austria's economic structure is entirely dependent on the success of its export industry.

Two sets of statistics serve to highlight the extent to which the Austrian economy was involved with the international economy. The first set of statistics indicates the per capita value of foreign trade: In 1929, it amounted to $120 for Austria, compared to $107 for Germany, $109 for France, $82

---

4 [The "Westwall" referred to military fortifications built as a defense line along Nazi Germany's western border with France. — Ed.]

5 [*Ersatz* items are substitute goods or resources manufactured to replace those no longer available from usual foreign markets. In Nazi Germany's case, such goods were needed because of government policies specifically designed to restrict trade and foreign exchange and develop domestic alternatives. In preparation for war, Hitler did not want to be dependent upon foreign suppliers. — Ed.]

for Czechoslovakia, $81 for the United States, $244 for Switzerland, and $161 for Sweden. There are unfortunately no accurate statistics for invisible import and export items such as the tourist trade, the invisible export of Viennese department stores, ready-made clothing, tailor-made clothing, etc. (which are particularly important for Austria and returned at least two hundred million schillings annually), and the export of all kinds of services. Inclusion of these items would certainly have raised the per capita value of Austria's foreign trade.

The second set of statistics giving some measure of the dependence of the Austrian economy on the international exchange of goods is the share of export goods in the total domestic output: In 1931, this share was estimated at twenty-five percent by a government-appointed economic committee (Dollfuss, Mises, Palla, and Schüller).[6] In other words, one quarter of the country's total domestic product was exported. It is estimated that exports accounted for forty-five percent of total industrial production.

C ❧❧❧

It is misleading to claim that we already underwent these experiences after the First World War and to say that then, too, everything seemed to be destroyed, yet a new start was easily and rapidly made.

It is true that the continuity of the production process was greatly disturbed, but it was not destroyed. No sooner had the armistice been signed than buyers for Austrian high-quality goods made their appearance and gave their orders. At the same time, suppliers of raw material and semifinished goods came to the fore and offered their wares with favorable conditions of payment. Had the absurd foreign-exchange policy of the Austrian government then in power and the trade unions' strike policy not imposed the greatest conceivable difficulties on industry, Austrian industry could have resumed its normal operation by 1919. The main accomplishment of Austrian entrepreneurs at that time consisted in overcoming the hurdles created by the government and the political parties. Today, we also

---

6 [In 1931, a report prepared for the Austrian government was coauthored by Mises, Engelbert Dollfuss, Edmund Palla, and Richard Schüller. It was called *Bericht über die Ursuchen der wirtschaftlichen Schwierigkeiten in Oesterreich*, or "A Report on the Causes of the Economic Difficulties in Austria."— Ed.]

lack what was available then: entrepreneurs with ties to customers and suppliers who know how to tackle all problems.

What counts most in industry is the entrepreneur: a man with a good brain, ideas, capacity for hard work, and perseverance; a man of integrity whom suppliers of raw materials can trust because he always pays on time; a reliable man who inspires confidence in customers because he always delivers a good product.

D ❧❧❧

In the "liberalist age," a country with little capital could import capital from other countries.[7]

Austria, which will be bereft of capital after the present war, can hardly count on capital import from elsewhere. Capitalists in countries well endowed with capital have had such unfortunate experiences with capital investments abroad that they will no longer dare to repeat the experiment. Not even the prospect of high interest rates will entice them, if they take into account the risk of losing the invested capital.[8]

But even if the capitalists themselves were willing to invest, their government will put obstacles in their way. The truth is that trade unions in

7 [The "liberalist age" refers to the period before the First World War, when the ideas of classical liberalism—individual liberty, free markets, and free trade in goods and capital—were still fairly predominant in political-economic policy in the major Western countries. —Ed.]

8 [In the period immediately following the end of the Second World War (May of 1945), Austria's Gross National Product was estimated to be 36 percent of its 1937 level and still only 67 percent of its 1937 level in 1947. In the words of one analyst, during this period the Austrian economy was characterized by "chaos, starvation, and general want." Prices for goods in Austria were distorted by price controls, resulting in a pervasive network of black markets. Monetary chaos led to high inflation. The country heavily relied upon foreign aid from the Allies, especially the United States, for feeding large segments of the population and infusing the economy with investment capital in order to foster private sector production hampered by production and price controls kept in place by the four occupying powers (the U. S., Great Britain, France, and the Soviet Union). Growth in production and employment in Austria between 1948 and 1951 was partly financed through foreign aid in the form of the European Reconstruction Program and the Marshall Plan. See Franz Nemschak, *Ten Years of Austrian Economic Development, 1945–1955* (Vienna: Association of Austrian Industrialists, 1955). Also, Fred H. Klopstock, "Monetary and Fiscal Policy in Post-Liberation Austria," *Political Science Quarterly* (March 1948), pp. 99–124. —Ed.]

all states attempt to block the export of capital. They want to raise the marginal productivity of labor in their own country and, thereby, increase wages.

E 〰〰〰

Fifty-four percent of the employed persons in Austria were engaged in agriculture and forestry, but Austrian agriculture prospered only because of the government's economic policy whereby the nonagrarian segment of the population was forced to buy agricultural products at prices that were a multiple of world market prices. Agriculture thrived on the exploitation of nonfarmers.

One example: In 1923, thirty-two hundred metric tons of butter were imported and one metric ton was exported. In 1932, seven hundred and twenty metric tons were imported and fourteen hundred were exported. These results were achieved through export subsidies. In 1935, the export subsidy was 175 percent of the price of butter across the border; when the butter price rose on the world market, the export subsidy was cut percentage-wise, falling to 110 percent that year and to 83 percent in 1937. The total sum expended remained almost the same, however, within the range of six to seven million schillings per year. Consequently, the quantity exported increased to seven thousand metric tons in 1937.

Austrian agriculture received far more subsidies by the state, under various guises, than it contributed in terms of direct taxes (property tax, building tax, and income tax). It not only did not share in the burden of the state budget, but was actually supported by the budget. It sold its products on the domestic market at prices that were far above those of the world market. The food prices in Austria were more than three times as high as in neighboring Hungary and Yugoslavia.

The new Austria will be unable to afford this farm policy. It will have to face the problem of finding some sort of income for the nonagrarian segment of the population. City dwellers, workers, cannot possibly afford to pay prices that make it worthwhile to grow agricultural products in remote mountain valleys. Through the destruction of the Austrian export industry, the major part of Austrian agriculture has lost its basis for existence.

The import of industrial products was also impeded or made more expensive by the policies affecting export trade. Protection given to industry was to some extent a concealed agricultural subsidy. The sugar and distilling industry and beer brewing and malt production were all protected in order to facilitate the sale of sugar beets, potatoes, and barley at prices greatly elevated above world market prices. With complete disregard for the true nature and basic needs of Austrian export industries, moreover, the government protected both the production of semifinished products, that were turned into finished products by the export industry, and the production of machines used by the export industry. The result was that the manufacture of ready-made clothing, shoes, and leather luxury goods was made more expensive because the prices of fabrics, upper leather, and smooth leather were artificially raised, despite their short supply and poor quality domestically. Iron was supplied at world market prices for the production of machines, equipment, and vehicles intended for export. But for machines that the Austrian export industry needed for its factories, this "favorable treatment" did not apply. For the delivery of these machines, which had high tariffs to protect them, machine manufacturers—mostly subsidiaries of companies in the German Reich—received much higher prices than those foreign competitors of the Austrian export industry had to pay.

The protective tariff from which the Austrian finished goods industry benefited could not compensate for the burden that was imposed on it by the protection of the semifinished goods industry and the machine industry.

F ❧❧❧

The most important unsubsidized export items created from domestic raw material were wood and cellulose.

In 1929, wood export came to 4.24 million metric tons, with a value of 238 million schillings; in 1937, 3.4 million metric tons had a value of 131 million schillings. In 1937, cellulose export amounted to 0.32 million metric tons and wood pulp to 40,000 metric tons (dry weight). The export value of cellulose and wood pulp amounted to 58.6 million schillings. Comprehensive figures for the contribution of wood products to Austrian foreign trade must include the export of cardboard, paper, and paper products, which added 0.3 million metric tons valued at 75.6 million schillings.

It will be impossible to maintain this major Austrian export item at its former level after the war. The National Socialists despoiled the existing forests by excessive timber cutting. It will be a matter of decades before the consequences of this depredation can be made good.

In 1929, magnetite export came to 0.42 million metric tons, valued at 18.4 million schillings. In 1937, exports came to 0.42 million metric tons valued at 15 million schillings.

Raw iron export came to 0.1 million metric tons, as against raw iron import of 50,600 metric tons.

In 1937, the total export of raw and used metals reached a value of 40 million schillings, as against imports valued at 89 million schillings. In evaluating the significance of iron ore extraction for export, one must also keep in mind the fact that the export of iron ware, machines, equipment, vehicles, and motors produced in Austria indirectly contributed to total iron export.

To grasp fully the order of magnitude of these figures, one must also look at import figures for 1937, in which import of critical food items alone had a value of 305 million schillings. In 1929, it attained a value of 691 million schillings; this decline implied significant cuts in the meat, bread, flour, legume, and fat consumption of the masses of the population.

These figures demonstrate beyond a doubt that Austria is an industrial country.

G

The significance of the Austrian tourist trade in the past and its future have been substantially overrated. Anyone who is not blinded by local patriotism must admit that Austria has less attraction for foreigners than other countries.

The Austrian Alps are not as high as the Swiss, French, and Italian Alps. There are few ski resorts at an elevation higher than fifteen hundred meters. Skiing in the woods is not to everyone's taste. Skiers prefer slopes located above the timber line, where the snow is suited for skiing in winters with little snow.

Vienna's museums are rich in treasures, but they cannot compete with those in Rome, Florence, Paris, and Madrid. The paintings that one admires in Vienna are of foreign provenance; Austrian art is not remotely of the same caliber as Italian, French, Spanish, and Dutch art.

Vienna, Salzburg, and Innsbruck are beautiful cities, but other countries are better supplied with such cities. Austria has few cathedrals, castles, and palaces rivaling those in France and the Iberian Peninsula, not to speak of Italy's architectural treasures. Anyone wandering through the streets of Paris, London, Rome, and Florence is surrounded by deeply impressive historical remnants. There lived the creators of our culture and there the major events of world history took place. Vienna is significant for foreigners as the home of great musicians, but other parts of Austria lack these associations. There is no historical event having taken place in an Austrian city that is still alive in the minds of our contemporaries. Is it any wonder that travelers prefer to go to Avignon, Arles, and Nimes, to Siena, Perugia, Assisi, and Ravenna rather than to Graz and Klagenfurt? Or that they are more interested in Michelangelo and Rafael, in St. Francis and Dante, in Cromwell and Napoleon than in the figures of our Austrian history?

The Danube is no less beautiful than the Rhine. Still, cultivated people have associations with the words Rheingold[9] and Lorelei[10] that give them a sense of familiarity with the Rhine, while Rüdiger von Bechelaren[11] evokes few such associations. The Austrian landscape is not blessed with the dignity that only a poet's masterpiece can confer.

The Austrian tourist trade was on the upswing between 1920 and 1937 because the international traveling public was in some way discovering a new country here. The attraction of the *Festspiele* in Salzburg[12]—the creation of two "non-Aryan" geniuses, Hugo von Hofmannsthal[13] and Max Reinhardt[14]—were an important factor in this respect.

The Germans were the major contingent of foreign visitors to Austria.

---

9 [*Das Rheingold* is the prologue in one act to the trilogy, *Der Ring des Nibelungen*, by Richard Wagner (1813–83), first produced in 1869.—Ed.]

10 [*Die Lorelei* is an unfinished opera in three acts by Felix Mendelssohn (1809–47). —Ed.]

11 [Rüdiger von Bechelaren (or Poechlarn) is a principal character in the *Nibelungenlied*, the longest epic poem written in Middle High German, which dates from the fourteenth century. He was a knight and a "noble figure."—Ed.]

12 [*"Festspiele"* is the annual music festival in Salzburg.—Ed.]

13 [Hugo von Hofmannsthal (1874–1929) was a well-known Austrian poet and essayist specializing in comedy and opera. He focused on three main themes: freedom and fate, change and constancy, and freedom and guilt in the human condition.—Ed.]

14 [Max Reinhardt (1873–1943) was a world-famous actor and theater director known throughout Europe for his productions of Shakespeare's plays. He immigrated to the United States in 1937 and operated the Max Reinhardt Workshop for Stage, Screen, and Radio in Hollywood, California. In 1938, the Nazis confiscated his property in Vienna.—Ed.]

The total number of overnight stays in Austria by foreigners in 1931–32 was 880,800, for which Germans from the Reich accounted for 393,800, Yugoslavs, Hungarians, Romanians, Czechs, Poles, and travelers from the Baltic countries altogether 338,900. Thus five-sixths of the travelers came from countries that will presumably have to curtail sharply their share of international travel after the war. The share from Western European countries (England, Belgium, Holland, Switzerland, France), the United States, and Canada was only 70,100, or less than 8 percent. These figures do not augur well for the future of the Austrian tourist trade.

The financial impact of the tourist trade can only be surmised. By estimating foreigners' expenditures in Austria in recent years at about two hundred million schillings, we are likely to err on the high side.

H ❧❧❧

Austrian economic policy did its utmost to destroy the underpinnings of the Austrian state.

A so-called "producer policy" protects less competent persons against the competition of the more competent by granting special privileges to the former. A more apt name would be "production-curtailing policy." Its net result is curtailing output and increasing production costs.

The goal of industrial policy has been to protect small artisan establishments against industrial factories working with the resources of modern technology. From 1883 on, it has vainly attempted, by increasingly harsh measures, to protect the shoemaker against the shoe factory, the baker against the bread factory, the butcher against large-scale slaughterhouses. The entire administrative apparatus at the federal, state, and local level has been geared to this anti-industrial struggle. It was a cause for celebration when an industrial enterprise was prevented from repairing its defective vehicles in its own workshops or from nailing together its own crates for shipping its products.

Proof-of-competency for setting up shop, a requirement found nowhere in the modern civilized world but in Austria, prevented the widow of a soldier killed by the enemy from earning her living as a seamstress or hairdresser. Many thick volumes contain trade agency decisions about the lines to be drawn between individual trades. There you can learn under what conditions a doll producer is entitled to provide dolls' heads with curls; whether a grocer is entitled to sell meat and may also prepare scrambled eggs; whether a candy store is allowed to sell lemonade and raspberry drinks; and whether shirtmakers may also turn out ladies' blouses, or whether this falls exclusively under the jurisdiction of tailors. Ministries, Länd [province] governments, district offices, and municipal magistrates devoted a substantial part of their activity to these and similar questions, which furthermore occupied chambers of commerce, industrial associations, trade promotion agencies, and hundreds of lawyers.

The incompetent and lazy in agriculture received similar protection. Special commissions were appointed to look into the transfer of agricultural property, so as to prevent "unqualified" persons from getting a foothold in agriculture. At the end of the 1920s, about one hundred Bulgarians immigrated to Austria, leased small pieces of fallow land in the vicinity of Vienna and other cities, and grew vegetables that they sold at markets. The farmers immediately complained about this unwanted competition, and the authorities intervened. The Bulgarians invoked existing Austro-Bulgarian agreements on which they based their rights. The Austrian government refused to back down, even after the Bulgarian government retaliated and expelled engineers and technicians working for Austrian machine factories, who were supposed to install and activate machines shipped to Bulgaria. The interests of large Austrian export industries were put at risk and the vegetable supply of urban dwellers was adversely affected (in 1931, a year of economic crisis), all for the sake of protecting backward Austrian vegetable growers against matching the Bulgarians' superior techniques and greater diligence.

I ❧❧❧

Taxation policy consisted in taxing away the capital of enterprises.[15]

Tax laws did nothing to protect entrepreneurs against arbitrary decisions by tax assessment offices, which were filled with a blind hate against "plutocrats." Corporate taxes paid by stock companies and limited partnerships, value-added taxes, and income taxes paid by entrepreneurs active in the export trade regularly drained away substantial portions of capital.

15 [On the rationales and consequences of antibusiness and confiscatory taxing policy in general, see Mises, *Human Action: A Treatise on Economics* (New York: Foundation for Economic Education, 4th ed., 1996), pp. 804–11. — Ed.]

It is useless to waste words on this subject. The new Austria will not be able to carry on the old taxation policy because no capital will be left to tax away and confiscate.[16]

J ∾∾∾

Every Austrian worker or employee was compelled to belong to a trade union. Anyone refusing to join a trade union could not have found employment anywhere. The trade unions relied on strikes or the threat of strikes to force entrepreneurs to fire unorganized workers.

Trade unions set wages and, under government pressure, entrepreneurs were forced to sign collective bargaining agreements ratifying trade union wages. These wage rates were far higher than the wages that would have been achieved on a free labor market. At these wage rates, only part of the workers could be employed. Mass unemployment was thus unavoidable. In 1937, 231,000 unemployed were receiving unemployment payments; unemployed persons registered at state employment offices for further action numbered 321,000.

The trade unions obliged their members to perform work on the "can-can't" principle. For example, typesetting is similar to typewriting; in both cases the work is normally done with all fingers of both hands. The apprentice typesetter has to learn to operate the composing machine with ten fingers. After the completion of his apprenticeship, however, he was allowed to use only one finger at work. This was the way the trade unions thought that they could create "work opportunities."

Austrian wages were lower than wages in Germany and in Western Europe (with the exception of France) and higher than in Czechoslovakia, Italy, and in Eastern Europe. Higher wages in the West reflected the more favorable natural production conditions in those countries and their industry's more abundant supply of capital. Western workers protected their higher wage level by keeping out immigrant foreign workers, just as Austrian workers defended their wage level by a stringent implementation of the worker protection code for Austrian workers against the threat of immigrant workers from Eastern European countries.

16 [On the taxation policies of the Austrian government in the interwar period and its negative effects on the private sector, see John V. Van Sickle, *Direct Taxation in Austria* (Cambridge, Mass.: Harvard University Press, 1931). The topic for this book had been suggested to Van Sickle by Mises in Vienna in 1919. — Ed.]

The only way to eliminate unemployment, or at least to reduce it to a minimum, would have been to lower the wage level to the point where entrepreneurs would have found it profitable to employ workers in larger numbers. The wage rate that entrepreneurs can afford to pay workers is determined on the one hand by the level of prices for the material means of production and on the other hand by the level of the product's sale price. Had the workers in the graphics industry received lower wages or had their performance been more efficient, the entrepreneurs could have increased their sales and hence employed more workers.

The trade unions celebrated each success achieved in their wage negotiations as a victory over the entrepreneur. What they in fact achieved was a victory over their fellow workers, whom they condemned to becoming or staying unemployed.

K ❧❧❧

These remarks would be incomplete if they were limited to economic matters and neglected the intellectual sphere.

Vienna was not only a center of industrial production and trade, Vienna was a city of intellectual and artistic achievement. This set it apart not only from the rest of Austria but from all the other eastern and southeastern European cities.

Let us pass over in silence those pseudospiritual forces that cried "Heil Hitler!" as soon as the first invaders appeared in Vienna; they well deserved the kicks they received from the National Socialists. The days of March 1938 demonstrated the true worth of their loud display of patriotism and Austrian chauvinism.[17]

If the world still considers enslaved and oppressed Austria a culturally significant country, this reputation owes nothing to the circles that previous governments treated with such incomprehensible generosity. It owes it to those intellectual movements that carried on their work without government support and often even in the face of government harassment.

17 [On the changes in the social, political, and economic situation in Austria following the German annexation in March of 1938, see Dieter Wagner and Gerhard Tomkowitz, *Anschluss: The Week Hitler Seized Power* (New York: St. Martin's Press, 1971); and Walter B. Maass, *Country Without a Name: Austria under Nazi Rule, 1938–1945* (New York: Frederick Ungar Publishing Co., 1979).—Ed.]

The leaders of these movements are not welcome in Vienna today, but it should not be forgotten that the intolerance manifested in the last years prior to the National Socialists' incursion had already driven many of them abroad.[18]

The venerable Vienna School of Medicine had already lost much of its prestige by basing appointments to its chairs on criteria other than merit. Nobel Prize winner Landsteiner,[19] for instance, was unable to establish himself in Vienna and immigrated in the 1920s to America, where Koller,[20] who had discovered the medical applications of cocaine, moved forty years earlier. The National Socialists have deprived the Vienna Faculty of Medicine of many talented people; some were forced to leave as "non-Aryans"; others left because they wished to stay loyal to Austria.

The psychoanalytic movement, which spread Vienna's fame worldwide, was always ignored by Austrian officialdom. Freud[21] barely managed to become a *Privatdozent*[22] at the University of Vienna, and Breuer was barely named corresponding member of the Academy of Sciences.[23] Others failed to attain even that much. Psychoanalysis and psychoanalytic research are in full swing everywhere but in Vienna.

The Austrian School of economics revolutionized thinking about the problems of human action. In the last decades, the government did noth-

18 [On the intellectual and cultural environment of Austria in general and Vienna in particular in the decades before 1938, see William M. Johnston, *The Austrian Mind: An Intellectual and Social History, 1848–1938* (Berkeley, Calif.: University of California Press, 1972); Hilde Spiel, *Vienna's Golden Autumn, 1866–1938* (New York: Weidenfeld and Nicolson, 1987); and Paul Hofmann, *Viennese: Spender, Twilight, and Exile* (New York: Doubleday, 1988).—Ed.]

19 [Karl Landsteiner (1869–1943) was the recipient of the Nobel Prize for Medicine in 1930 for the development of blood-grouping techniques used in transfusions.—Ed.]

20 [Carl Koller (1857–1944) demonstrated the medical uses of cocaine as a local anesthetic in eye operations. He immigrated to the United States and lived in New York. —Ed.]

21 [Sigmund Freud (1856–1939) is considered the founder of modern psychoanalysis; he left Austria in 1938 and moved to England.—Ed.]

22 [A *Privatdozent* in the German and Austrian systems of higher education was an unsalaried university lecturer, permitted to teach with the approval of the university faculty on the basis of demonstrated work of scholarly merit.—Ed.]

23 [Josef Breuer (1842–1925) was a leading Viennese psychiatrist and a developer of the method of hypnosis for psychiatric application.—Ed.]

ing to promote its expansion. Today, all the representatives of this school have transferred their activity abroad.[24]

Opinions may differ about the Positivist "Vienna Circle," but there is no question that it contributed to Austria's reputation. It, too, has been expelled.[25]

Vienna's continued reputation as a theatrical center after the war was entirely due to Max Reinhardt. Currently, he is active in Hollywood, where many of the best performers and directors have moved.

Although great Viennese musicians are a thing of the distant past, the

---

24 [The Austrian School of economics was founded in 1871 with the publication of Carl Menger's *Grundsätze der Volkswirtschaftslehre*, or *Principles of Economics*. Leading members of the Austrian School in the late nineteenth century included Eugen von Böhm-Bawerk and Friedrich von Wieser. The early Austrian economists emphasized the development of marginal utility theory and its application for explaining value and price; the concept of opportunity cost; the time-structure of production; and the time-preference theory of the rate of interest. In the period between the two world wars, the two prominent and senior members of the Austrian School in Vienna were Mises and Hans Mayer. The younger generation of Austrian economists during this time included Gottfried Haberler, Friedrich A. Hayek, Fritz Machlup, Oskar Morgenstern, Paul N. Rosenstein-Rodan, Richard von Strigl, Ewald Schams, and Leo Schonfeld. In the 1920s and 1930s, the Austrian economists focused on such themes as the formalization of the logic of human action and choice; the theory of price formation and market equilibrium; the problem of imperfect knowledge; the formation of expectations and interpersonal plan-coordination; the theory of capital formation, the processes of production, and the rate of interest; and the theory of money and business cycles. Many leading members of the Austrian School left their homeland in the 1930s: Hayek (1931 to England and 1948 to the United States); Mises (1934 to Switzerland and 1940 to the United States); Machlup (1934 to the United States); Haberler (1934 to Switzerland and 1936 to the United States); Morgenstern (1938 to the United States); and Rosenstein-Rodan (1929 to England and 1947 to the United States). Hans Mayer (1879–1955), one of the senior Austrian economists at the University of Vienna, remained in Austria and collaborated with the Nazis following 1938. See Mises, "The Historical Setting of the Austrian School of Economics," [1969] in Bettina Bien Greaves, ed., *Austrian Economics: An Anthology* (Irvington-on Hudson, N.Y.: Foundation for Economic Education, 1996), pp. 53–76; and Earlene Craver, "The Emigration of the Austrian Economists," *History of Political Economy*, Vol. 18, No. 1 (1986), pp. 1–32.—Ed.]

25 [The "Vienna Circle" was organized in 1924 by philosopher Moritz Schlick (1882–1936), who was shot to death by a student on the steps of the University of Vienna. The Circle was composed of a group devoted to or interested in Positivist philosophy, which argued that only sense perceptions were a permissible basis of knowledge and precise thought. Among the prominent members were Rudolf Carnap, Kurt Gödel, Felix Kaufmann, Carl Menger, Jr., Otto Neurath, and Karl Popper.—Ed.]

State Opera—in contrast to the *Burgtheater*—maintained its fame down to our times. Vienna was second to none for its concerts. There, too, the National Socialists have wrought great havoc.

It should be mentioned, finally, that the invaders have plundered public museums and libraries, carried off invaluable items from the imperial *Schatzkammer*,[26] and ravished the most precious private art and book collections. It remains doubtful that these losses can ever be repaired.

II   *The Program*

A ❧❧❧

The new Austria must unequivocally espouse free trade both in its foreign and in its domestic economic policies. It will not be in a position to "encourage" or subsidize anybody, because it will have no resources at its disposal to do so.

Free trade does not imply the elimination of all tariffs. What it does imply is that no attempt will be made to raise domestic prices by imposing import duties, to give domestic producers a chance to sell their wares more advantageously than their foreign competitors. Only two kinds of import duties are therefore compatible with free trade:

1. Duties levied on articles for which consumption taxes are imposed (alcoholic beverages, tobacco, and tobacco products); these duties must be set at exactly the same level as domestic taxes for these products.

2. Retaliatory tariffs, which apply to imports of all or certain commodities from countries that adopt a hostile policy toward Austrian exports. Retaliatory tariffs must be imposed at any given time only against a limited number of countries, to maintain Austria's supply of each of these individual articles at world market prices.

Singling out luxury articles for import duties, on the other hand, is a very bad idea. Austrian exports have largely consisted of commodities that might well, with some ill will—of which there is no lack—be characterized as luxury items. It is quite unlikely that this situation will ever change. A country that is as dependent as Austria on the export of luxury items must not give other countries a bad example on this score.

26 [This term refers to the imperial treasury and crown jewels. —Ed.]

Prohibiting specific imports for reasons of sanitary and veterinarian regulations is defensible, but must not be abused for protectionist purposes. The import of weapons and ammunition is a governmental prerogative.

Prohibiting exports is defensible in periods of political tension only on military grounds.

B ❧❧❧

The currency must be backed by gold.[27]

The note-issuing bank must be strictly obligated to redeem on demand in gold at legal parity its notes and liabilities on their bills of trade. It must publish a weekly report of its status.

Money exchanges with other countries must not be subject to any restriction.

C ❧❧❧

Domestically there must be complete freedom of commercial activity.

The right to free commercial activity can legitimately be restricted in only three cases: the production and dissemination of weapons, ammunition, and explosives; retail trade in medications and poisons; and activities involving sanitary and veterinarian regulations.

D ❧❧❧

The central government is the only authority entitled to levy taxes. Municipalities are not authorized to collect their own taxes, but will receive their funding from the central government.

---

27 [On the case for a gold standard, see Chapter VI, "A Noninflationary Proposal for Postwar Monetary Reconstruction," in this volume; and Mises, *Human Action*, pp. 471–76; "Gold vs. Paper" (1953) in Bettina Bien Greaves, ed., *Economic Freedom and Interventionism: An Anthology of Articles and Essays by Ludwig von Mises* (Irvington-on-Hudson, N.Y.: Foundation for Economic Education, 1990), pp. 82–86; and "The Gold Problem" [1965] in *Planning for Freedom* (South Holland: Libertarian Press, revised 4th ed., 1980), pp. 185–94.—Ed.]

The following will be the types of taxes levied:

1. Excise taxes for alcoholic beverages, tobacco, and tobacco products.

2. A sales tax, which applies exclusively to the transfer of goods and the receipt of services by the ultimate consumer. The transfer of goods to persons or enterprises that resell them either unprocessed or after processing or use of them in their profession or trade remains tax exempt; exports must also remain tax exempt.

3. A wage tax, modeled after the social insurance tax. This tax, which was introduced in Vienna by the Social Democrats, later adopted by all Christian Social and *Grossdeutsch* Provincial (*Länder*) governments and then maintained by the Christian Socialists in Vienna between 1934 and 1938, should be acceptable to all concerned.

4. A progressive tax on higher consumption levels, based on housing expenditures. No tax is to be levied on housing expenditures of the less affluent.

5. A tax on ownership of higher-priced automobiles for personal use.

6. A tax on lottery winnings.

7. A playing-card stamp.

8. Administrative fees for the performance of specific administrative services. Fees for the issuance of patent rights, for registration of brands and samples, the determination of weights and measures, and official stamps must be adequate to cover related administrative expense.

9. Lastly, a moderate tax on net profits paid out to shareholders of stock companies and partners in limited partnerships, for annual disbursements exceeding 6 percent of capital assets. Disclosed or undisclosed capital must remain tax exempt to avoid interfering with capital formation.

It should be pointed out that with the exception of the wage tax, which the employer is not allowed to deduct from wages, and of the tax on excess distributions of earnings, all earnings are exempt from taxation. This is essential in view of the economic situation of the new Austria. The taxation policy of the old Austria was misguided in that it ignored Emperor Charles V's[28] principle and led to killing the goose that laid the golden

---

28 [Charles V (1500–1558) became king of the Habsburg domains in 1519 and was elected emperor of the Holy Roman Empire in 1521—after accumulating debts in the neighborhood of twenty million (1960s) dollars to pay bribes and expenses for propaganda, wages of agents, secretaries, couriers, and payments of troops needed to win the election against the king of France. He also was Charles I, king of Spain (1516–56).—Ed.]

eggs. The new Austria must not kill the goslings that many years hence will be laying eggs.

This taxation system has the great advantage that tax collection will be done at very small expense.

The government budget will have to adapt its expenditures to the revenues it is able to collect.

E ❧❧❧

The government must divest itself of or abandon enterprises whose operations are not self-supporting. The new Austria will not have enough resources at its disposal to run up deficits in poorly managed railroads, timberland, mines, and factories.

F ❧❧❧

Public servants who retired before March 1, 1938, will receive their pensions, but only if they can prove that they did nothing to promote National Socialism. The same principle applies to public servants pensioned off or dismissed by the National Socialists.

Public servants employed at the time of the liberation will keep their position on a provisional basis. Their reinstatement will have to be decided by the government, case by case, in line with the country's best interests. For any public servant who is definitively reinstated, length of service will count from the day of liberation.

Not only undeniable budgetary considerations, but also vital political considerations speak in favor of this arrangement. It would be disastrous if the new government were to accept any obligations toward those who served the Nazi regime.

At a much later date, it will be feasible to count the years of service prior to 1938 for mid-level and low-level government employees who behaved decently. Academically trained civil servants as well as military officers may not, under any circumstance, benefit from such favors, inasmuch as they violated their special obligation to remain loyal.

The new state will not be vindictive and will throw the mantle of Christian forgiveness over the past. But it will not reward felony and will force plunderers to give up their loot.

G

The central government will have sole administrative responsibility. The costly duplicate administration by both the central government and autonomous local authorities will come to an end.

District (*Kreis*) authorities will be set up by the central government, one in each province (*Länd*) and a separate one in Vienna. Precinct administrations will be eliminated. In the age of automobiles and buses, every citizen can reach each provincial capital more easily, rapidly, and cheaply than he could reach precinct offices ninety years ago when they were first established. The chief district officer and his staff can travel to each locality within the district without having to stay overnight anywhere.

Each district authority's territory will be divided into police districts in which police officials will handle public security matters with the help of the police and *gendarmerie*. No other task may be assigned to police officials.

The district administration is the seat of the lowest level tax assessment office.

Thus only two administrative levels will be involved in all administrative procedures—aside from those relating to police matters—and administrative costs will be greatly reduced.

H

Whether large or small, municipalities will have to devote themselves exclusively to those tasks that are assigned to them by legislation. They will have to concentrate on road maintenance, fire protection, the administration of municipal enterprises, and other useful matters and will have to avoid being at cross-purposes with the central government's policies. They will have to get along with the income derived from the earnings on municipal assets and municipal enterprises plus the allocations that they receive from the central government. Municipalities will need the permission of the central government to raise money and this permission will be contingent on their using this money for investments whose eventual earnings will cover interest and amortization of the borrowed amount.

No elected municipal official will be able to receive a salary or compensation for his services, nor may he sell any goods to the municipality or have a contract with it.

With the elimination of the provincial (*Länder*) legislatures and the administrators appointed by them and with the sharp restriction on the power of municipalities, the major source of corruption and of the squandering of public funds will run dry.

I ❧❧❧

The educational system must be thoroughly restructured.[29]

Elementary education will be under the control of the central government. All matters concerning elementary education will be under the overall control of the Office of Education, but directly supervised by the school inspector of the district authority. All institutions of higher education will be under the direct supervision of the Office of Education.

The gymnasiums[30] and other secondary schools will expand their curricula. English and French instruction will be part of the compulsory program. Students will be held to substantially higher standards of achievement. Only gifted and hardworking students deserve to have the state devote special resources to their education. Higher standards will reduce crowding in these institutions, so that the number of secondary schools can be reduced. This reduction is essential not only for budgetary reasons, but also because of truly suitable teaching personnel being in short supply.

As expenditures for universities and for the salary of university professors kept going up, the professors' scholarly qualifications kept declining. The chair of sociology at the University of Vienna was held by a man who did not know a word of any classical or modern foreign language. Many doctors of law knew less about Austrian legal institutions than any intelligent newspaper reader. One might run across doctors of philosophy with the right to teach history and German in gymnasiums who had never heard of Dante, Voltaire, and Pasteur, and who did not know the main provisions of the Austrian constitution.

The University of Vienna will have to be rebuilt almost from scratch

---

29 [On the educational system and its curricula before and during the period between the two world wars in Austria, see Ernst Papanek, *The Austrian School Reform: Its Bases, Principles, and Development—The Twenty Years Between the Two World Wars* (Westport, Conn.: Greenwood Press, 1962); and on the nature and philosophy of higher education in German-speaking central Europe during this time, see Abraham Flexner, *Universities: American, English, and German* (New York: Oxford University Press, 1930), pp. 305–61. —Ed.]

30 ["Gymnasiums" were high schools with a classical emphasis.—Ed.]

with the help of teaching personnel from Western Europe. It may also be possible to bring back some of those Austrians who are now teaching in Anglo-Saxon countries. American foundations will undoubtedly do their share in financing the reorganization of the University and of research institutions.

The universities in Graz and Innsbruck, which have long since ceased to be worthy of this name, will be abolished.

J ❧❧❧

The judicial system, like all other branches of the administration, was over-staffed. A 1930 report of the Austrian Ministry of Justice indicates that the number of citizens per judge in different countries was the following:

Austria	4,487
Germany	6,651
Sweden	7,600
Norway	8,300
Italy	9,770
Denmark	13,430
France	20,000

In many rural district courts, fewer than ten decisions per year were handed down in civil cases.

The elimination of the provincial (*Länd*) courts of appeal will lead to a two-tier judiciary. The number of district courts must be substantially re-duced. Vienna tribunals will extend their jurisdiction to all of Lower Aus-tria. At the seat of the remaining district authorities, a provincial tribunal will be established, with jurisdiction for the entire province (*Länd*).

K ❧❧❧

The whole post, telegraph, and telephone service will be merged into a single postal administration in Vienna. Postal administrations in the cap-itals of the individual provinces (*Länder*) are superfluous and will be eliminated.

All administrative branches will have to be operated much more eco-nomically than before 1938. That will be all the easier to implement as the new state will be under no obligation to reappoint functionaries who served under the Nazi regime.

The French system of competitive examinations is to be applied in filling public service jobs. Notwithstanding its weaknesses, this system is incomparably superior to patronage, nepotism, and corruption.

L ❧❧❧

Citizens are entitled to establish organizations at will, as long as the objectives of the organizations are not in violation of the law.

Compulsory organizations—notably commerce, trade, and industrial chambers, labor chambers, agricultural chambers, industrial guilds, etc.—on the contrary, are to be abolished. Only the lawyers' chamber is to be retained because of its functions with respect to judicial policies.

Any organization using direct or indirect means in order to compel citizens to join its ranks will be dissolved by the courts. Persons charged with exerting this kind of compulsion will be permanently barred by the courts from belonging to organizations and from receiving financial support from organizations.

M ❧❧❧

After the collapse of the National Socialist regime, Austria probably will be occupied by Allied troops and placed under military administration.[31]

This military administration will be faced with a disastrous situation: an undernourished, badly dressed, and badly shod population, lacking food supplies and fuel; factories that are completely shut down, railroads and roads in a state of dilapidation, and possibly even bridges and tunnels that have been destroyed. Food will undoubtedly be distributed—with the help of the Quakers and the Red Cross—but the Czechs and Poles will be given priority over the Austrians.

The wretchedness of the situation will make the Allies all the more eager to transfer responsibility to the legitimate government. It is to be hoped that they will offer a small amount of credit to this government as well. Thereafter, the Allies will move on to their own problems, however, and will advise Austria to take care of its own.

---

31 [Between 1945 and 1955, Austria was divided into four Allied occupation zones—American, British, French, and Soviet. Located within the Soviet zone, Vienna was also subdivided into four zones, with the center of the city jointly administered and policed by the four Allied Powers.—Ed.]

What is to happen at that point? The masses will urgently demand to be given food. Where is it to come from?

Factories—where today weapons are being turned out with too little equipment—will be idle. There will be a shortage of raw materials. There will not be a penny in the whole country, nothing but totally valueless Reichsmark notes. All banks, savings banks, and insurance companies will be insolvent. Real estate will be totally worthless, with no tenant able to pay rent. Agriculture will be without seed grains or fertilizers and will have a diminished livestock.

A few people from other countries will appear on the scene to buy up jewelry and other objects that are easy to carry off. This will alleviate the lot of the middle classes for a while, but it will do nothing to solve the problem of feeding the masses.

Restitution claims against the German Reich will probably be upheld, but it will be years before payments are received. Others will obviously have stronger claims, and Austria will have to make room for them.

If no preparations are made for these difficult days ahead, the new government will collapse before it has begun its rule.

Now is the time to take the requisite steps.[32] Capitalist and entrepreneurial circles in other countries must be contacted and informed that free market principles will prevail in the new Austria. Preliminary negotiations must tackle the establishment of a note-issuing bank and must deal with the takeover of railroads and state-owned timberland, the creation of branches of foreign banks, etc. Then, when the day of liberation has arrived, an agreement can be quickly put into place. The entrepreneurs who have been expelled from Austria must be sought out and urged to be ready to resume their activities in Austria.

Cultural propaganda must be initiated as well. The bad reputation that Austria has unhappily acquired in the world must be dispelled. It must be clearly proclaimed that the future government will no longer treat badly all those Austrians who can accomplish great things and that it has no intention of letting the French, English, and Americans be derided from the lecterns of its universities. Every effort must be made to utilize the good-

---

32 [It is worth noting that as early as May of 1940, Mises is anticipating the liberation, occupation, and reconstitution of a new, free Austria by the victorious Allies. This was a time when the armies of Nazi Germany were in the process of overrunning Holland, Belgium, and France, and the likelihood of Germany not only being stopped but totally defeated seemed to many to be highly improbable. With France occupied, Great Britain was standing alone against Hitler, for the Soviet Union was still unofficially allied with Nazi Germany and the United States was a neutral power.—Ed.]

will Austria has generated through the cultural achievements of its sons.

And finally, Western public opinion must be alerted to the significance of a free, independent, and economically and militarily self-sufficient Austria for peace and order in Europe, especially in the Danube area.

French methods of cultural propaganda must be studied and imitated where appropriate. Everything possible must be done to efface the memory of the previous governments' arrogance toward the foreign press and to build up Austria's reputation. Anyone officially representing Austria must be selected more carefully than in the past. The press attaché working at the London Embassy at highly critical times was a man who had previously been working for the German news service. For many years the Austrian delegate to the International Committee of Intellectual Cooperation[33] was a National Socialist who was an ex-minister![34] The chairman and the majority of the members of the Austrian National Committee to the International Institute of Intellectual Cooperation[35] were National Socialists![36]

33 [The International Committee of Intellectual Cooperation was established by the League of Nations in 1922 to support and encourage intellectual cooperation and contacts between nations. Among its first standing members were the French philosopher Henri Bergson, the Polish physicist Madame Curie, and the German physicist Albert Einstein; see Gilbert Murray, "Intellectual Cooperation," *The Annals of the American Academy of Political and Social Science*, Vol. 235 (September 1944), pp. 1–9.—Ed.]

34 [This man was Henrich Ritter von Srbik (1874–1951). Beginning in 1922, he was a professor of history at the University of Vienna. From 1929 to 1930, he was Austria's minister of education. After the annexation of Austria in 1938, he served as a member of the German Reichstag and as president of the German Historical Commission. From 1938 to 1945, he was also president of the Viennese Academy of Science under the Nazis.—Ed.]

35 [The International Institute of Intellectual Cooperation was founded in 1928, with its headquarters in Paris. Its stated purpose was to offer solutions for peaceful change in response to international political and economic conflicts. Participants included such leading classical liberals of the interwar period as Lionel Robbins and Theodore Gregory of Great Britain, Charles Rist and Louis Baudin of France, William Rappard, Paul Mantoux, and Michael Heilperin of Switzerland, Moritz J. Bonn of Germany, Oskar Morgenstern of Austria, and Jacob Viner, Frank Graham, and Eugene Staley of the United States. Mises attended the May 1936 meeting of the International Institute of Intellectual Cooperation in Madrid, Spain, as a representative of the Graduate Institute of International Studies in Geneva, Switzerland (at that time, he served the Institute as a professor of international economic relations). The meeting in August of 1939 in Bergen, Norway, was held under the darkening clouds of war in Europe, and the Institute suspended operations soon afterwards; see *The Intellectual Studies Conference: Origins, Functions, Organization* (Paris: International Institute of Intellectual Cooperation, 1937).—Ed.]

36 [The chairman of the Austrian National Committee to the International Institute of Intellectual Cooperation was Alfons Dopsch (1868–1953). Dopsch was a professor of eco-

On the day of liberation, diplomatic representatives must be sent to all the important capitals. Only men with great personal prestige based either on their scholarly contributions or on other personal distinctions must be chosen for these positions in the West. They alone can create the esteem that Austrian representatives would otherwise lack in the first years of the new state's existence. Here, too, the French system can serve as a model.

Even if all goes as well as can be hoped, the new state will not be able to count on regular tax revenues in the first years of its existence.

In 1918–1919, the Renner[37] government had substantial credits for relief at its disposal. The Western powers delivered food supplies on credit; the government sold these food supplies to the population at prices that were below the market price and purchase cost and used the proceeds to cover current government expenses.[38] It also relied on a policy of unlimited inflation.[39] The new state will not be able to resort to such tactics. The

---

nomic and cultural history at the University of Vienna. The secretary of the Austrian National Committee was Eric Voegelin (1901–85), a leading conservative philosopher and political theorist best known for *The New Science of Politics* (1952) and a four-volume treatise, *Order and History*. Voegelin was dismissed from his university position by the Nazis in 1938 and immigrated to the United States, where he became a professor at Louisiana State University. The Institute's Committee of Coordinating Institutions in Vienna represented the *Hocheschule für Welthandel* (College for International Trade); the *Konsularakademie* (Consular Academy); the *Rechts und Staatwissensschaftliche Fakultät* (Law and Political Science Faculty) of the University of Vienna; the *Seminar für Kultur und Wirtschaftsgeschichte* (Seminar for Culture and Economic History) at the University of Vienna; and the *Österreichisches Institut für Konjunkurforschung* [Austrian Institute for Business Cycle Research], which Mises founded in 1926 and which he served as acting vice president. —Ed.]

37 [Karl Renner (1870–1950) was a leading Austrian socialist who headed two coalition governments of the new Republic of Austria between the fall of 1918 and the summer of 1920. In April of 1945, he formed a provisional government that proclaimed the reestablishment of Austria as a democratic republic; in November of that year, he was elected president of Austria, a position he held until his death. —Ed.]

38 [On the form and amount of Allied financial aid and food relief to Austria in the immediate post–World War I period, see David Strong, *Austria (October 1918–March 1919): Transition from Empire to Republic* (New York: Octagon Books, [1939] 1974), pp. 241–73. —Ed.]

39 [On the economic conditions in Austria immediately after the First World War and the phases of the Great Austrian Inflation between 1918 and 1923, see J. van Walre de Bordes, *The Austrian Crown: Its Depreciation and Stabilization* (London: P. S. King and Son, 1924). —Ed.]

relief credits at its disposal will be very small and the population, which will be bereft of all resources, will not be able to pay for the food supplies, which will have to be distributed free of charge. Inflation will be impossible, as no one will be willing to turn over commodities in exchange for the government's printed notes.

At the very start, the government will therefore have to rely exclusively on the advances paid by foreign buyers of railroads, timberland, and so on.

There will be hard times ahead before the new machinery of the export industry can be set in motion.

III   *Rebuttal to the Anticipated Objections*

A ❧❧❧

It can be expected that these proposals will be indignantly rejected by all those who have had their share of responsibility for Austrian policies in the last twenty years. The old parties are incapable of conceiving of the state as anything but an instrument of coercion that takes things from the propertied classes to bestow them on other citizens and that puts all conceivable obstacles in the path of entrepreneurs.

The new Austria will have neither entrepreneurs nor property owners from whom anything can be taken. The old policies can therefore no longer be sustained.

People will say that there are forests, ores, and magnetite mines. These are, in fact, important assets for the new Austria. However, their exploitation will first require considerable investment, which can only be made by foreign capital, as no domestic capital will be left. It will be very difficult to acquire the necessary capital from elsewhere. But certainly foreign capital will be impossible to attract if it is threatened by the confiscatory policies of the old system.

People will propose the nationalization of timberland and mines. Well, the state is already the largest owner of woodland in Austria, owning over four hundred thousand hectares of forests. It operated this property so incompetently that it not only brought in no revenues, but even created a substantial deficit, which had to be covered by tax money.

People will talk about the existence of large-scale landholdings and will insist that these be taxed, broken up, or nationalized. The fact is, however, that the earnings of Austrian agriculture depended on protection and subsidies and its earnings were extracted by putting an antisocial burden on the food consumption of the masses. It will be years before Austrian agriculture makes a positive contribution to the economic structure.

People will point to urban real estate. In truth, the houses are value-less, as there is no one who can pay rent. It will not even be easy in the first years to set high enough rents for existing apartments to pay for the main-tenance costs of the buildings.

B ❧❧❧

Some people will undoubtedly propose full socialization in line with the Russian model.

No other country can rival Russia's abundance of natural resources. It has more than its share of the most fertile fields. It is endowed with the right soil for growing wheat and rye, oil-producing plants, tropical fruits, and cotton and with ample space for raising beef, pigs, and sheep. It is blessed with limitless forests full of fur-bearing animals. It has the richest sources of iron and manganese ore, gold, platinum, and mineral oil. The socialist system is incapable of exploiting these treasures.[40] A few years ago, millions died of starvation in the Ukraine, the famous bread basket of Eu-rope.[41] The Russian people have the lowest standard of living of all Chris-tian peoples. The Russian experience does not speak in favor of socialism.

How could a socialist Austria feed its population? How could it pay for foreign raw materials and food supplies, without which it could not survive?

If Austria were to follow the Russian model, it could at best feed a mil-lion people in the Bolshevist style. What should the remaining 5.5 mil-lion people do?

40 [On Mises's view of Russia and Soviet socialism, see *Liberalism in the Classical Tradi-tion* [1927] (Irvington-on-Hudson, N.Y., and San Francisco, Calif.: Foundation for Eco-nomic Education and Cobden Press, 1985), pp. 151–54.—Ed.]

41 [Leading historians of the Soviet period have estimated that as many as seven to twelve million people may have died during the forced collectivization of the land in the early 1930s; many of those millions had lived in Ukraine; see Robert Conquest, *The Harvest of Sorrow: Soviet Collectivization and the Terror-Famine* (New York: Oxford University Press, 1986); and Miron Dolot, *Execution by Hunger: The Hidden Holocaust* (New York: W. W. Norton and Co., 1985).—Ed.]

C ❧❧❧

The Social Democratic leaders will certainly try to rouse opposition to this program among trade unions and the Western European and American labor parties and at the International Labor Office. It would be terrible if trade unions were not allowed to set wages as they pleased through strikes and the threat of strikes, and if unemployment support were withdrawn; such antisocial measures must not be tolerated, they will say. But if Western labor parties sincerely wish to improve the lot of Austrian workers, the most effective step they can take is to eliminate the laws that prevent Austrian workers from immigrating to the United States and the British Dominions seeking work there. Low wages in relatively overpopulated Austria are the counterpart to the high wages in these relatively underpopulated countries. There are millions of hectares of uncultivated soil in America, Australia, and New Zealand that is far more fertile than the best soils in Austria. Austrian workers must work in a country with particularly unfavorable production conditions, because they are kept away from production sites that are better endowed by nature. It is not the greediness of Austrian entrepreneurs that condemns Austrian workers to a lower standard of living, but the selfishness of Western workers.[42]

In the West, unemployment insurance is paid out of the proceeds of high inheritance and income taxes. In the new Austria there will be no heirs to pay taxes and income taxes will have to be paid exclusively out of worker income.

Austria's only heritage is misery, and it is Austria's task to extricate itself from this misery and move to a new prosperity.

D ❧❧❧

Some will propose following Hitler's prescription of autarchy and public works (labor service) to keep the unemployed at work.

We do not propose here to demonstrate that Hitler's policy is bound to ruin any country as it has already ruined the German Reich. Let it suffice

---

42 [On the issue of free immigration and international equalization of market-determined wages, see Mises, "The Freedom to Move as an International Problem," [1935], reprinted in Richard M. Ebeling and Jacob G. Hornberger, eds., *The Case for Free Trade and Open Immigration* (Fairfax, Va.: Future of Freedom Foundation, 1995), pp. 127–30.—Ed.]

to point out the following: the German Reich is much more abundantly provided with raw materials and food than Austria, and it can cover a far greater part of its nutritional needs domestically, thanks to the natural fertility of its soil, than is possible for mountainous Austria. It was able to meet part of its import needs by the export of domestically extracted raw materials (e. g., coal). When Hitler came to power, Germany disposed of an industrial base that far outstripped Austria's in size, productivity, and capital equipment. It is Austria's special problem that it must more heavily rely on the import of food supplies than Germany, that it earns less from the export of raw materials than the German Reich, and that its industry is totally ruined today. An autarchic Austria could offer its children not bread but only stones.

The problem is not to find work for the unemployed to keep them from being bored. The problem is to find them productive work, something that can never be achieved by public works or labor service. Only the export industry can achieve this goal. A blouse producer selling an assortment of blouses abroad does more for Austria and Austrian workers than all the trade unions and social policy-makers put together.

E ᔥᔥᔥ

Finally, people will again raise the question of Austria's viability as a separate state.

There is no denying that nature has been niggardly toward Austria. For that very reason Austria must pay by means of its export of industrial goods for the food supplies and raw materials from abroad that are required for the consumption needs of its sons and daughters. This state of affairs is not merely the result of the Treaty of Saint-Germain.[43] Even under the old Austro-Hungarian monarchy, nobody presented the inhabitants of the territory that constituted the Austrian state between 1919 and 1938 with gifts or tributes. When the inhabitants of Vienna or Graz had coal delivered

---

43 [The Treaty of Saint-Germain was signed by Austria and the Allied Powers in 1919. It ended the state of war between them and formally dissolved the territory of the former Austro-Hungarian empire into a new, small Republic of Austria, the independent states of Hungary and Czechoslovakia, a re-created Poland, an enlarged Romania, and a Serb-dominated Yugoslavia. — Ed.]

from Silesia,[44] grain from Hungary, or tropical fruits from Gorizia,[45] they had to pay for these items, and they could do so only by selling the commodities that they had produced. This is not a matter of "exchange rates." In a country whose government does not engage in inflationary practices and that is not trying to conceal the consequences of inflation by foreign exchange controls, there is no foreign exchange problem and no "shortage of foreign currency."

From a purely budgetary point of view, the dissolution of the old monarchy was not unfavorable for post-Saint-Germain Austria. In effect, the territory that constituted Austria between 1919 and 1938 contributed to the administrative costs of the other parts of the monarchy, rather than receiving contributions from them. If one insists on the existence of tributes, one would have to say that the Viennese were obliged to pay tribute to the Dalmatians,[46] the Galicians,[47] and the Hungarians. From the point of view of trade policies, the Treaty of Saint-Germain had disastrous consequences, because each one of the new states closed itself off from the other states. The consequences of this policy, however, were far more catastrophic for Czech industry and Hungarian agriculture than for Austria. Large segments of the Bohemian-Moravian-Silesian industry and the larger part of Hungarian agriculture were incapable of selling their products outside their tariff-protected zone. Austrian export industries, on the other hand, could compete on the world market and might have been thriving between 1919 and 1929, despite all foreign tariff barriers, had they not

44 [Austrian Silesia was the northern region of the province of Moravia that was incorporated into the new nation of Czechoslovakia at the end of the First World War. Since 1993, it has been a part of the Czech Republic.—Ed.]

45 [The city of Gorizia was part of the Austro-Hungarian empire before the First World War. It was annexed by Italy at the end of the war as a result of the Treaty of Saint-Germain. It is north of the Gulf of Trieste at the northern end of the Adriatic Sea.—Ed.]

46 [Dalmatia, which lies on the east shore of the Adriatic, was also part of the Austro-Hungarian empire. It was annexed by the new state of Yugoslavia at the end of the First World War as a result of the Treaty of Saint-Germain. Since 1991, it has been part of the Republic of Croatia.—Ed.]

47 [Galicia was the easternmost area of the imperial Austrian domains under the Austro-Hungarian empire, containing the city of Lemberg (now Lvov), the birthplace of Ludwig von Mises. It was incorporated into the re-created state of Poland at the end of the First World War. Most of Galicia, including Lemberg, was annexed by the Soviet Union in September of 1939 as a result of the military conquest and division of Poland between Nazi Germany and the USSR. Since 1991, it has been part of the Republic of Ukraine.—Ed.]

been hampered domestically in all their moves by Austrian economic policies. The misery in the Sudeten-German industrial area[48] and the decline in the standard of living in large parts of Hungary, Yugoslavia, and Galicia, were actually consequences of the commercial situation that arose after the dissolution of the Austro-Hungarian customs union. In the first months after the war, Czechs and Hungarians believed that their surplus coal, sugar, and wheat assured them of a permanent superiority over Austria. It did not take them long to realize that the export market for these items was highly unfavorable.[49]

One must bear in mind a circumstance that has received too little public attention. The Great Depression, which began in 1929, had a far more devastating effect on the prices of raw materials and agricultural products than on the prices of industrial products. Consequently, a country with Austria's economic structure was less affected by the crisis than countries relying on the export of agricultural products and raw materials. The catastrophic situation of the Austrian economy was not a result of the degradation of its position on the world market, which required the import of food supplies and raw materials, but the consequence of Austria's economic policy.[50]

No word is strong enough to characterize the absurdity of the economic policy pursued by the successor states. However, Austria's agrarian protectionism was not an iota less absurd than Hungary's, Poland's, Romania's, or Yugoslavia's promotion of industrial development. Austria bears

48 [The Sudetenland was the westernmost area of Bohemia bordering on Germany. It was incorporated into Czechoslovakia at the end of the First World War. In September of 1938, the area was annexed by Nazi Germany as a result of the Munich agreement between Germany, Great Britain, France, and Italy. It was returned to Czech control at the end of the Second World War, and the approximately three million German-speaking residents were expelled.—Ed.]

49 [On the consequences resulting from the policies of economic nationalism and protectionism in the post–World War I countries of the former Austro-Hungarian empire, known as a group as "the successor states," see Leo Pasvolsky, *Economic Nationalism of the Danubian States* (New York: Macmillan Co., 1928); Antonin Basch, *The Danube Basin and the German Economic Sphere* (New York: Columbia University Press, 1943); and Frederick Hertz, *The Economic Problem of the Danubian States: A Study in Economic Nationalism* (London: Victor Gollancz, 1947).—Ed.]

50 [On the reasons for the duration and severity of the Great Depression, see Mises, "The Causes of the Economic Crisis" (1931) in Percy L. Greaves, ed., *Von Mises, On the Manipulation of Money and Credit* (Dobbs Ferry, N.Y.: Free Market Books, 1978), pp. 173–203.—Ed.]

as much responsibility as the other states for the failure of all efforts to organize economic cooperation between the Danubian states.

When people in Austria kept referring to the need for an "expansion of the economic territory" and used this need as an argument for the *Anschluss*, they were as insincere as most of the people in the rest of the world (for example, in the League of Nations, the International Chamber of Commerce, etc.) who called for a "reduction of obstacles to trade." Every country was eager to have import duties in other countries reduced, but at the same time refused to reduce its own. Similarly, these Austrian proponents of the *Anschluss* wished to secure duty-free access for Austrian products to the German market, but at the same time refused to guarantee free access to Austrian markets for their German competitors. In the second half of the 1920s, the government and the political parties put pressure on the Austrian trade and agricultural chambers to take a stand on the idea of a union with Germany, whereupon each agricultural branch and many industrial groups requested an intermediate custom border for their products. They all asserted that they would welcome this customs union, but each group requested special protection for its products. When the projected customs union broke down because of the opposition of the Western Powers,[51] many industrialists—including those that belonged to the *Grossdeutsch* [the Greater Germany] party and who vociferously supported the union with Germany—breathed a sigh of relief, as did the agrarian leaders. The *Anschluss* could never have come about by peaceable agreement between the two states, but only as it did in reality, by the influx into Austria of S.A. and S.S. men[52] in disguise, in whose wake followed the German army.

The union of the Eastern European states is a political necessity to allow them to stand up in self-defense against Germany, Russia, and Italy.

---

51 [In March of 1931, the German and Austrian governments signed a protocol for the establishment of an Austro-German customs union. Under opposition from the governments of Great Britain, France, Italy, and Czechoslovakia, the customs union was prevented from operating after the World Court at the Hague found it to be inconsistent with international agreements that Austria had signed in 1922; see Mary Margaret Ball, *Postwar German-Austrian Relations: The Anschluss Movement, 1918–1936* (London: Oxford University Press, 1937), pp. 100–185.—Ed.]

52 [The "S.A." were the "*Sturmabteilung*," or "Storm Troopers" or "Brownshirts," of Hitler's National Socialist movement in Germany. The "S.S." were the "*Schutzstaffel*," or "Blackshirts," who came to be the most feared Nazis.—Ed.]

This political union is contingent on an economic union.[53] But even an economic union will not relieve Austria of the need to put its own house in order.

The slogans about Austria's "lack of viability" and the need for an *Anschluss* played such a disastrous role between 1918 and 1938 because they were used to excuse and justify the greatest follies in economic policy. "Our economy is not viable in any case. Our only salvation lies in doing what is forbidden by the Treaty of Saint-Germain," it was said. "We are bound to come to a miserable end, it is inevitable. Those who blame our economic policy are choosing the wrong target; they should be blaming the Treaty of Saint-Germain." In the face of this fatalism, all attempts by people with some understanding to adopt a more sensible economic policy were doomed to failure. Anyone sincerely interested in preserving Austria had to conclude that only the *Anschluss* could shake the country out of its comfortable "do nothing" mentality; only the *Anschluss* could eliminate Austria's only excuse for its self-destructive policies.

No matter whether Austria is surrounded by states closed off by tariff walls or finds itself in a free market world; whether it is part of the German Reich, a new "Great Power Hapsburg monarchy," or a differently structured Danubian federation; whether it becomes part of the British Empire or a member of the Federal Union planned by Mr. Streit[54] or of Coudenhove-Kalergi's Paneuropa;[55] under all circumstances Austrians must fend for themselves. Come what may, they will have to pay for what they wish to consume. But the only way they can pay is by the sale of industrial products and, to a limited extent, by the export of raw materials and the proceeds of the tourist trade.

F ❧❧❧

There is no other path for Austria's reconstruction than the one described in this program.

It is an arduous path. In the new Austria there will be no room for

53 [See Chapter IX, "An Eastern European Union: A Proposal for the Establishment of a Durable Peace in Eastern Europe."—Ed.]

54 [See Chapter I, "Postwar Reconstruction," footnote 40.—Ed.]

55 [See Chapter IV, "The Fundamental Principle of a Pan-European Union," footnote 1.—Ed.]

comfortable ministerial seats or sinecures. There will be no room for parasites who thrive on the handouts that they receive from the state at the expense of other citizens.

For decades Austria has pursued a policy of capital consumption.[56] The time has come for new capital formation and for the creation of a new export industry. Only then can a new Austria take shape.

---

56 [On the problem of capital consumption in Austria in the years after the First World War, see Nicholas Kaldor, "The Economic Situation in Austria," *Harvard Business Review* (October 1932), pp. 23–34; and Fritz Machlup, "The Consumption of Capital in Austria," *The Review of Economic Statistics* (January 15, 1935), pp. 13–19. On the general process by which such capital consumption can come about, including in Austria during this period, see F. A. Hayek, "Capital Consumption," [1932] in Roy McCloughry, ed., *Money, Capital, and Fluctuations: Early Essays by F. A. Hayek* (Chicago: University of Chicago Press, 1984), pp. 136–58. —Ed.]

CHAPTER IX

An Eastern Democratic Union: A Proposal for the Establishment of a Durable Peace in Eastern Europe[1]

I   *Peace Within a World of Nationalism*

In a world of free trade and democracy, no special institutions and provisions are needed in order to ensure undisturbed peaceful cooperation among all nations. In such a world, where there are neither trade barriers nor migration barriers, where the activities of governments are limited to the protection of the lives, the health, and the property of individuals against violent or fraudulent aggression, and where neither the laws nor the administration nor the tribunals discriminate between different groups of citizens or between citizens and foreigners, it is without importance to the individual where the frontiers of his country are drawn. Every individual has the opportunity to live and to work where it suits him best. Nobody can derive any advantage from a change in the political distribution of the earth's surface. No citizen can be enriched by a victorious war, which makes his country larger at the expense of other countries. War does not pay. Nations become peaceful because they consider warfare a useless waste of both blood and wealth.

Our world is very different from this liberal free-trade utopia. We are living in an age when governments are eager to further the short-term interests of some groups of citizens at the expense of other groups of citizens and of foreigners. Ours is an age of economic nationalism. Economic nationalism is a policy which intends to improve the lot of greater or smaller groups of citizens by putting impediments in the way of foreigners. Foreign products are withheld from the domestic markets; foreign labor is banned

1 [This paper was written in October of 1941.—Ed.]

from competition on the domestic labor market. Whether these measures really can attain the ends which the governments want to attain or whether they do not, in the long run, hurt in some way or other the citizens whom they want to benefit is immaterial. The decisive point is that the great majority of our contemporaries firmly believe in the efficacy of these measures of economic nationalism. There is, therefore, no hope that the world will, in the near future, try to embark upon a policy of free trade.[2]

Such is the stark reality we have to face. We should not deceive ourselves by false illusions. All the arguments brought forward in order to demonstrate the disadvantages of warfare and the benefits of undisturbed peace are vain in an age of economic nationalism. Under present conditions, the pacifists are mistaken when they declare that a victorious war does not pay. It is true that the individual citizens of Germany did not gain anything in 1871 by the conquest of Alsace-Lorraine.[3] This was in the days of a more or less free trade Europe. But today it is different. For instance, a conquest of Australia by the Japanese would improve the lot of every individual Japanese wage earner. It would give a great number of Japanese the opportunity to work in Australia, where the natural opportunities for production are much more favorable than in the overpopulated Japanese home islands. It would therefore raise the level of wages and the standard of living for all Japanese wage earners, both for those who could immigrate to Australia and for those who remain in their old country.

Whereas in a world of universal and absolute free trade every nation is eager to maintain peace, in a world of economic nationalism those nations that believe themselves strong enough are ready to profit from every opportunity to attack weaker nations. In such a world, there is no solidarity of interests but a permanent latent conflict of interests that becomes manifest as soon as a good chance for prey appears. It is useless to fight this militarist bellicosity by mere moral condemnation. Both the Covenant of the League of Nations[4] and the Briand-Kellogg Pact[5] failed, because the

2 [On the meaning and practice of economic nationalism, see Chapter I, "Postwar Reconstruction," footnote 17, and Chapter VII, "A Draft of Guidelines for the Reconstruction of Austria," footnote 49.—Ed.]

3 [See Chapter I, "Postwar Reconstruction," footnote 10.—Ed.]

4 [The Covenant of the League of Nations was signed in April of 1919. Its twenty-six articles formed an agreement among the member governments to establish a system of collective security for the maintenance of peace and the settlement of disputes among nations. —Ed.]

5 [See Chapter I, "Postwar Reconstruction," footnote 6.—Ed.]

warlike nations considered them an insincere protection of the unfair privileges of the weak. The principle of collective security could not work in a milieu where every nation waged a permanent economic war against all other nations.[6]

We may hope that this unsatisfactory state of things will one day be replaced by a mentality of free trade and goodwill. But we have to realize that it would be foolish to believe that trade barriers and immigration barriers will be abolished directly after this war. We have to try to discover means that could make peace durable even in this age of radical nationalism.

Nations inspired by the spirit of nationalism recognize only one argument in favor of peace, namely, that there is but little hope of success for their armed forces in waging war. What is wanted, therefore, is some way to build up a political structure that would prevent the nations calling themselves "dynamic" because of the use of their powers for aggression.

It is very probable that the British empire, the American republics, and some of the democracies of Western Europe will arrange, after the war, for permanent political and military cooperation in order to assure their security against German and Japanese aggressions. Whether constructed according to the pattern laid out by Mr. Clarence Streit[7] or in another way, such a union could peacefully settle conflicts in all countries from the left bank of the Rhine westward to the western boundaries of the British sphere of influence in Asia. But just that part of the earth in which both world wars have originated would remain outside. A special scheme for a durable peace in Eastern Europe is a necessary condition for the satisfactory working of all plans to make the world safe for peace.

II   *The German Problem*

The following proposals for a new political constitution of Eastern Europe are based on two assumptions.

The first assumption is a total defeat of Nazism. We do not have to worry about what will happen if the Nazis should end their total war by a total victory. They will exterminate some of the vanquished nations, expel

---

6 [On the failure of attempts to reestablish freer trade in the period between the two world wars, and its relationship to the preparations for war, see William E. Rappard, *The Common Menace of Economic and Military Armaments* (London: Cobden-Sanderson, 1936), and *Postwar Efforts for Freer Trade* (Geneva: Geneva Research Centre, 1938).—Ed.]

7 [See Chapter 1, "Postwar Reconstruction," footnote 40.—Ed.]

others from Europe, and enslave the remaining ones. In the "New Order," the members of the Nazi Party will rule over slaves.

The second assumption is that the victorious British empire and its allies will not use their total success to exterminate the German nation.[8] We assume that the victors will neither kill all Germans nor expel them to the Arctic Circle; of course, they do not even consider such a barbaric plan. But then the German problem remains unsolved.

This German problem consists in the firm conviction of the German nationalists that the German nation is the strongest military power on earth. The German philosophers, historians, and would-be economists who have expounded these doctrines for more than eighty years base their statements on the following arguments:

A. The Germans are the most numerous among the European nations.[9] It is a mistake to believe that the Russians or the Americans are more numerous than are the Germans. From the total figures of the inhabitants of European Russia, the non-Russians (Ukrainians, White Russians, Mongolians, and others) have to be deducted; the remaining numbers of the Great Russians are inferior to those of the Germans. The Americans are not a homogeneous nation, but a minority of Nordics amidst Negroes, Jews, Slavs, Italians, and other "inferior" races.

B. The Germans own that country that dominates strategically the whole of Europe and some parts of the two adjacent continents. They enjoy in warring the advantages of standing on interior lines.

C. The Germans are a warlike nation; they are heroes, whereas the other white nations are peddlers (*Händler*), who stick to pacifism and cowardice.[10]

D. The genuine Germans have always been socialists in their soul and have, first under the guidance of the Hohenzollerns[11] and later under Adolf

---

8 [At the time when this monograph was written in October of 1941, Great Britain and the Soviet Union were the two primary military powers fighting Nazi Germany. The United States was still a neutral power, not entering the war against Nazi Germany until December of 1941, following the Japanese attack on Pearl Harbor.—Ed.]

9 [Before 1939, the ten leading countries in terms of population in Europe (excluding the Soviet Union) were: Germany, 77,028,433; France, 63,849,000; Great Britain and Northern Ireland, 46,605,753; Italy, 44,530,000; Poland, 35,090,000; Spain, 23,950,821; Yugoslavia, 15,703,000; Czechoslovakia, 15,096,025; Hungary, 13,412,667; Netherlands, 8,728,722.—Ed.]

10 [See Chapter I, "Postwar Reconstruction," footnote 52.—Ed.]

11 [The House of Hohenzollern was a royal German family that ruled Brandenburg (1415–1918), Prussia (1525–1918), and Germany (1871–1918). Its rule came to an end with the abdication of Kaiser Wilhelm II in 1918 at the close of the First World War.—Ed.]

Hitler, freed themselves from the domination of Western and Jewish ideas; their mind has only superficially or temporarily been infected by "Christianism," humanitarianism, capitalism, utilitarianism, liberalism, democracy, and Bolshevism.

E. Strong as they are, the Germans have therefore the sacred duty to conquer and rule the world. As supermen they will tame the underdogs, to whom the appellation "human" should be denied. Such is the will of the German God, who gave power to his chosen people, the Germans.

The main accent lies on the first of these five points. "We are a nation of one hundred million, therefore, we are chosen to own the earth." It is necessary to realize that German nationalism differs from the nationalism of other nations only in the fact that the Germans believe themselves to be the strongest of all nations. They are not prepared to endure the disadvantages that the economic nationalism of other nations imposes on them, because they feel themselves strong enough to do away with these discriminatory measures. They say, "Smaller nations may acquiesce in the actual distribution of the resources of the earth; we, the big German nation, cannot tolerate this state of affairs." The Nazis are full of contempt for the Norwegians and the Danes, for example, because they themselves are many and these "Nordic" nations are small.

As long as the world follows a path of economic nationalism and as long as there are eighty million Germans living in Europe and twenty million in non-European countries, the spirit of aggression will dominate the political thought of Germany. Nazism is not a new doctrine. It has a long history. Fichte,[12] List,[13] Lassalle,[14] Lasson,[15] Lagarde,[16] Lang-

12 [Johann Gottlieb Fichte (1762–1814) was a German philosopher who developed a theory of transcendental idealism; he was also a leading German nationalist who advocated a controlled economy and national economic self-sufficiency.—Ed.]

13 [Friedrich List (1789–1846) was a German political economist who formulated a five-stage theory of economic development. He argued that, for an industrializing nation like Germany in the nineteenth century, economic protectionism was essential to national development.—Ed.]

14 [Ferdinand Lassalle (1825–64) was a leading proponent of the German theory of state socialism; he was also a founder of the German Workers Association, which was the forerunner of the German Social Democratic Party.—Ed.]

15 [Adolf Lasson (1832–1917) was a German philosopher who argued that intuition and mysticism were superior to rational methods for the understanding of man and nature.—Ed.]

16 [Paul Anton de Lagarde (1827–91) was a professor of Oriental languages at Göttingen. He advocated German national regeneration through religious and politically conservative

behn,[17] Wagner,[18] Treitschke,[19] Schmoller,[20] and Chamberlain[21] were its sponsors. The doctrine was completely laid out in the course of the nineteenth century. Spengler,[22] Spann,[23] Sombart,[24] Hitler, and Rosenberg[25] did not add any new ideas; they only repeated and emphasized the old slogans.

Nothing can prevent a new German aggression but an organization of

programs. His book *German Studies* was highly anti-Semitic, stating that "the Jews are aliens in every European state, and as aliens they are nothing but carriers of decomposition."—Ed.]

17 [Julius Langbehn (1851–1907) was known as the "Rembrandt German," due to his book *Rembrandt as Teacher* (1890); he emphasized the irrational elements in culture in contrast to naturalistic or rationalist ideas. He said that good, clean Aryan blood "is the blood that contains the most moral 'gold.'"—Ed.]

18 [Richard Wagner (1813–83), a leading composer of German Romanticism, was best known for *The Flying Dutchman, Die Walküre*, and *Der Ring des Nibelungen*.—Ed.]

19 [Heinrich von Treitschke (1834–96) was a prominent German historian and Prussian state historiographer. He was known for his strong German nationalist beliefs and anti-Semitism.—Ed.]

20 [Gustav von Schmoller (1838–1917), a prominent economist in imperial Germany at the University of Berlin, was a leader of the "Socialists of the Chair." He defended and glorified Prussian political and military power. He was also a founder of the *Verein für Sozialpolitik* (Association for Social Policy) and a prominent spokesman for the German Historical School.—Ed.]

21 [Houston Stewart Chamberlain (1855–1927) was an Anglo-German author whose book *The Foundations of the Nineteenth Century* argued for the idea of German racial superiority and anti-Semitism. He greatly influenced the development of Nazi ideology.—Ed.]

22 [Oswald Spengler (1880–1936) was a German historian best known for *The Decline of the West* (1918–22), in which he argued that cultures go through life cycles and that Western culture had entered its period of decline.—Ed.]

23 [Othmar Spann (1878–1950) was a University of Vienna economist who developed a theory of society and the economic order called "Universalism," which argued that collectivist groupings were naturally prior to and superior to individuals.—Ed.]

24 [Werner Sombart (1863–1941), a professor at the University of Berlin after 1917, was a prominent proponent of the German Historical School. At first, he was sympathetic to the Marxian critique of capitalist society. In the 1930s, he became an apologist for the Nazi regime in Germany.—Ed.]

25 [Alfred Rosenberg (1893–1946) was a German Nazi leader. The racist ideas in his book *The Myth of the Twentieth Century* (1930) were incorporated into National Socialist doctrine by Adolf Hitler. He was responsible for many Nazi atrocities in Eastern Europe after 1941. He was convicted at the Nuremberg trials as a war criminal and was hanged.—Ed.]

Europe which makes it hopeless for Germany to embark on a new war of conquest. The political and military union of the Western democracies will stop Germany at its western and northern frontiers. Special provisions are needed to stop it at its eastern and southern frontiers.

The German danger has to be seen not in the spirit of aggression which inspires most of the Germans of our time, but in the military strength of Germany, which makes such an aggression a dreadful menace. The other nations that today share a similar mentality of aggression are less dangerous. They all would be innocuous but for the constellation created by Nazified Germany's "dynamism."

To carry out a scheme for a durable peace is not the outcome of hostility or hatred against Germany, Italy, or Japan, the three aggressor nations of our times. The blessings of peace will benefit these nations in the same way they will favor the rest of mankind. The purpose of all plans for a lasting peace which involve the existence of these three nations is exactly this: to give to the vanquished nations after the war the opportunity to again become incorporated into the great human society of free nations. Germans and Italians were, from time immemorial, foremost among the shapers of our civilization. We may hope that they will one day remember that this civilization, which they despise today, was to a great extent an achievement of sons of their own peoples.

It is the aim of the following plan to make it unnecessary for the victorious Allies to consider any proposal which intends to treat the vanquished peoples in the same way in which the Nazis wish to treat the conquered in case of their own total victory.

III   *The Clash of Linguistic Groups*

The term "Eastern Europe" as used in this paper includes the whole territory between the eastern boundaries of Germany, Switzerland, Italy, and the western borders of Russia. It reaches from the shores of the Baltic to those of the Black, Adriatic, and Aegean seas. We shall revert later to the problem of the precise delimitation of this territory.

This vast territory was, in the Europe of the Congress of Vienna,[26] di-

26 [The Congress of Vienna (1814–15) settled the peace terms following the defeat of Napoleon. It redrew the boundaries of the nations of Europe which resulted in Austrian, Prussian, and Russian domination of Central and Eastern Europe.—Ed.]

vided among Russia, the Hapsburg empire,[27] Prussia, and Turkey. With the dissolution of the Ottoman power in Europe,[28] with the disintegration of the Austro-Hungarian empire,[29] and with the curtailment of Russian power,[30] the peoples of this part of the world obtained autonomy and self-government. But this independence resulted in anarchy and finally in a new partition of the territory involved among the three mighty neighbors, Germany, Russia, and Italy.[31] The order established by the treaties of 1856,[32] 1878,[33] and 1919[34] collapsed catastrophically.

27 [The House of Hapsburg was the ruling house of Austria from 1282 to 1918.—Ed.]

28 [The Ottoman, or Turkish, empire was a vast state founded in the thirteenth century. At its height, it included Asia Minor, most of Arabia, parts of Persia, the Balkan region of southeastern Europe, and parts of North Africa, including Egypt and Libya. In the last decades of the nineteenth century and the first two decades of the twentieth century, Ottoman rule was displaced in southeastern Europe by the establishment of independent nations.—Ed.]

29 [The Austro-Hungarian, or Dual, Monarchy emerged from the constitutional compromise of 1867 between the House of Hapsburg and Hungary; it established a jurisdictional division in the Austrian empire. The Austro-Hungarian empire was formally dissolved as a result of the Treaty of St. Germain in 1919, following World War I.—Ed.]

30 [As a result of the Treaty of Brest-Litovsk between imperial Germany and Lenin's new Bolshevik government in March of 1918 and the Treaty of Versailles in June of 1919, Russian political control over parts of Eastern Europe, including Poland, Finland, Estonia, Latvia, Lithuania, and Bessarabia (annexed by Romania), was ended.—Ed.]

31 [This refers to the annexation by Nazi Germany of Austria in March 1938 and Czechoslovakia in 1938 and 1939; the Italian annexation of Albania in April of 1939; the new partition of Poland between Nazi Germany and Soviet Russia in September of 1939; the annexation of the Baltic republics of Estonia, Latvia, and Lithuania by the Soviet Union in June of 1940; the partial partition of Romania by the Soviet Union, Hungary, and Bulgaria in June and August of 1940; and the partition of Yugoslavia and Greece in May of 1941 between Nazi Germany, Italy, Bulgaria, and Hungary.—Ed.]

32 [The Congress of Paris of 1856 was held by Great Britain, France, the Ottoman empire, Sardinia, Russia, Austria, and Prussia to negotiate peace after the Crimean War (1853–56). It also adopted the Declaration of Paris, which attempted to codify an international law of the sea, limiting the conduct of belligerents and the protection of neutral trade in times of war.—Ed.]

33 [The Congress of Berlin was held in 1878 to invoke a Concert of Europe to halt Russian expansion into the Ottoman empire following the Russo-Turkish War of 1877–78. It established new boundaries and new political jurisdictions in the Balkan region of Europe. —Ed.]

34 [The Congress of Peace in Paris in 1919 resulted in the Treaty of Versailles that ended the Allied Powers' war with Germany, and the establishment of the Covenant of the League of Nations for an international organization for the maintenance of world peace.—Ed.]

Eastern Europe is the central seat of trouble and unrest. Both world wars arose in this territory. The units or groups that are bitterly fighting one another in Eastern Europe apply to themselves, in their own languages, terms that correspond to the English words "nation," "nationality," or "people." They consider a community of language as the characteristic feature of a nation. The issue in these fights is always the right to use the national idiom. The terms "Germanization," "Polanization," "Magyarization," etc., always mean to induce people, by violence or other methods of pressure, to replace their mother tongue with German, Polish, Hungarian, etc.

These are not struggles among races. No distinct bodily features which the anthropologist could establish with the aid of the scientific methods of his branch of knowledge separate the men belonging to different groups. If you present one of these men to an anthropologist he will not be able to decide whether the man is a German, a Czech, a Pole, or a Hungarian.

Neither have the men belonging to one of these groups a common descent. The right banks of the Elbe river were eight hundred years ago inhabited by Slavs and Baltic tribes only. They became German in the course of the processes which the German historians call the "colonization of the East."[35] There was an immigration of Germans from the west and from the southwest into this area, but the main stock of its present population are the descendants of the indigenous Slavs and Baltic peoples who, under the influence of the church and school, turned to the use of the German language. Prussian chauvinists, of course, assert that the native Slavs were radically exterminated and that the whole present population are the descendants of German settlers. There is not the slightest proof for this doctrine, which some Prussian historians developed in order to justify the Prussian claim for hegemony in Germany. But even they never dared to deny that the purely Slav ancestry of the princely families and of most of the aristocratic families is beyond doubt. Queen Louisa of Prussia,[36] whom all German nationalists consider as the paragon of German womanhood, was a scion of the ruling house of Mecklenburg, whose originally Slavic character has never been contested. Many noble families of the Ger-

35 [The "colonization of the East" refers to the expansion of German political and linguistic control over regions east of the Elbe River from the eleventh through the nineteenth centuries.—Ed.]

36 [Queen Louisa of Prussia (1776–1810) was the daughter of Prince Charles of Mecklenburg-Strelitz; she married Frederick William III (1770–1840) in 1793 and ascended the throne as Queen of Prussia in 1797.—Ed.]

man northeast can be traced back to Slav ancestors. The genealogical trees of the families of the middle classes and of the peasantry cannot be established as far back as those of the nobility; this alone explains why the proof of Slavic origin cannot be provided for them.

Shifting from one of these linguistic groups to another occurred not only in earlier days. It happened in the nineteenth century and today is so frequent that nobody ever remarks upon it. Many outstanding personalities in the Nazi movement in Germany and Austria, and in the Czechoslovakian, Polish, and Hungarian districts claimed by Nazism, were the sons of parents whose language was not German. Similar conditions prevail in the nationalist parties of all Eastern European linguistic groups. In many cases, the change of loyalties was accompanied by a change in the family name. But many radical nationalists have retained their foreign-sounding family names that clearly show their alien origin.

Whenever the question is raised whether a group has to be considered as a distinct nation, and therefore as such should be entitled to claim political autonomy, the issue is whether the idiom involved has to be considered as a distinct language or only as a dialect. The Russians maintain that the Ukrainian idiom is only a dialect, like the Plattdeutsch in Northern Germany or the Provençal of the "Felibriges" in southern France.[37] The Czechs propose the same argument against the political aspirations of the Slovaks and the Italians against the Rhaeto-Romanic idiom. (Only a few years ago the Swiss government gave to the Romansh the legal status of a national language.)[38]

There is only one case in Eastern Europe where the characteristic feature that separates two nations is not language, but religion and the alphabetical types used in writing and printing. The Serbs and the Croats speak the same language, but whereas the Serbs use the Cyrillic alphabet, the Croats use the Roman. The Serbs adhere to the orthodox creed of the Oriental Church; the Croats are Catholic.

Religious issues, moreover, play only a subordinate role in these strug-

37 [The French language is comprised of North French and South French (or Provençal). Provençal is spoken in the lower Rhône Valley and the French Riviera. It was used extensively by a number of French writers in the nineteenth century, whose followers became known as the "Felibriges."—Ed.]

38 [The Swiss Federal Constitution of 1848 declared that the three main languages of the country were German, French, and Italian. In 1938, a federal popular vote formally recognized Romansh as a fourth national (though not federally official) language.—Ed.]

gles of linguistic groups. It is, on the contrary, the linguistic issue which dominates religion. As soon as a linguistic group of the Oriental Church succeeded in obtaining some degree of political or cultural autonomy, it freed itself from the religious rule of the patriarch of Constantinople and founded an autonomous church. No dogmatic differences motivated these changes; they were purely political.

At the turn of the sixteenth and seventeenth centuries, Ukrainian bishops acknowledged the Pope's supremacy. This Uniat Oriental Church was the main instrument in the poor Ukrainian serfs' fight against their oppressors.[39] When Russia conquered the greater part of the Ukraine, it violently persecuted this church in order to break Ukrainian resistance against Russification. Finally, the Czars succeeded in exterminating the Uniat Church on Russian soil. This church survived only in those parts of the country which were under the rule of the Habsburgs.[40]

All those parts of Eastern Europe, which in the Middle Ages acknowledged the supremacy of the Pope, were some hundreds of years ago terribly shaken by religious struggles. But times have changed. Today Catholics and Protestants of different denominations jointly cooperate within each linguistic group. Loyalty to the nation means more to them than the community of religion.

Only a few words have to be devoted to the Pan-Slavic idea. The Russian governments—both that of the Czars and that of the Soviets—favored, at different times, a doctrine that assigned to the Russians, as the most numerous Slavic nation, the task of freeing all Slav brethren from the yoke of the Germans, Turks, Italians, and Hungarians. As far as Pan-Slavism means more—namely, the establishment of a unitary state including all Slavic peoples under Russian hegemony—it was nothing more than a poor disguise for Russian imperialism.[41] The Poles and the Ukrainians, who knew what Russian rule meant, always bitterly opposed it. Neither are the other Slavic peoples ready to surrender to Russia.

Nowadays, some authors recommend a union of all Slavs as the best

39 [The Uniat is an Eastern Christian Church in communion with the Roman Catholic Church, but it maintains its own language, rites, and code of canon law.—Ed.]

40 [Today, the Uniat Church is most evident in the western region of Ukraine.—Ed.]

41 [Pan-Slavism was developed in the mid-nineteenth century by Russian intellectuals who argued that Russian culture was inherently distinct from and incompatible with the cultures of Western Europe. They also advocated the unity of the Slavic peoples of Eastern Europe under Russian leadership.—Ed.]

solution of the problems of Eastern Europe. Such a union would mean an alliance of the Slavs for the sake of the oppression of the Germans, Lithuanians, Estonians, Letts, Hungarians, Romanians, Italians, and Greeks living in Eastern Europe. It would not abolish the existing struggles, but would instead perpetuate them.

IV   Present-Day Conditions in Eastern Europe

If you ask representatives of the nations of Eastern Europe what they consider would be a fair determination of the boundaries of their own countries, and if you mark these boundaries on a map, you will discover that the greater part of this territory is claimed by two nations and that a not-negligible part is claimed by three nations. Every nation knows how to justify its claims with linguistic, racial, historical, geographical, economic, social, or religious arguments. No nation is prepared to renounce the least of its claims for reasons of expediency. Every nation is ready to resort to arms in order to satisfy its pretensions. Every nation, therefore, considers its immediate neighbors as mortal enemies and relies on its neighbors' neighbors for armed support of its own territorial claims against the common foe. Every nation tries to profit from every opportunity to satisfy its claims at the expense of its neighbors. The history of the last twenty years proves the correctness of this description.

These claims are not claims of governments or of "ruling" and "exploiting" classes, as current opinion would have us believe; these are claims of whole nations and of every member of the respective linguistic groups. The governments are sometimes prepared to renounce some of these claims temporarily, in order to adjust the conduct of foreign policy to immediate political necessity.

The wealthy classes are peace-loving because they do not want to suffer material losses. The radical nationalists, supported by the general consent of the large majorities, rebuke the governments for their cowardice and moderation and the capitalists and entrepreneurs for their selfish materialism. Extreme nationalism is not the work of bribed propagandists; it is a mentality created by the teachings and writings of sincere poets, writers, and scholars.[42] The teachers and the youth are the most enthusiastic

---

42 [On the intellectual origins of modern nationalism, see Carlton J. H. Hayes, *The Historical Evolution of Modern Nationalism* (New York: Richard R. Smith, Inc., 1931).—Ed.]

supporters of chauvinism and nationalism. The nationalism of public opinion is intractable and intransigent and eliminates from the public scene every politician and every political party suspected of being lenient in the matter of "national" concerns. The most radical nationalists terrorize the moderate men because everybody knows that the voters favor the most radical program.

Years ago it could be asserted that only the intellectuals were nationalists, whereas the uneducated masses were more or less indifferent. This is no longer true since the spread of education has caused the disappearance of illiteracy. Besides, in our age of economic interventionism and its consequence—economic nationalism—every citizen has a personal interest in the result of these struggles between linguistic groups. Every peasant and every worker wishes that the area in which no discrimination is applied against him should be broadened. Every Czech shoe worker derived an immediate advantage from the fact that shoes manufactured in Czech plants could easily be sold in the sheltered markets of Slovakia and Carpatho-Russia.[43] Every Croat peasant was injured by the fact that the Yugoslavian government's export agency discriminated against the Croats in purchasing cereals for sale to Germany. Austrian immigration barriers worked their harm on all Czechs, Hungarians, and Yugoslavs, who were barred from the Austrian labor market, where wages were higher than in their own countries.

It is impossible to draw boundaries in Eastern Europe that would clearly separate linguistic groups. A great part of this territory is linguistically mixed, that is, inhabited by men of different languages. Every territorial division would therefore necessarily leave minorities under foreign rule. These minorities are the bearers of permanent unrest, of irredentism[44] and hatred.

To dispose of the problem of minorities in a peaceful way, two methods had been suggested.

One method was the protection of minority rights by international law and its enforcement by international tribunals. The method failed. The economist has to recognize that such a system could be successfully applied only in a world of free trade and an unhampered market economy. It must necessarily fail and it did fail in our age of economic interven-

---

43 [Carpatho-Russia, also known as Carpatho-Ukraine or Ruthenia, was the easternmost region of Czechoslovakia from 1918 to 1939; it was annexed by Hungary in March of 1939 and incorporated into the Soviet Union as a part of Ukraine in 1945.—Ed.]

44 [See Chapter I on "Postwar Reconstruction," footnote 34.—Ed.]

tionism. A law cannot protect anybody against measures dictated by alleged considerations of economic expediency. All measures of government interference in business can be and are used in countries inhabited by different linguistic groups for the sake of injuring the minorities. Customs tariffs, foreign exchange regulations, taxation, subsidies, labor legislation, and so on may be utilized for discrimination although this cannot be proved in court procedure. The government can always explain such measures as being dictated by purely economic considerations. If licenses are denied to members of the minority but, on the other hand, are granted to members of the privileged group, the interference of an international tribunal is in vain. A system of foreign exchange regulation can be used to strangle all business activities of the minority. By means of subsidies, the minority has to contribute to the bounties paid to its competitors who belong to the ruling linguistic group. Where the export trade of agricultural produce is nationalized and a government agency is the only buyer on the export market, discrimination in making purchases and in prices paid is practiced against the minority. With the aid of government interference in business, life for the minorities without formal violation of legal equality can be made unbearable. In our age of interventionism, there is no legal protection available against an ill-intentioned government.

The impracticability of protecting minorities by international tribunals led to the proposal of another solution—the transplantation of minorities. This method could work only in a world in which all parts offered the same natural opportunities for production. In our actual world, where the natural conditions for production are unequally distributed, the execution of such a plan would only aggravate existing inequalities and therefore intensify the desire for territorial expansion. When Hitler withdrew some German minorities from the East, he did so because he believed that he has much more fertile land to offer them.[45]

The reform most commonly suggested recommends to these nations the formation of an economic union. An economic union would, under present conditions of government interference in business, have to include a complete unification of all branches of economic policy. It would shift the political center of gravity to the executive office of the union and reduce the national governments to the level of provincial and local auxiliaries. We may witness today how in all federations the power of the member states is gradually shrinking and that of the federal authorities in-

45 [See Chapter I, "Postwar Reconstruction," footnote 37.—Ed.]

creasing. This is not an accident. It is rather the unavoidable consequence of economic interventionism.

The Western nations are unjust when they ridicule the anarchic conditions in Eastern Europe and the inability of their rulers to find a way for peaceful neighborliness. These Eastern nations do nothing else than imitate the economic policies of the Western democracies. They apply the same measures of economic nationalism. This means they discriminate against foreigners because they believe that in this way they can further the welfare of their own citizens. They have invented nothing; they have only taken over ideas from others. It is not their fault that the contradictions and deficiencies of economic nationalism are more glaring under the conditions in which they have to live.

There is general agreement today that the principle of unlimited sovereignty cannot be maintained in a world where the international division of labor results in a mutual dependence of every nation on all other nations. Notwithstanding this consensus, nothing was done to limit the power of each nation, even the smallest one, to behave as if it were alone in the world. This contradiction is to be explained by the confusion that the term "limited sovereignty" involves. The concept of sovereignty, that is, supreme power, does not allow for any limitation. A power may be supreme only if unlimited. If the power of a nation is limited so as to exclude only some measures, the remaining power can be used for the annihilation of this restriction. If, for instance, customs tariffs are excluded or limited, it is possible to use other powers to render this limitation meaningless. It is possible, for example, to use the measures of veterinarian policy or measures for fighting animal diseases in a protectionist way, not to mention foreign exchange controls and other methods. A pure limitation of sovereignty is not enough when the spirit of economic nationalism is allowed to survive. A total suppression of local sovereignty is necessary in order to insure goodwill and cooperation. To make Eastern Europe peaceful it is indispensable to vest the whole sovereignty in one democratic body ruling the entire area, which for more than twenty-five years has been a theater of continual warfare and destruction.

The world as a whole is not yet prepared to renounce national sovereignty in favor of a world government. The commonwealth of free nations and free men is today only a utopian concept. Great ideological changes have to take place before a mentality of universal peace and worldwide cooperation can replace the present-day spirit of conquest and mutual hatred.

But Eastern Europe cannot wait any longer; something has to be done immediately. A return to the conditions of 1933 is out of the question.[46] Conditions in which every sovereign state is looking for an opportunity to annex some territories belonging to its neighbors and every government considers a large number of its citizens as pariahs cannot be maintained.

We may assume that every linguistic group is honest in believing that its own claims are better founded than those of the competing groups. But we cannot agree with the repeated assertions of some linguistic groups that the yoke that they impose on other groups is more fair and reasonable and less harsh than the yoke imposed on them. The judgment of the oppressed has not less weight than that of the oppressors. No linguistic group should be permitted to inflict harm on members of other groups. No "protectorate" can be considered as justified, if the "protected" do not want the alleged protection.[47]

We have to realize that the principle of nationality, as developed in Western Europe, is simply inapplicable in Eastern Europe, where the linguistic groups are inextricably mingled. The political system of Eastern Europe, therefore, cannot be built up as a replica of that in the West. New standards have to be applied.

The foremost aim of a new order in Eastern Europe is to eliminate the problem of linguistic minorities. To be a member of such a linguistic minority means to be an outlaw. Every Slovak will say that this was the status of Slovaks in Hungary (before 1918)[48] and in Czechoslovakia (from 1918 to 1939); every Hungarian will say that this was the status of Hungarians in Czechoslovakia and is today in Slovakia; every Czech will say that this is today the status of Czechs, both in those territories that the Reich has annexed since 1939, and in the Bohemia-Moravia Protectorate. It is the same with similar cases all over Eastern Europe. There were and are autonomy and democracy only for the members of the ruling linguis-

---

46 [The year 1933 saw Adolf Hitler come to power in Germany. —Ed.]

47 [After Nazi Germany's annexation of Czechoslovakia's Sudetenland in September of 1938 as a result of the Munich agreement, Hitler ordered the occupation of the remainder of Czechoslovakia in March of 1939. The western regions of Bohemia and Moravia were made a "protectorate" under German rule, and the eastern region of Slovakia was made an independent country under German protection. —Ed.]

48 [Slovakia was under the rule of Hungary as part of the Austro-Hungarian empire. —Ed.]

tic majorities; the members of the minorities have the disadvantages, but not the privileges, of citizenship.

It is immaterial to enter into a discussion of the claims of all these linguistic groups concerning their respective cultural values. It is of no concern whether Hungarian civilization is higher than that of the Romanians or of the Croats. The fact that Goethe, Kant, and Beethoven were Germans does not justify the methods applied by the Nazis against the Czechs and the Poles. Mussolini may be right or wrong that Dante means more for humanity than Walter von der Vogelweide,[49] but what relationship has this comparison of two poets to the problem of the oppression of the German-speaking inhabitants of Bozen and Brixenz?[50] It is grotesque that both Germans and Poles claim Copernicus for their own nation. It is beyond doubt that Copernicus wrote in Latin. There were at that time neither German nor Polish books on mathematics and astronomy; all the lectures which were delivered at the Italian, German, and Polish universities were delivered in Latin.

We do not have to discuss the question whether it is of any value for mankind that the Czech, Polish, Ukrainian, or Serb civilizations should survive. The only fact which we have to face is this: There are people who wish to use freely the language which their parents have taught them. This legitimate desire has to be satisfied.

It is not true that, in order to develop its own civilization, a linguistic group needs a government whose sovereignty can be used to inflict harm on other linguistic groups. No Hungarian can derive any advantage from the fact that a Slovak or a Romanian is denied the right to use his native tongue.

The treaties of 1919 brought large minorities of Germans, Russians, and Ukrainians under the rule of Czech and Polish majorities. This state of things could not be maintained except by a power strong enough to prevent both the Reich and the Soviet Union from interfering. It was based on the readiness of the French and the British to fight for the Czechs and the Poles.

49 [Walter von der Vogelweide (1170–1230) is still considered to be one of the most gifted German poets and "singers of love."—Ed.]

50 [Bozen (Bolzano) and Brixenz (Bressanone) are cities in the south Tyrol, a region that was part of the Austro-Hungarian empire until 1919, when it was annexed by Italy as a result of the peace treaties that ended World War I.—Ed.]

Of course, neither Germany nor Russia has a right to oppress the Poles or the Czechs. But their title is no worse than the title of the Czechs against the Germans in the districts of Eger and Reichenberg[51] or of the Poles against the Ukrainians in Eastern Galicia.[52]

We do not mention these deplorable events of the past in order to blame anybody or in order to discover some nation's guilt. It is immaterial to establish who the first aggressors were. It is without consequence whether Bohemia in the early Middle Ages was inhabited by Germans or Slavs or whether the Germans came to Bohemia only in the late Middle Ages as colonists. An argument like that between Hungarian and Romanian scholars concerning the question of whether the Romanian settlement in Transylvania took place earlier or later is futile. It is useless to inquire whether the century-old hatred between Poles and Russians was inaugurated by Polish or by Russian aggression. Let bygones be bygones. We do not have to revenge crimes of the past, but to build up a future in which people can enjoy the blessings both of peace and of freedom.

V The Requisites for a Permanent Settlement of the East European Problem

In order to make Eastern Europe safe for peace, it is necessary to establish a state of affairs under which war does not pay. The average citizen should not expect any profit from a war in which his own linguistic group would be victorious over one of the other linguistic groups. Within this area, borderlines must lose their present meaning. They must not have more importance, in the future, than the frontiers between the forty-eight states of the United States of America or between the counties of England.

The whole territory of Eastern Europe has to be organized as a politi-

51 [Eger (Cheb) and Reichenberg (Jablonic) are in the region of the Czech Republic bordering on Germany formerly known as the Sudetenland. Before 1945 this region was home to a predominantly German-speaking population.—Ed.]

52 [Eastern Galicia was the northeastern region of the Austrian part of the Austro-Hungarian empire before 1918. It was annexed by Poland as part of the peace treaties ending World War I; its population was heavily Ukrainian and Jewish. Eastern Galicia was annexed by the Soviet Union in September of 1939 as a result of the Nazi-Soviet invasion and partition of Poland; it is now the western region of independent Ukraine.—Ed.]

cal unit under a strictly unitary government. Within this area, every individual has to have the right to choose the place where he wishes to live and to work. The laws and the authorities have to treat all natives—that is, all citizens of Eastern Europe—in the same way and on an equal footing without privileges or discrimination against individuals or groups.

Within the frame of this new political structure—let us call it the *Eastern Democratic Union (EDU)*—the old political units may continue to function. A dislocation of the historically developed entities is not required. Once the problem of borders has been deprived of its disastrous political implications, most of the existing national bodies can remain intact. Having lost their power to inflict evils on their neighbors and on their minorities, they may prove very useful for the progress of civilization and welfare.

There will be, for instance, a Kingdom of Romania and a Polish Republic. But these former sovereign states will now have to comply strictly with the laws and with the administrative provisions of the EDU. There will be no constitutional limit to the power of the EDU which could be used by an ill-intentioned local government to frustrate the laws and regulations issued by the EDU.

This shows us why the aims of the EDU cannot be realized in the constitutional form of a federation (*Bundesstaat*).[53] Under a federated system, the constitution assigns some branches of government activity to the federal government and other branches to the local governments of the member states. As long as the constitution remains unchanged, the federal government does not have the power to interfere with questions which are in the jurisdiction of the member states. Such a system can succeed and has succeeded only with homogeneous peoples and where there exists a strong feeling of national unity and where no linguistic, religious, or racial discrepancies divide the population.

Let us assume that the constitution of a supposed East European Federation grants to every linguistic group the right to establish schools where its own language is taught. Then it would be illegal for a member state to hinder directly and openly the establishment of such schools. But if the building code and the administration of public health and fire fighting are in the exclusive jurisdiction of the member states, a local government could use its powers to close a school on the grounds that the building does not comply with the requirements fixed by these regulations. The federal authorities would be helpless because they would not have the

53 [A federal state or centralized confederacy.—Ed.]

right to interfere, even if the grounds given prove to be only a subterfuge. Every kind of constitutional prerogative granted to the member states could be abused by a local government. If the fight against crime should be assigned to the member states, they could be slow in protecting the members of a minority group. If they should have the right to establish foreign exchange control, they could discriminate against the members of the minority groups in complying with the demands for foreign exchange.

If we want to abolish all discrimination against minority groups and if we want to give to all citizens actual and not only formal equality, we have to vest all powers in the central government only. This would not cripple the right of a loyal local government eager to use its powers in a fair way. But it would hinder the return to methods whereby the whole administrative apparatus of the government is used to inflict harm on minorities.

A federation in Eastern Europe could never succeed in abolishing the political implications of the frontiers. In every member state there would remain the problem of minorities. There would be oppression of minorities, hatred, and irredentism. The government of every member state would continue to consider its neighbors as adversaries. The diplomatic and consular agents of the three big adjacent powers would try to profit from these quarrels and rivalries and might succeed in disrupting the whole system.

The main objectives of the new political order which has to be established in Eastern Europe are:

A. This new system of government has to grant to every citizen full opportunity to live and to work freely without being molested by the hostility of any linguistic group inside or outside the boundaries of Eastern Europe. Nobody should be prosecuted or disqualified on account of his mother tongue or his creed. Every linguistic group should have the right to use its own language. No discrimination should be tolerated against minority groups and their members. Every citizen should be treated in such a way that he will call the country without any reservation "my country" and the government "our government."

B. No linguistic group should expect any improvement of its political status by a change in the territorial organization. The difference between a ruling linguistic group and oppressed linguistic minorities has to disappear. There must not be any "irrendenta."

C. The system has to be strong enough to defend its independence against aggression on the part of its neighbors. Its armed forces have to be able to repel without foreign assistance an isolated aggression of either Germany, Italy, or Russia. It should rely on the help of the Western democracies only against a common aggression by at least two of these neighbors.

VI   *The Abandonment of Economic Nationalism*

The EDU will have to renounce all hostility against any linguistic group. This includes the elimination of all measures of economic nationalism. Economic nationalism is, as already mentioned, a policy that intends to improve the conditions of some groups of citizens by inflicting evils on foreigners; it is a policy of discrimination against foreigners. Foreign goods are excluded from the domestic market or only permitted after having paid an import duty. Foreign labor is disbarred from competition on the domestic labor market. Foreign capital is liable to confiscation. But, at the same time, all these measures hurt the economic interests of some groups of citizens. An import duty for shoes, for instance, may benefit the people interested in this particular branch of industry, but it injures all consumers of shoes.

It was feasible in linguistically homogeneous nations to justify import duties in the eyes of the consumers. The German protectionists, for instance, succeeded in convincing the majority of the German voters that it is expedient for them to pay a much higher price than the world market price for wheat in order to increase the revenue of the German wheat producers. But in a country inhabited by different linguistic groups, such a justification would not be considered satisfactory. Those linguistic groups whose industrial production is backward will never acquiesce to an import duty on shoes that would benefit the shoe production of those linguistic groups whose industrial production has reached a higher stage of development. They will call such foreign trade policy an exploitation of their own group. The history of the Austro-Hungarian customs union provides us with ample evidence for the correctness of this statement.[54] Sometimes even within linguistically homogeneous nations the discussion concerning foreign trade policy favors the spirit of disintegration. Both in the Dominion of Canada and in the Commonwealth of Australia, purely agricultural western sectors oppose the protectionist policy of the more industrialized sectors and even ventured to propose a dissolution of the customs union.

If the EDU would embark on a policy of protectionism its existence would be doomed.

---

54 [On the conflicts between nationality groups in Austria-Hungary over tariff and customs policies, see Gustav Gratz and Richard Schüller, *The Economic Policy of Austria-Hungary During the War* (New Haven: Yale University Press, 1928) and David F. Strong, *Austria (October 1918–March 1919): Transition from Empire to Republic* (New York: Columbia University Press, 1939), pp. 19–28. — Ed.]

The EDU will therefore be a country of free trade. There will be no protective tariffs nor other measures for the protection of home industries against foreign competition. There will be neither foreign exchange controls nor inflationary measures. There will be neither subsidies nor bounties and no migration barriers. There will be a stable currency system with stable rates of foreign exchange.

All objections raised against such a policy of free trade on the part of a single country within a world of economic nationalism and protectionism are futile. It would be a waste of time to refute again the popular fallacy that such a country would not be able to continue any domestic production and only import from abroad.

The far greater part of Eastern Europe is mostly interested in the export of food and raw material. These agricultural, forest, and mining interests cannot suffer any disadvantage from a policy of free trade. On the other hand, it is obvious that none of the industrial interests of this territory can assume that the excessive protectionism of the past could be continued even if the EDU should not be formed.

Let us consider the two types of foreign trade policy applied in this territory before 1938 in referring to Austria as an instance of agricultural protectionism and to Hungary as an instance of industrial protectionism.

In Austria, the nonagricultural section of the population was exploited for the benefit of agriculture. Food prices in Austria were maintained at a level of much more than 200 percent of world market prices. The peasants got from the treasury much more as bounties than they had to pay as taxes. In the mountain districts, the peasants got a premium for tilling the land regardless of whether climatic conditions would allow wheat to ripen. For butter, the government, paradoxically enough, paid export subsidies that were much higher than the world market price of butter. It will be impossible to continue these methods after the war to the disadvantage of the impoverished nonagricultural population.[55]

Hungary, on the other hand, exploited the agricultural population for the benefit of industrial production. The prices of manufactured goods were much higher than in the world market and in the countries of Western Europe and America. A system of more or less concealed export pre-

---

55 [See *Austria—Public Finances* (Geneva: League of Nations, 1936–37) in three reports prepared by the Financial Organization of the League of Nations.—Ed.]

miums and tax exemptions furthered the export of manufactured goods which were unavailable to the masses of peasants and poor agricultural workers. It is obvious that such a policy will have to be abandoned sooner or later.[56]

The main economic problem which the peoples of Eastern Europe have to face is relative overpopulation.[57] In respect to the natural conditions which this territory offers for production and in respect to the density of population in areas much better endowed by nature, all these countries are overpopulated. The abolition of migration barriers in other parts of the world would result in an emigration of scores of millions from Eastern Europe and would create a tendency toward an equalization of the marginal productivity of labor; wages and farmers' income in Eastern Europe would rise. (Of course, the tilling of the poorer soil would be discontinued.) Migration barriers force these peoples to stay at home and put a check on the improvement of their standard of living. But this problem cannot be solved by any scheme limited to the domestic organization of Eastern Europe. It is a world problem.

The second economic problem of these countries is scarcity of capital. It is unlikely that foreign capital will be available for them. Private investors will have more promising offers for the employment of their funds; foreign governments will consider domestic investment as more useful than the export of capital to Eastern Europe.

Even with a smoothly functioning political organization, Eastern Europe will remain a poor country with a standard of life which Americans and Britons will judge as very low.

But all these sad facts cannot be considered valid objections to the scheme proposed. For Eastern Europe to improve its economic conditions, there is no other method left other than the establishment of a durable peace and the abandonment of the policies that wasted the economic resources and the capital accumulated in previous years.

---

56 [See *Quarterly Reports on the Financial Position of Hungary* (Geneva: League of Nations, 1936–38)—Ed.]

57 [On the concept of "relative overpopulation," see Mises, "Freedom to Move as an International Problem" (1935) in Richard M. Ebeling and Jacob G. Hornberger, eds., *The Case for Free Trade and Open Immigration* (Fairfax, Va.: Future of Freedom Foundation, 1995), pp. 127–30; and Lionel Robbins, "The Optimum Theory of Population," in T. E. Gregory and H. Dalton, eds., *London Essays in Economics: In Honour of Edwin Cannan* (London: George Routledge and Sons, 1927), pp. 103–34.—Ed.]

VII   *Outlines of the New Order*

A ❧ The Area of the EDU

The EDU has to include the territories which in 1933 formed the sovereign states of Albania, Austria, Bulgaria, Czechoslovakia, Danzig, Estonia, Greece, Hungary, Latvia, Lithuania, Poland, Romania, and Yugoslavia.

It has to include the whole territory which in 1913 belonged to the Prussian provinces: Eastern Prussia, Western Prussia, Posen, and Silesia.[58] The three first-named provinces were once parts of Poland. They were appropriated by the princes of the House of Hohenzollern,[59] but this conquest did not make them a part of the Holy Roman Empire. The fact that the rulers of these countries were at the same time electors of Brandenburg had legally and constitutionally no other significance than the fact that the kings of England were electors (and later kings) of Hanover. Neither did these provinces belong to the German Confederation from 1815–1866.[60] They remained the "private property" of the Hohenzollern family. Only after the battle of Königgrätz in 1866[61] did the King of Prussia incorporate them by his own sovereign decision into the Norddeutscher Bund[62] and later, in 1871, into the Deutsches Reich.[63]

Silesia was part of the Holy Roman Empire only as an adjunct of the Kingdom of Bohemia. In the sixteenth and seventeenth centuries, it was ruled by dukes who belonged to a branch of the Piasts, the old royal family of Poland. When Frederick the Great embarked on the conquest of Silesia in 1740, he tried to justify his claims by pointing out that he was the legitimate heir of the Piast family.

---

58 [These German territories approximate the areas of pre-1938 Germany east of the Oder-Neisse Rivers that were annexed by Poland and the Soviet Union after the Second World War.—Ed.]

59 [See footnote 11.—Ed.]

60 [The German Confederation was established as a loose association of thirty-eight princely states in 1815; it was dissolved in 1866 following the Seven Weeks' War between Prussia and Italy against Austria.—Ed.]

61 [The battle of Königgrätz (Sadowa) on July 3, 1866, was the decisive military engagement between Prussia and Austria that brought the Seven Weeks' War to a close with a Prussian victory.—Ed.]

62 [This was the Northern German confederation that was dominated by Prussia.—Ed.]

63 [The German empire was established under Prussian leadership in 1871, following the Prussian victory over France in the Franco-Prussian War of 1870–71.—Ed.]

These four provinces are inhabited by a linguistically mixed population. They returned many Polish members to the old German Reichstag. In Eastern Prussia, there is a not-negligible Lithuanian minority.

Italy has to cede to the EDU all the European countries that it has occupied since 1913, the Dodecanese Islands[64] and the eastern part of the province of Venice—Venetia—a district inhabited by people speaking a Rhaeto-Romanic idiom.[65]

Thus the EDU will include about seven hundred thousand square miles with about one hundred and twenty million people using seventeen different languages. Such a country, when united, will be strong enough to defend its independence against its three mighty neighbors, Russia, Germany, and Italy.

B ᴥ THE CONSTITUTION

Every adult will have the right to vote. The parliament—one chamber only, with about six hundred members—has to be a fair representation of all citizens. The cabinet has to be responsible to the parliament.

The parliament's first task will be to make a constitution. It will decide whether the head of the EDU should be an elected president or a hereditary ruler.

The parliament will be the only legislative body. All local and provincial councils will be advisory boards only. Every attempt to give more power to provincial institutions and to local boards would necessarily revive the problems of borders and of minorities.

C ᴥ THE LOCAL GOVERNMENT

The former independent states in the framework of the EDU will be nothing more than provinces. Retaining all their honorary forms they will have to comply strictly with the laws and administrative provisions of the EDU. But so long as they do not try to violate these laws and regulations, they will

64 [The Dodecanese Islands, off the coast of Turkey, include the Isle of Rhodes, which was occupied and annexed by Italy during the Balkan Wars of 1912–13; it was transferred to Greek jurisdiction at the end of the Second World War. —Ed.]

65 [This region, including the cities of Trieste and Fiume, had been part of the Austro-Hungarian empire before 1918 when it was annexed by Italy as a result of the peace treaties ending World War I. Most of the region was transferred to Yugoslavian jurisdiction at the end of World War II and is now part of the Republic of Slovenia. —Ed.]

be free. The loyal and law-abiding government of each state will not be hindered, but will be strongly supported by the central government.

Special commissaries of the EDU will have to oversee the functioning of every local government. Against all administrative acts of the local authorities, all parties will have the right to appeal to this commissary and to the central government, provided that such acts are not liable to be appealed to a tribunal. All disagreements between the commissary and the local government or between different local governments will be ultimately adjudicated by the central government, which is responsible to the central parliament only. The supremacy of the central government will not be limited by any constitutional prerogatives of local authorities. Disagreements will be settled by the central government and by the central parliament, which will judge and decide every problem in the light of its implications for the smooth working of the total system. If, for instance, there arises a dispute concerning questions of the City of Wilno[66]—one of the innumerable neuralgic points of the East—the solution will be sought not only between the Polish and the Lithuanian local governments or between the Polish and Lithuanian members of the central parliament, the central government and the central parliament will try to find a solution which will do justice to similar cases arising in Budweis,[67] in Temesvar,[68] or in Salonica.[69]

In this way it may be possible to have a unitary government with a high degree of administrative decentralization.

66 [The City of Wilno (Vilna or Vilnius) was in dispute between the newly independent states of Lithuania and Poland at the end of the First World War. The Lithuanians claimed it as their historic capital; the Poles claimed it due to its large Polish population. The city was occupied by a Polish Army in 1920. In the early 1920s, the League of Nations tried to resolve the dispute by means of a plebiscite, but the Lithuanian and Polish governments could not decide on the districts or the terms under which the plebiscite would be held in the Wilno region. The city and the surrounding area remained under Polish control until 1939, when, following the Nazi-Soviet dismemberment of Poland, it was transferred to Lithuania by the Soviet Union. See Paul Mantoux, "A Contribution to the History of the Lost Opportunities of the League of Nations," in William E. Rappard, ed., *The World Crisis* (Freeport, N.Y.: Books for Libraries Press, [1938] 1969), pp. 3–35.—Ed.]

67 [Budweis (Ceske Budejovice), a city in the southern border area of the Czech Republic that had a large German population before 1945.—Ed.]

68 [Temesvar (Timisoara), a city in the western part of Romania that has a large Hungarian-speaking population.—Ed.]

69 [Salonica (Thessalonika), a city in northern Greece that had a large Turkish population before the First World War.—Ed.]

D The Budget and the Power to Tax

All financial powers will be vested in the central government and in the central parliament.

The parliament will allocate to every local government for its expenditures a lump sum according to the population of its area. It will, in addition, supervise the spending of this money.

It is further advisable to give to every local government the revenue derived from taxes on real estate situated in its jurisdiction. But, in any case, the laws regulating these taxes have to be enacted by the central parliament.

With regard to provisions for government bonds issued prior to the establishment of the new order, an international agreement between the EDU and the representatives of the foreign bondholders will be necessary. New loans will be floated only by the central government or, with its permission, by the bigger cities.

E The Linguistic Problem

The most delicate problem of the EDU will be the linguistic problem.

All seventeen languages will be treated on an equal basis. In every district, county, or community the tribunals, the government agencies, and the municipalities will have to use all the languages in their district, county, or community that are used by more than 20 percent of the population.

English has to be used as an international subsidiary language for dealings between the members of different linguistic groups. All laws have to be published in English and in all seventeen national idioms. This system may seem strange and complicated. But we have to realize that it worked rather satisfactorily in old Austria, which boasted eight languages. Contrary to a widespread error, the German language had no constitutional preeminence in imperial Austria.

F Religion

The peaceful coexistence of different denominations can easily be secured by the adoption of the system which has succeeded in the United States of America.

G ✥ Education

The governments of Eastern Europe abused the system of compulsory education in order to force minorities to give up their own languages and to adopt the language of the majority. The EDU will have to be strictly neutral in this respect.

There will be private schools only. Every citizen and every group of citizens will have the right to run educational institutions. If these schools comply with the standards fixed by the central government, they will be subsidized by a lump sum for every pupil.

The curriculum of secondary education will include the teaching of English.

The local governments will have the right to take over the administration of some schools. But even in this case, the budget of these schools has to be kept independent of the general budget of the local government, and no public funds may be used except those allocated by the central government as subsidies for these schools.

H ✥ Economic Policy

It is necessary to deny to the government the power to benefit one linguistic group at the expense of others. There will be neither subsidies nor licenses which can be granted or denied *ad libitum.*

To the general principle that no measures of protectionism should be applied, only one exception should be permitted. The importation of commodities from countries that do not treat the imports from the EDU according to the most favored nation standard[70] or do not allow any imports at all may be prohibited or taxed.

I ✥ Measures for the Period of Transition

The first president and the members of the first cabinet have to be appointed by the League of Nations. They will have to hand over their functions to the parliament as soon as it is constituted.

70 [The "most favored nation" principle came into increasing use in international trade agreements following the Anglo-French tariff reduction treaty of 1860. It requires that any agreed-upon reduction in the tariffs between two countries be automatically extended to all the other nations with whom they have respective trading agreements. Its purpose is to assure nondiscrimination against other trading partners in the arena of international exchange. — Ed.]

For a period of transition, foreign citizens—with the exception of Germans, Italians, Russians, and the subjects of totalitarian states—will be eligible for all public and judiciary offices and functions.

J ✨ THE WORKING OF THE SYSTEM

A foreign visitor, more interested in sightseeing than in the study of constitutional and economic problems, will notice the disappearance of the customs barriers and of the variety of national currency systems, but in all other respects it will be impossible for him to observe any change. He will say, "Now I have visited Hungary and I want to go to Romania." He will not see the EDU; he will not have the opportunity to meet the agents of the EDU.

There will be the old national flags and anthems. Every member state will have its own postage stamps issued by the unitary postal system of the EDU. There will be coins of every member state, coined with the national emblems and—in monarchies—with the portrait of the king (as in the German Reich from 1873 until 1914). Of course, all these coins will be minted by order of the EDU's government and will be legal tender in the whole territory of the EDU. Every member state and every linguistic group will be free to cultivate intellectual relations with foreign countries and to represent its own civilization abroad.

The individual citizen will have to renounce all claims for privileges that could harm other individuals or groups. But he will be free to use his own mother tongue and to bring up his children with the aid of schools where this language is taught. He will not have to consider himself a citizen of minority status because all authorities and tribunals will treat him in a fair way.

VIII *The Political Chances of the Proposed Plan*

We have to realize that the politicians and the statesmen of these Eastern nations are united today on only one point: the rejection of such a proposal. They do not see that the only other alternative is the partition of their territories among Germany, Russia, and Italy. They do not see it because they firmly rely on the invincibility of the British and the American forces. They do not imagine that the Americans and the British have any other task in this world than to fight an endless sequence of world wars on their behalf.

It would be merely an evasion of reality if the refugee representatives of these nations would try to convince us that they have the intention of peacefully disposing of their mutual claims in the future. It is true that the Polish and the Czech refugees have made an agreement concerning the delimitation of their common boundaries and a future political cooperation. But this scheme will not work when actually put into practice. We have ample experience to prove that all agreements of this type fail because the radical nationalists never accept them. All endeavors at an understanding between Germans and Czechs in old Austria met with disaster because the fanatical youth rejected what the more realistic, older leaders had proposed. Refugees are, of course, more ready to compromise than men in power. During the First World War, the Czechs and the Slovaks and, likewise, the Serbs, the Croats, and the Slovenes came to an understanding in exile. History has proved the futility of these alleged agreements.

Besides that, we have to realize that the area which is claimed both by the Czechs and by the Poles is comparatively small and of minor importance for each group. There is no hope that a similar agreement ever could be effected between the Poles, on the one hand, and the Germans, the Lithuanians, the Russians, or the Ukrainians on the other—or between the Czechs, on the one hand, and the Germans or the Hungarians or the Slovaks, on the other.

What is needed is not delimitation of specific borderlines between two groups, but a system where the drawing of borderlines no longer creates disaffection among minorities, unrest, and irredentism.

Democracy can be maintained in the East only by an impartial government. Within the EDU, no single linguistic group will be sufficiently numerous to dominate the rest. The most numerous linguistic group will be the Poles; they will comprise about 20 percent of its population.

It is not unlikely that some critics will call the EDU a reconstruction of the old Austrian empire on a broader scale. This is true as far as old Austria (but not Hungary!) was the only power among those ruling in this area which tried to treat all citizens on an equal footing. In the Turkish empire, all Christians were pariahs. In Russia, Prussia, and Hungary, the governments were eager to force all subjects to give up their mother tongues and to become Russians, German-speaking Prussians, or Magyars. In Austria, the Constitution of 1867 granted to every citizen the right to use his own language and provided equality in the use of all languages in court procedures, in the administration, and in educational institutions. The system failed because the striving for full national independence of every linguistic group hindered its success. Some details of the suggested constitution for the EDU are based on precisely the lessons which this Austrian failure teaches us and, at the same time, on the shortcomings of the League of Nations' protection of minorities.[71]

There is no precedent that we could use in framing a new political system for Eastern Europe. The Swiss Confederation cannot be considered a useful pattern. In Switzerland, the cooperation of the three (or four) linguistic groups was undisturbed as long as its economic policy was based on free trade. With the trend toward economic interventionism, conditions changed. Today, there is a not-negligible Nazi Party in the German-speaking cantons and a powerful pro-fascist group in the Ticino.[72] The French-speaking cantons strongly oppose what they call the policy of Berne.[73] Switzerland will have to face serious problems in a not-too-distant future.

There was still another linguistically mixed democratic country in Europe: Belgium. Here, too, the linguistic diversion disrupted political unity. The military defeat of Belgium was to a great extent due to the irredentism of the Vlames.[74] Belgium will have to solve its linguistic problems in the future.

We do not have to discuss in this context the general problem of government interference with business. It suffices to realize the fact that the system of interventionism can never work satisfactorily where different linguistic groups are determined to use it as a weapon in their wars of mutual extermination.

More serious would be the objection that the territory assigned to the EDU is too large and that the different linguistic groups involved have nothing in common. It seems strange, indeed, that the Lithuanians should have to cooperate with the Greeks although they never before have had any mutual relations other than diplomatic ones existing among all nations of the world.

But we have to realize that the EDU has to create peace in a part of

71 [On the League of Nations' rules and procedures for protection of minority groups, see William E. Rappard, et al., "The Problem of Minorities," *International Conciliation*, No. 222 (September 1926); and Raymond N. Kershaw, "The League and the Protection of Linguistic, Racial and Religious Minorities," in William E. Rappard, ed., *Problems of Peace*, 3rd Series (London: Oxford University Press, 1929), pp. 156–77.—Ed.]

72 [This is a southern region of Switzerland with a predominantly Italian-speaking population.—Ed.]

73 [This is the north-central region of Switzerland, with a predominantly German-speaking population.—Ed.]

74 [Vlames (or Vlaams or Flemish) are the Dutch-speaking members of the Belgian population.—Ed.]

the world riddled by age-old struggles among linguistic groups. Within the area assigned to the EDU, there cannot be discovered any undisputed borderline. If the EDU has to include both the Lithuanians and the Poles, because there is a large area where Poles and Lithuanians live inextricably mixed and which both nations vigorously claim for themselves, it has to include the Czechs and the Ukrainians, too, because the same conditions as between the Poles and the Lithuanians prevail between the Poles and the Czechs and between the Poles and the Ukrainians. Then the Hungarians have to be included for the same reasons, next the Serbs, and, consequently, all other nations which claim parts of the territory known as Macedonia, that is, the Bulgarians, the Albanians, and the Greeks.

For the smooth functioning of the EDU it is not required that the Greeks should consider the Lithuanians as friends and brothers. (Although it seems probable that they would have more friendly feelings for them than for their immediate neighbors.) What is needed is nothing less than the conviction of the politicians of all these peoples that it is no longer possible to oppress men who happen to speak a foreign language. They do not have to love one another, but to stop inflicting harm on one another.

The EDU will include many millions of German-speaking citizens and some hundreds of thousands of Italian-speaking citizens. It cannot be denied that the hatred engendered by the methods used by the Nazis and the fascists during the present war will not disappear at once. It will be difficult for Poles and Czechs to meet for collaboration with Germans.

But none of these objections can be considered valid. There is no other solution for the East European problem which could give to these nations a life of peace and political independence.

Conclusion

The third point of the Atlantic Declaration[75] establishes as a common principle in the national policies both of the United States and of the British empire that "they respect the right of all peoples to choose the form of government under which they will live; and they wish to see sovereign rights and self-government restored to those who have been forcibly deprived of them." The sixth point expresses the "hope to see established a

75 [The Atlantic Charter was issued by Franklin D. Roosevelt and Winston Churchill on August 14, 1941, as an eight-point declaration of principles for the postwar era. —Ed.]

peace which will afford to all nations the means of dwelling safely within their own boundaries, and which will afford assurance that all the men in all the lands may live out their lives in freedom from fear and want."

These principles are incompatible with the conditions that have prevailed for ages in Eastern Europe. There were many millions of people who were forced to live under governments that they had not chosen. There were countries where 20 percent, 30 percent, or even 40 percent of the population were Irredentists and expected to be redeemed by the armed interference of foreign powers. These millions considered themselves as having been forcibly deprived of their sovereign rights and self-government. They believed that they were prevented from living out their lives in freedom from fear and want.[76]

The proposed scheme for an Eastern Democratic Union is the only plan that could adjust political and economic conditions in Eastern Europe to the requirements of the Atlantic Declaration. Its execution would impose on no nation any sacrifice other than the renunciation of the power to inflict harm on other linguistic groups. But it would, on the other hand, secure them against the risk of falling victim to oppression by other nations. It would make Eastern Europe safe both for peace and democracy.

76 [This refers to President Roosevelt's "Four Freedoms" speech before Congress on January 6, 1941: freedom of religion and speech, and freedom from fear and want. — Ed.]

CHAPTER X

Mexico's Economic Problems[1]

Introductory Remarks

A ❧ INTERNATIONAL CONDITIONS AND DOMESTIC POLICIES

In this age of international division of labor, the destiny of every nation is linked with that of all other nations. The fate of Mexico does not depend upon the Mexicans alone. If the other nations do not succeed in substituting peaceful collaboration for their present-day antagonisms and hatreds, the doom of every country is assured, whatever its policies may be. No individual people can withdraw from the disastrous consequences of world anarchy and international chaos.

But, on the other hand, even the most satisfactory solution of the problems of international life cannot free a nation from the necessity of adopting, for its own sake, an appropriate domestic economic policy.

The distinctive mark of a sound economic policy is that it aims at the establishment of a durable system resulting in a continuous improvement of the nation's well-being. There can hardly be imagined a worse principle of government than that of the short-run policies of the last decades. It brought about economic depression, unemployment of millions of workers, social unrest, revolutions, and wars. It led to the disintegration of world trade and the international money market. Lord Keynes's dictum, "in the long run we are all dead," is nothing but a new version of the mischievous motto of Madame de Pompadour, "*après nous*

---

1 [This monograph was written by Mises in June of 1943 and submitted to a market-oriented business association in Mexico City. — Ed.]

le déluge."[2] A policy which, indifferent about tomorrow, strives after ephemeral success and carelessly sacrifices the future is not progressive but parasitic. Nothing can inflict more harm upon the masses and frustrate more effectively all attempts to raise their standard of living than capital consumption.

There is but one means to improve the economic well-being of a whole nation and of each of its individual citizens: The progressive accumulation of capital. The greater the amount of capital available, the greater the marginal productivity of labor and, therefore, the higher the wage rates. A sound economic policy is a policy that encourages savings and investment and thereby the improvement of technical methods of production and the productivity of labor.[3]

B ❧ Natural Conditions

There was a time when people exaggerated in a rather fantastic way the natural wealth of Mexico and the chances of its future prosperity. Today, this unfounded optimism has given way to an equally groundless pessimism. Mexico borders on one of the world's industrially most advanced and richest countries, the United States of America. If one compares the economic conditions of these two countries, the result is rather unfavorable for Mexico. But it is different if Mexican affairs are viewed with regard to other countries, for instance, other Latin American countries or the countries of Southern and Eastern Europe. Mexico is still on the eve of the Industrial Revolution, and it is a mistake to apply to Mexican problems the standards of the predominantly industrial countries.

It would be useless to deny that Mexico, as far as its economic condi-

---

2 [John Maynard Keynes, "A Tract on Monetary Reform," in D. E. Moggridge, ed., *The Collected Works of John Maynard Keynes*, Vol. IV (New York: Macmillan Co., [1924] 1971), p. 65. For Mises's and others' view of Keynes's emphasis on the short run, see Chapter III, "Europe's Economic Structure and the Problem of Postwar Reconstruction," footnote 21. —Ed.]

3 [On the significance of savings, investment, and capital formation, see Mises, "Capital Supply and American Prosperity," (1952) in *Planning for Freedom* (South Holland, Ill.: Libertarian Press, 1980), 4th rev. ed., pp. 195–214; "The Economic Role of Saving and Investment," (1963) in Bettina Bien Greaves, ed., *Economic Freedom and Interventionism: An Anthology of Articles and Essays by Ludwig von Mises* (Irvington-on-Hudson, N.Y.: Foundation for Economic Education, 1990), pp. 26–30.—Ed.]

tions are concerned, is a backward country. But history has demonstrated that it is possible to overcome economic backwardness in a short time. Germany, when compared with Great Britain, was a backward country around 1830. Some fifty years later, German industry was paramount on the European continent and in a position to compete very successfully on the world market. Mexico's industrial future is not hopeless, provided that the country adopts an adequate domestic economic policy.

The geographic situation of Mexico is propitious. It lies in the center of the American continent; it has access both to the Atlantic and to the Pacific ocean; it is midway between Europe and West Africa on the one hand and Australia and East Asia on the other. Climatic and geological conditions are less favorable. In the greater part of the country, the soil is dry and barren.

A nation's main asset is the character and the gifts of its citizens. It is a common error, especially among many entrepreneurs, to doubt the ability of populations in non-industrialized countries to work in modern factories. Experience has proved these judgments to be unfounded. It is beyond doubt that the Mexicans are endowed with the spirit of workmanship. The achievements of craftsmen and artisans meet with the admiration of all experts. The workers in the already existing industrial factories and in the mines are not less efficient than those of other countries. It is true that the agricultural technique of the peons is rather poor, but one should not forget that these people had to fight against many odds. We may wonder whether other races or nations would have succeeded better on the rocky soil on which they have to till.

It has been said that the Mexicans do not have the capacities required by modern entrepreneurs. It is a fact that many important factories and shops are operated by foreigners. But economic history has shown that, with the exception of Great Britain, all countries owe their early industrial development primarily to foreigners and immigrants. Present-day chauvinism wrongly tends to belittle the role played by foreigners or the sons of foreigners in the evolution of all modern nations.[4]

It is a very fortunate condition that Mexico is not menaced by racial and linguistic struggles. Antagonism between the various political parties is deplorable. But it is not worse than those of all other countries.

4 [On the positive historical impact of immigrant groups for the economic development of the countries into which they have moved, see Thomas Sowell, *Migrations and Cultures: A World View* (New York: Basic Books, 1996).—Ed.]

C ❧ MEXICO AND THE WAR

The Second World War brings about special economic conditions that are apt to confuse a cool appreciation of the country's situation. The increase of government expenditure caused by the war is, for Mexico, only slight when compared with the enormous increase in Great Britain and in the United States. Mexican territory is perfectly safe from invasion; the losses of its commercial shipping are happily not great. On the other hand, the war means good business for mining, for various branches of agriculture, for some other branches of Mexican export trade, and offers many Mexican workers the opportunity to find well-paid jobs in the United States. For Mexico, the war is on the whole economically more advantageous than disadvantageous. But these conditions will not last. With the return of peace, the nation will have to face serious economic problems.

It is an illusion to believe—as Brazilian coffee planters, Argentinean cattle breeders, and North American farmers do—that after the war Europe will be able to buy large quantities of American products. The impoverished peoples of Europe will lack the means to pay for those commodities. It is very unlikely that conditions for the marketing of wheat, meat, wool, cotton, coffee, rubber, and oil will be satisfactory.

The Second World War will change the world's economic conditions in a much more radical way than was done by the First World War. All countries, after the war, will suffer from poverty and a lack of capital. Decades will be needed for the reconstruction of the shattered apparatus of production. Great Britain and France and the other predominantly industrial countries of Europe will hardly ever be restored to their previous level of productive capacity, wealth, and competitive power. Their foreign assets are gone, the equipment of their factories and farms is used up, their markets are lost. Nobody can foresee how conditions will be.

D ❧ ECONOMIC FREEDOM

Modern industry is an achievement of private business. Not governments but entrepreneurs and capitalists have transformed the world of craftsmen and artisans, of horses, sailing ships, and windmills, into the world of steam power, electricity, and big-scale production for the satisfaction of the needs of the masses. If business had not succeeded in freeing itself from the tutelage of governments and from the restrictions imposed by old statutes and privileges, from the operation of guilds and traditional prejudices and fallacies, the masses would not be better off than two hundred years ago. Capitalism has poured a horn of plenty over all strata of the population. It is an accomplishment of capitalism that today there are living in the advanced countries many more people than in the centuries preceding the Industrial Revolution, and that every single citizen enjoys a much higher standard of living than the well-to-do of earlier ages.

Popular doctrines have badly distorted these facts. The stereotypical description of capitalism is as inappropriate as would be the description of a motorcar as an instrument for the killing of pedestrians. All the so-called mischief of capitalism is the outcome of policies designed to check its operation and to interfere with the working of the market and the price system, for the alleged advantage of the poor. Economic depressions are the inextricable outcome of the endeavors to enforce easy money policies by credit expansion and inflation; such policies result for a short time in the creation of an artificial boom but must later end in a slump and in depression. Unemployment is the effect of the attempts of governments and trade unions to fix minimum wage rates at a higher level than that formed on the unhampered labor market.

It is not true that Russian experience has proved the feasibility of socialism. The Soviets try in a rather unsatisfactory way to imitate what the capitalist nations have achieved in the field of technical improvement, and they use for their economic calculations the prices fixed on the markets of capitalist countries. Without the aid of these prices, their actions would be aimless and planless.[5] The Russians themselves have contributed nothing to technical progress. Russia's soil is much better endowed by nature than that of any other nation. It offers the most advantageous conditions for the growing of all kinds of cereals, fruits, seeds, and plants. Russia owns immense pastures and almost inexhaustible forests. It has the richest resources for the production of gold, silver, platinum, iron, copper, nickel, manganese, and all other metals, and of oil. But for the despotism of the czars and for the deplorable inadequacy of the communist system, its population could long since have enjoyed the highest standard of living. But the Russian masses are much poorer than those of any other European or American country. Only a few years ago, many millions were literally

5 [See Mises, *Socialism* (Indianapolis: Liberty Fund, [1951] 1981), pp. 117–18 & 535–36. —Ed.]

starved to death in the Ukraine, Europe's most fertile area.[6] It is a fable that the Soviet regime has improved the lot of the Russian people. A comparison of the description of Russian economic conditions by Marxian authors published thirty and forty years ago and the reports on present-day Russian affairs rendered by the admirers of the Soviet methods unmasks the fallacies of these legends.

If history and experience could teach us anything in the field of social organization, they would teach that capitalism is a more efficient method of economic management than is socialism. It is an illusion to assert that the Russian experience has refuted the economic theories concerning the impracticability of public ownership of the means of production.

For many decades the most characteristic feature of the economic policies of all nations has been hostility toward capitalism. We do not have to deal with the disastrous consequences of this alleged "progressivism." Neither are we concerned with the problem of whether or not these policies will lead to a manifest failure in a not-too-distant future. We have only to emphasize that their application by the poorer and economically not yet developed countries is suicidal.[7]

What Mexico needs most is capital, either foreign or domestic. The repudiation of the national debt and the expropriation of foreign investments deter the foreign capitalist. The methods of taxation prevent the accumulation of domestic capital. The total abandonment of such acts is the first requisite of the country's economic regeneration.

It is hopeless to build up a prosperous industry in a country that considers every entrepreneur as an exploiter and tries to penalize his success. A policy of shortening the hours of work, of raising costs by forcing the entrepreneur to provide housing facilities for the workers, and of fixing minimum wage rates either by direct government interference or by giving a free hand to trade union pressure is vain in a country whose industrial production has still to be created.

It is a sad fact that a country in which the natural conditions for pro-

6 [See Chapter VIII, "A Draft of Guidelines for the Reconstruction of Austria," footnote 39.—Ed.]

7 [On the problems of underdeveloped Third World countries under the influence of socialist and interventionist ideas in the immediate post–World War II period, see Mises, "The Plight of the Underdeveloped Nations," (1952) in Richard M. Ebeling, ed., *Money, Method, and the Market Process: Essays by Ludwig von Mises* (Norwell, Mass.: Kluwer Academic Press, 1990), pp. 166–73.—Ed.]

duction are less favorable than in other countries and that suffers from a comparative shortage of capital has but one means to compete with countries better endowed by nature and richer in capital: A lower price of labor. In a world without migration barriers, there prevails a tendency toward an equalization of wage rates in different countries. In the absence of free mobility of labor, wage rates must necessarily be lower within an area in which natural resources are poorer and capital is more scarce. There is no means available to alter this state of affairs. If the government or the trade unions are not prepared to submit to the facts, they do not improve the conditions of the masses, instead they impair them. They hinder the development of the processing industries and force those people who could find a more remunerative employment in factories to remain extremely poor peons.

It is indispensable to see things as they really are, not as one would wish them to be. The allegedly progressive measures on the part of the Mexican government and the alleged blessings of trade unionism not only do not contribute to the welfare of the Mexican people, they seriously make their conditions worse.

The only way toward an improvement of Mexico's economic situation is economic liberalism, that is, the policy of *laissez-faire*. It is a common weakness of man to envy the success of luckier fellow citizens.[8] But an honest patriot should not look askance at the wealth of efficient entrepreneurs. He must understand that in the framework of capitalist society, the only means to acquire riches is to provide the consumers in the cheapest way with all the commodities they ask for. He who serves the public best profits the most.

What Mexico needs is economic freedom.

I   *Agricultural Conditions*

Out of a total of 5,351,800 gainfully employed workers, 3,626,000 people, or almost 70 percent (according to the census of 1935), were employed in agriculture. Mexico is, therefore, a predominantly agricultural country.

But things appear different if we consider the value of the annual output. While the total value of the products of agriculture, cattle breeding, and forestry amounted to 723 million pesos, the value of the products of

---

8 [On the role of envy in creating antimarket sentiments, see Mises, *The Anti-Capitalistic Mentality* (Princeton, N.J.: D. Van Nostrand Co., 1956). —Ed.]

processing industries, mining, and oil drilling was 1,365 million pesos. It is true that the above-mentioned figures do not include the agricultural products consumed by the farmers in their own households. But it is well known that the standard of living of these farmers is very low.

In 1939, the last year that can be considered as somewhat "normal" and "peaceful," the country imported products valued at 186 million pesos and exported products of agriculture, cattle breeding, and fishing valued at 117 million pesos. These export figures were specifically:

coffee	34 million pesos
henequén[9]	23 million pesos
fish	13 million pesos
cotton	5 million pesos
bananas	17 million pesos
chicle[10]	19 million pesos
ixtle[11]	6 million pesos
TOTAL	117 million pesos

If we deduct these figures from the total import figure of 186 million pesos, there was a deficit in the foreign trade balance regarding agricultural products totaling 69 million pesos.

In order to understand the problem of Mexican agriculture, it is necessary to consider separately the conditions of the lowlands and the highlands, the former producing "exotic" crops, and the latter producing products of the type grown and bred in the temperate zones of the earth.

Some parts of Mexico offer the opportunity for the production of coffee, bananas, and cotton. It is very probable that it would be technically possible to expand further the production of these crops. But it is rather doubtful whether such an expansion would pay. World market conditions will probably be rather unfavorable for these three crops. There are, on the one hand, countries that can produce them under more favorable physical conditions than Mexico. On the other hand, one has to expect a

9 [Henequén is a tropical American plant that has large, thick, sword-shaped leaves producing a rough, reddish fiber used in making rope and twine. —Ed.]

10 [Chicle is the coagulated milky juice of the evergreen tree known as sapodilla. It is the principal ingredient in chewing gum. —Ed.]

11 [Ixtle, or pita, is one of several plants of the genus Agava that yields strong leafy fibers used in making cordage and paper. —Ed.]

fall in the demand. Europe will be too poor to buy the quantities it previously used to consume. With regard to cotton, one has, moreover, to realize that modern technology has developed new textiles that can replace cotton goods. Prospects are better with regard to *henequén, ixtle,* and *chicle.* It is even possible that these three crops will pay much better in the future. But it is not possible to form a definitive opinion.

With regard to the products of highland agriculture, Mexico is more an importing than an exporting country. In 1939, Mexico imported 54,000 tons of maize and 51,000 tons of wheat. The quantities imported of these two vital grains change from year to year according to the crops harvested in the country. In 1940, the imports amounted only to 8,271 tons of maize and 1,225 tons of wheat. But the fact remains that Mexican domestic agriculture is even in good years not efficient enough to supply the whole nation with its main diet. This unsatisfactory state is the outcome of the agrarian reforms of the Mexican revolution.[12] The detrimental effects of these reforms become manifest if we compare conditions of the years preceding the reform with those of 1937.[13]

YEAR	CULTIVATED AREA (HECTARES)	CROPS (TONS)	AVERAGE OUTPUT PER HECTARE (KILOGRAMS)
MAIZE			
1907	8,600,000	5,075,000	584
1937	2,999,000	1,634,000	545
WHEAT			
1907	560,000	313,000	554
1937	502,000	325,000	648
BEANS			
1907	978,000	198,000	202
1937	507,000	104,000	177

12 [The Mexican Constitution of 1917 declared that private ownership of land was no longer a right but a privilege, and that the state possessed the authority to seize land and redistribute it in the national interest. The size of agrarian holdings was restricted, and the old *hacienda* (estate) system was ended. An extensive distribution of land took place over the next several years under a system of *ejido* (rural community) land rights; qualified residents within communities were given "use rights" for farming, but not private ownership. —Ed.]

13 Cf. Sr. Antonio Manero, *El Economista* (November 1, 1942).

The gloomy significance of these figures becomes even more apparent if we realize that the country's population increased from 13,545,000 in 1900 to 18,852,000 in 1936.

There is no doubt that the agrarian reform resulted in economic disaster. The old *hacienda* system, which the revolution brushed away, was certainly unsatisfactory not only from the social and political viewpoint, but no less from the economic viewpoint. But it is necessary to appreciate things in an unbiased and sober way in order to understand the main problems of Mexican agriculture.

The country's agriculture is primitive and backward. But it is inappropriate to compare it either with conditions in countries whose soil is much more fertile (for instance, Canada and the United States) or with countries whose agriculture could enjoy the protection of high tariffs. The former countries produce at much lower physical costs and are, therefore, in a position to withstand the competition on the world market and to export a part of their crops. The latter countries could compensate their physical inferiority by the high prices obtained on the sheltered domestic market. It is true that the agriculturists of the predominantly industrial countries of Europe (especially those of Germany, Austria, and Switzerland, but also those of France and Great Britain) succeeded in growing wheat, rye, and potatoes, in breeding cattle, and in dairying under extremely unfavorable natural conditions. But we have to realize that natural conditions in these countries, although unfavorable enough, are still better than those of the greater part of Mexico.

The main factor is that these European farmers, cattle-breeders, and dairymen had the opportunity to sell their products at a domestic market in which—as a result of an excessive protectionism—prices were much higher than on the world market. Agricultural expansion in the predominantly industrial countries of Europe was essentially parasitic. It was based on a ruthless spoliation of the industrial section of the population to the benefit of the agricultural section. The high state of agricultural technique, the intensity of exploitation, and the great returns per hectare tilled were not achievements of the farmers but rather the outcome of an economic policy that heedlessly sacrificed the welfare of the nonagricultural population. The characteristic feature of Mexican agriculture (and of agriculture in other countries in a similar position, for instance, Spain) is that such a policy is unfeasible. Mexico's nonagricultural population is neither numerous nor wealthy enough to bear the burden of such a system.

It is, therefore, a mistake for both Mexicans and foreigners to hold up

European agriculture as a model for Mexican farming. The evolution of agriculture in Western and Central Europe in the last decades was unsound and detrimental to these nations' vital interests. Moreover, it will be impossible for these countries to continue such policies after the present war to the disadvantage of an impoverished nonagricultural population. European agriculture is on the eve of an extremely serious crisis.

The agrarian consequences of the Mexican revolution would have been much more propitious if the statesmen had considered as the main goal of their interference the creation of a class of free landholders, husbanding on soil that is fully their own property and that their children will inherit. The poorer a soil is, the more important it is that the farmer is imbued with the consciousness of full ownership. He must be made sure that every melioration will improve his own material well-being and that of his children. A fanatical sense of property is the main prerequisite of a peasant's devotion to his task. Free landholders are enthusiastic in the support of private ownership. They are unflagging in their efforts if they know that they will reap the fruit of their toil and trouble.

It was a mischief that the Mexican socialists became fascinated by the Marxian doctrines and wanted to imitate the Russian methods of collective farming. We do not have to deal with the problems of Russia, but it is indispensable to realize that natural conditions are different in both countries. Russia's agriculture operates on the earth's most fertile soil in plains offering favorable opportunities for big-scale farming. Mexican agriculture, on the other hand, is forced to utilize barren soil in stony upland. Here mechanical devices are of little use. The essential factor of production is the human one: The farmer's stubborn and fanatical devotion to his task. This mentality cannot thrive within the frame of a collective farm.

The prospects of Mexican farming in the highlands lie exclusively in individual farming by free landholders supported by farmers' cooperatives. The cooperatives have to organize on a cooperative basis the buying of agricultural equipment, seed, fertilizers, and other implements; they have to rent machinery and to market the products. They have to provide the credit necessary. But the individual farmer has to be the master on his own farm.

Various government agencies in Mexico have done a good job in encouraging the formation and the operation of cooperatives and in spreading technical education. If they pursue these endeavors and abandon the spurious attempts to follow the Russian example, they will contribute a good deal to the improvement of conditions.

It is a very comforting fact that the volume of agricultural production was in a steady upward movement during the last decade. It increased by no less than 46 percent between 1934 and 1942.[14] One can fairly assume that the disastrous consequences of the revolution are now overcome and that agriculture will develop as much as market conditions allow.

But let us not forget that the fundamental problems of Mexican peasantry cannot be solved solely by measures limited to agricultural issues. Mexican agriculture is overcrowded. The more the technical methods of exploitation improve, the more it will become obvious that too many people are employed in agriculture. A reduction of the nation's agricultural sector is indispensable. This, however, can only be achieved by progress in industrialization. The future of Mexican agriculture depends on the expansion of the country's processing industries.[15]

II   The Processing Industries

A ❧ TWO WAYS TOWARD INDUSTRIALIZATION

The main economic problem of Mexico is the building up of processing industries. Mexico is a comparatively overpopulated country. The opportunities for the development of its—comparatively poor—natural resources are limited. As emigration is almost impossible under present-day institutional conditions, there are millions of people living on the verge of extreme poverty. There is but one means available to improve the lot of these poor peons: They must be given better-paid jobs in the processing industries.

Conditions in Mexico for the processing industries are in many regards less propitious than in many other countries. Most of the machinery, raw materials, and half-manufactured articles have had to be imported

14 Banco de Mexico, *Vigesima primera asamblea general*, p. 34.

15 [Between 1940 and 1978, the agricultural component of Mexico's total output fell from 19 percent to 9 percent, while industry's share of total output increased from 25 percent to 36 percent; the service sector's component fell from 56 percent to 55 percent during this period. In 1940, about 65 percent of the work force was employed in agriculture; that decreased to 40 percent by 1977. Industrial employment increased from 15 percent to 25 percent of the labor force. The rest of the shift in employment was absorbed by the service sector of the Mexican economy.—Ed.]

from abroad. There is a lack of skilled workers and a shortage of capital. But, on the other hand, there is plenty of cheap labor.

We have to emphasize again and again that the comparative cheapness of labor is the only condition that makes industrialization of Mexico possible. But for this factor, it would be hopeless for Mexican factories to stand the competition with older industrial countries, as all other items of the production costs are higher in Mexico. But what, from the point of view of North American industrial conditions, has to be qualified as cheap labor, has to be appreciated in a different way from the point of view of Mexican conditions. Even when earning not more than a fraction of what the North American workers earn, the workers of the Mexican factories would be much better off than in their present agricultural employment and would enjoy a much higher standard of living than under present circumstances. The establishment of every new factory brings about a tendency to raise the income of all Mexican proletarians. It improves the standards of living both in agriculture and in all branches of hired labor.

It may be fairly assumed that there prevails unanimity both in Mexico and abroad with regard to the urgent necessity for the nation to develop its processing industries as much as possible. However, one may wonder whether people understand why only an expansion of the processing industries can improve the conditions of the masses. Many Mexican patriots are entangled today in the almost universally accepted neomercantilist fallacies. Yet, these popular errors have resulted in a manifest failure in the policy endeavors of all predominantly agricultural nations to raise standards of living by the advancement of domestic industrial production.

The essential feature of modern industrial production is specialization. The further specialization goes on, the cheaper the products can be delivered. Specialized production requires a broadening of the market. It is beyond doubt that the citizens of the United States of America would never have enjoyed their high standard of living if each of the forty-eight states had tried to insulate its own state's market from the markets of the forty-seven other states. Great Britain and prewar Germany were prosperous countries because conditions made it possible for their industries to embark upon specialization.

The goal of Mexico's industrialization has to be the raising of the average Mexican's standard of living by acquiring a place within the international community of modern industrialism. The mutual exchange of products between Mexico and other countries has to be intensified. Mexico has to be made ready to contribute its share to the international division of labor by producing more goods for which its national market is too narrow and that have to be sold abroad, thereby giving Mexicans the greater means by which they can buy foreign products. Mexico has to play a greater role on the world market.

But the mercantilist sees things in a different way. In his eyes, industrialization means the country's withdrawal from the world market. He aims at national autarky. The realization of his plans would not raise, but would lower the domestic standard of living. The mercantilist rejoices if he succeeds in substituting a more expensive domestic product for one cheaper and better manufactured abroad. He does not realize that his policy of economic nationalism makes his countrymen poorer, not richer.

B ❧ The Closed Door Method of Industrialization[16]

The predominantly agricultural nations have entirely misunderstood the meaning of modern industrial production and the nature of the advantages that their own countries could possibly derive from a development of the processing industries. They did not realize that what they needed was their incorporation into the community of the international division of labor and of the mutual exchange of commodities and services. Their notion of industrialization was not production for the world market, but, on the contrary, commercial insulation of their own countries.

The policy that the countries of Southern and Eastern Europe and

16 [What Mises criticized in 1943 as the "closed door method of industrialization" became widely advocated in underdeveloped Third World countries in the post-World War II era under the heading of the "import-substitution" method of industrial development. Two of its leading proponents were Argentinean economist Raul Prebisch (1901–86) and German-born British economist Hans Wolfgang Singer (1910–), both of whom were extremely influential in legitimizing the idea through their positions within United Nations development organizations. For criticisms of "the closed door" import-substitution approach by later market-oriented economists, see Gottfried Haberler, "Critical Observations on Some Current Notions in the Theory of Economic Development," in *L'industria*, No. 2 (Milan, 1957), pp. 373–83, and "Terms of Trade and Economic Development,"(1961) in Anthony Y. C. Koo, ed., *Selected Essays by Gottfried Haberler* (Cambridge, Mass.: MIT Press, 1985), pp. 453–72; Peter T. Bauer, *Dissent on Development* (Cambridge, Mass.: Harvard University Press, 1976), pp. 233–71; I. D. M. Little, "The Developing Countries and the International Order," in Ryan C. Amacher, Gottfried Haberler, and Thomas D. Willett, eds., *Challenges to a Liberal International Economic Order* (Washington, D.C.: American Enterprise Institute, 1979), pp. 259–78; and Paul Craig Roberts and Karen Lafollette Araujo, *The Capitalist Revolution in Latin America* (New York: Oxford University Press, 1997), pp. 107–9. — Ed.]

Latin America espoused was hyperprotectionism and prohibition of imports. They were anxious to promote the growth of domestic production by barring access to the cheaper commodities of foreign plants. Thus the policy that was designed as a method of improving the domestic standard of living resulted in a considerable rise of domestic prices for manufactured goods. The consumers had to forego many goods because they were too dear.

Moreover, the outcome of this state of affairs was a drop in the export of foodstuffs and raw materials. As the industrial nations of Western and Central Europe sold minor quantities of manufactures, their means to pay for the imports of badly needed foodstuffs and raw materials were reduced proportionally. Their own protectionism tried to substitute for goods previously imported the dearer products of some domestic production. However, in dealing with the problems of Mexico, we do not have to dwell upon the inadequacy of the policies of the predominantly industrial nations. Even if the European nations concerned had adopted a more reasonable policy, a fall in the exports of raw materials and foodstuffs on the part of the predominantly agricultural nations would still have resulted from their own protectionist policies.

The politicians responsible for the protectionist policies of the agricultural countries boasted of the apparent success of their programs. They triumphed when the statistics of foreign trade showed a fall in the import of various manufactured goods. But unfortunately they did not take into consideration the drawbacks from their policies. They did not realize that this system doubly hurt the agricultural sector of their own nation by rendering manufactures more expensive and by restricting the exports of their own agricultural products. It is true that many people could find jobs with the sheltered plants, but what these people gained, on the one hand, as producers was lost, on the other hand, by the higher prices of all manufactured goods.

Thus such industries artificially brought up in a hothouse, as it were, do not contribute anything to the general improvement of a country's economic prosperity. Instead, they impair that well-being. Even if they succeed in exporting a part of their products, they still are more or less parasitic. Their exports are based on the fact that they are in a position to sell the greater part of their output at higher prices on the sheltered domestic market.

Some countries have openly subsidized industrial enterprises. This is a rather awkward method, but its effect is not different from that of the more current measures of protectionism. In paying higher prices for the domestic product, the consumers are forced to subsidize the sheltered industry.

The closed door method cannot be justified by the infant industry argument. The weakness of the enterprises concerned and their inability to compete with the superior factories of the other countries have nothing to do with their youthful age. They are due either to the fact that the natural conditions of production are utterly unfavorable in this branch of production or that the domestic market is too narrow to make big-scale production pay. The protectionist believes there is ample justification for protectionism and the establishment of a domestic line of production because (a) in some branches of industry, there are no domestic factories and (b) the total supply is imported from abroad. It does not occur to him to investigate whether conditions are so unfavorable that domestic production will never pay unless it is openly or indirectly subsidized.[17]

The worst outcome of protection is that it raises the cost of production for all other branches of domestic production, especially in those branches that could successfully compete on the world market if not for the checks put upon them by the higher price of some producer goods.

What a nation that up to now mainly produced foodstuffs and raw materials needs in order to raise its standard of living are processing industries that can export and thereby provide the means of payment for greater imports. Its citizens are eager to consume more of those commodities that the highly specialized big-scale factories of the most advanced countries are manufacturing. Their aim is to obtain more of these cheap goods, not to be forced to content themselves with the dearer and less perfect goods of an artificially reared domestic hothouse production.

If Mexico, Hungary, or Italy were part of the United States or Germany, or if an international statute were to declare tariffs as unlawful, no one would believe that the best way to make these nations more prosperous would be to force their citizens to abstain from buying the goods produced by the more efficient industrial factories of New Jersey or Saxony. Everyone would understand that what these people need is to be able to produce something that would enable them to buy more of those U. S. or

17 [On the "infant industry" argument and other protectionist rationales, see Mises, "The Disintegration of the International Division of Labor," (1938) in Richard M. Ebeling, ed., *Money, Method, and the Market Process*, pp. 113–36.—Ed.]

German goods. Their businessmen would be anxious to embark upon only such projects that could succeed without the aid of protective measures.

The closed door method leads a nation into a blind alley. It perpetuates the low standard of living.

C ❧ The Open Door Method of Industrialization

The inferences drawn from Ricardo's theory of foreign trade are irrefutable.[18] All the desperate attempts of would-be economists to refute Ricardo's statements have lamentably failed. Even if all other nations cling to protection, every country serves its own interests best by free trade.

It has been asserted again and again that conditions have changed since the days of Ricardo and that under present conditions his conclusions are no longer valid. This, too, is a fallacy.

Ricardo assumes that there is no mobility of capital and labor, but that there is some mobility given for commodities. (If there is no mobility at all for commodities, then every nation lives in perfect autarky, and there is no question of foreign trade.) The conditions assumed by Ricardo changed in the course of the nineteenth century. Labor and capital could, to some extent, move from country to country. Millions of workers moved from the comparatively overpopulated countries to the comparatively underpopulated countries offering more favorable conditions for production and thereby higher wage rates.[19] An international capital market came into being. Today things have changed, and the state of affairs is by and large the same again as in the days of Ricardo. Migration is almost impossible. The international capital market has disintegrated. The capitalists shun foreign investment because discriminatory taxation, expropriation, confiscation, foreign exchange controls, and repudiation of debts make it too risky. The governments of those nations whose capitalists could consider foreign investment are ready to put an embargo upon capital export because they view it as contrary to the interests of the most influential domestic pressure groups, labor and farming.

18 [See Chapter V, "Aspects of American Foreign Trade Policy," footnote 4.—Ed.]

19 [It has been estimated that about sixty million people emigrated from Europe between 1850 and 1940, settling in the United States, Latin America, Asiatic Russia, Canada, Australia, New Zealand, and South Africa; see R. R. Palmer and Joel Colton, A History of the Modern World, 8th ed. (New York: McGraw-Hill, 1992), pp. 592–95.—Ed.]

In a world of perfect mobility of capital, labor, and products, there prevails a tendency toward an equalization of the material conditions of all
countries. Those parts of the earth's surface that offer more favorable natural conditions of production attract more capital and labor than those offering less propitious ones. There are more densely populated countries
and less densely populated. Freedom of migration and of investment tend
to make the difference of comparative overpopulation and comparative
underpopulation disappear. They tend toward an equalization of wage
rates and rates of interest and concomitantly of standards of living.

In a world of immobility of men, some countries are comparatively
overpopulated, others comparatively underpopulated. There are conspicuous differences in wage rates and in standards of living. Of course, the
productivity of labor must necessarily be lower in a country where natural
conditions of labor are less favorable. The restrictions imposed upon the
free mobility of capital intensify this outcome.

Mexico is such a comparatively overpopulated country. There is no
doubt that, with perfect mobility of labor, its population would be lower
than it is today. Mexico's economic policy has to adjust itself to this fact.
The country can successfully develop only those branches of the processing industries in which wages form comparatively a greater part of the total
cost of production than in the others. The expansion of such industries
will raise the standard of living within the country. However, wage rates
and the standard of living will never reach the level of other countries that
are more favored by nature and comparatively underpopulated.

The advantage derived from foreign trade lies entirely in importing,
not in exporting. An increase in exports is only the means to increase imports. A reduction of imports is not a blessing, but a calamity. What is
needed is an expansion of exports in order to increase the imports. As natural factors limit the expansion of exports of food and raw materials, and
as world market conditions do not favor the expansion of exports of cotton
and the products of the tropical belt, the exports of manufactured goods
have to be increased. Industrialization for an increase of exports has to be
the goal of economic policy, not industrialization for the purpose of restricting imports.

It is a fallacy to believe that exporting raw materials is an unsatisfactory
state of affairs and that it is especially so with regard to the "extracting"
branches of production, for example, mining. If domestic conditions are
unfavorable for the working up of these materials into finished goods, it

would be contrary to purpose to foster the processing industries concerned by protection.

It is highly probable that Mexico could develop its metallurgical industries without any protection. It is not protection that is needed for this purpose, but the abandonment of policies that consider every industrial establishment as a cow that can be milked even when badly treated.

D ❧ The Transition from the Closed Door Policy to the Open Door Policy

Although the open door policy best fits the interests of Mexico—as those of any other country—we have to realize that a sudden change would do more harm than good. It would be inexpedient to institute the necessary reforms by the use of measures that, although beneficial in the long run, would for the immediate future bring more hardship than benefits.

Some of the industries already existing in Mexico can be qualified as self-supporting. Although founded and developed under the shelter of protectionism, they will be able to do very well under free trade, too. This is especially the case with the textile and metallurgical industries. The former are favored by the cheapness of labor, the latter by their proximity to the mines. A third group of industries that will be left more or less untouched by free trade are those producing mostly for local demand: The production of building materials on the one hand, the factories producing beer and other beverages, bakeries, canneries, printing offices, and so on, on the other hand. There need be no fear that any factory in these activities will be forced to discontinue production. Some factories, it is true, will have to rearrange their lines of production in order to attain a higher degree of specialization.

A sound industrialization program for Mexico has to repeal all import duties. But as far as products that are already produced within existing factories are concerned, the tariffs have to be abolished only by a gradual process. Every year, a tariff reduction of 10 percent has to take place. Thus the enterprises will be in a position to adjust their operations to the new system of free trade.

It would not be necessary to make special provisions to encourage the establishment of new industries if Mexico had not acquired a sinister reputation as an anticapitalist country. The mere fact that labor is cheap would be incentive enough for the capitalists. Only the fact that the Mexican government is considered, not without some reason, as hostile to private enterprise creates the requirement for some definite measures.

The government, the parliament, and all political parties have to pledge themselves, in a solemn way, to an unconditional policy of domestic free trade, private enterprise, and private property. They have to promise:

1. They will never again expropriate [the property of] capitalists and entrepreneurs, whether they be foreign or native.

2. They will not adopt methods of taxation designed to confiscate business profits.

3. They will not take recourse to foreign exchange controls or foreign exchange restrictions and will not hinder the transfer of funds to foreign countries.

4. They will neither directly nor indirectly interfere with the management of law-abiding private enterprise.

If these declarations are proclaimed in such a way that they inspire confidence in the capitalists, the effects produced will be very satisfactory.

Of course, one cannot expect that large-scale investments will be made immediately. In the beginning, only those industries will expand that require comparatively small investments. The garment industry and the producers of leather fancy goods and various small articles will be the first to profit from the new system. Spinning and weaving mills and furniture and stationery shops will follow. Mexico's industry will probably always consist of relatively medium-sized factories. But European experience has proved that medium-sized factories can very successfully compete on the world market.

The ambition of Mexico has to be the export of manufactured goods, not the prevention of the imports of such goods. This is not a utopian goal. Mexico has plenty of the most important factor of industrial production: Labor. What it lacked in the past was only a policy that makes it possible for the enterprising businessmen to start and to develop promising projects.

Free trade means the absence of any import duties, with the exception of those collected as a compensation for a domestic excise tax. They should not be more burdensome than this domestic duty. All the qualms concerning the feasibility and expediency of such a policy on the part of only one country while the other countries cling to protection are unfounded and have long since been irrefutably dispelled by economists. However, one further exception to this general rule of free imports is indispensable.

If a protectionist country discriminates against imports from Mexico, or if a country that has nationalized its foreign trade, whether openly or by foreign exchange control, purposely does not buy Mexican products or does not allot to importers the amount of foreign exchange needed for the imports of Mexican goods, the Mexican government must have the right to retaliate. There need be no fear that such a provision will result in a rise of domestic prices in Mexico, and, therefore, will be equivalent to a disguised return to protectionism. Free importation of the merchandise concerned from other countries will still be permitted. Moreover, the countries applying such an unfriendly policy toward Mexico will probably very soon abandon their discriminatory procedures in order not to lose their own prospects on the Mexican market.

The law providing for such cases would have to run this way: The administration is empowered to prohibit the importation either of all commodities or of some commodities or to penalize such imports by the imposition of import duties, whenever the commodities concerned are produced in a country that discriminates against the importation of commodities made in Mexico or sold by Mexican merchants or transported on Mexican ships or planes in a more burdensome way than against those made in or imported from other countries or imported on the ships or planes of another nation. The administration is further empowered to conclude agreements with such countries in order to abolish such discrimination against Mexican trade, shipping, and aircraft, and to renounce in such agreements the exercise of this power of retaliation with regard to the contracting nation for the duration of the agreement.

The administration has the same right to prohibit or to penalize imports with regard to countries that have, whether openly or by other means, nationalized foreign trade or dealings in foreign exchange, if these countries pursue in these transactions a policy detrimental to Mexican economic concerns. The administration is further empowered to conclude with such countries bilateral exchange agreements that entitle the contracting nation to import to Mexico, free from import duties, a quantity of commodities corresponding to the value of Mexican goods exported to the same country and to the services received from the Mexican mercantile marine and mercantile aircraft.

In this way, Mexico will be in a position to secure for its trade the most favored nation treatment and to fight successfully economic nationalism on the part of nations that have nationalized foreign trade.[20]

20 [See Chapter IX, "An Eastern Democratic Union," footnote 70.—Ed.]

E • The Political Consequences of the Open Door Policy

An industry that is sheltered by import duties is extremely weak in its dealings with public opinion, government agencies, and trade unions.

The public considers such an industry parasitic since it charges high prices. If its business is profitable, people ask either for a price ceiling or for the imposition of higher taxes. Trade unions ask for higher wage rates. Government and parliament are prone to solve every budgetary embarrassment by putting additional burdens upon the entrepreneurs. They argue this way: Business profits are the outcome of import duties imposed on the part of the legislature. It is only fair to allot a part of the income derived from this privilege to the treasury.

In a protectionist country, the entrepreneurs do not count at all on the political scene. The President of the United States [Franklin D. Roosevelt] has assembled two groups of main advisers for all nonmilitary duties of the administration. These groups are his true cabinet, while the orthodox regular cabinet, formed by the heads of the ten big departments of the executive, has lost its former importance. (Incidentally, there is nothing in the Constitution about this "regular" cabinet; it was built up by custom and seems to have lost its status by custom again.) Now, these new presidential advisory boards are a labor group, consisting only of trade union representatives, and a farm group, consisting only of farmers' representatives. The banks and the bankers, and the merchants and the manufacturers are not in a position to advise the president; they do not sit in his councils; they have not only no opportunity to influence the nation's policy, they do not even have the opportunity to be heard regularly by the man who determines the course of affairs. Such are conditions in the world's paramount industrial nation.[21]

It is different with unprotected industries. With regard to them, everyone is fully aware that increasing production costs means impairing their ability to compete. It is obvious that with higher costs, sales both on the domestic and on the foreign market must drop, that production must shrink, and that workers will lose their jobs. Government will look twice before risking such disastrous consequences. It will consider very carefully all the

---

21 Cf. T. R. B., "Washington Notes: The Men Who Run America," *New Republic* (April 26, 1943), p. 565.

problems involved and will try to avoid disturbing the smooth operation of the factories as much as possible. It will be anxious to get advice from the entrepreneurs.

III   *The Extractive Industries*

A MINING

The main assets of Mexico's extractive industries are rich natural resources and cheap labor. But exploitation is fettered by the shortage of capital and by the special taxes imposed upon the entrepreneurs.

It is rather difficult to predict the postwar evolution of the country's mines and oil wells. Technological improvements may alter conditions radically. Nobody can foretell how such changes will affect the profitability of Mexican mines. At any rate, it is advisable for the enterprises to accumulate reserves out of the good wartime earnings in order to be in a position to make investments, if need be. A company that can finance investments without appeal to the capital market is in a comparatively favorable position, especially under the conditions to be expected for the first years following the peace.

Mining and oil drilling have always been very risky. There is but little doubt that they will be exposed to chance in the future, too. It is a bad mistake on the part of public opinion to assume that the operation of mines and oil wells requires very little entrepreneurial skill, foresight, and practical ability. The outcome of this fallacy was the belief that no harm could be done by nationalizing them or by singling them out for special taxation.

Government management of mines and oil wells has failed everywhere, not only in Mexico. If there ever was a nation that had succeeded in training a staff of highly efficient civil servants, it was Prussia in the time of the Hohenzollern. However, the operation of coal mines by the Prussian government proved extremely unsatisfactory. The 1919 report of the German Commission for Socialization, whose members were biased in favor of nationalized business, provides a devastating description of the shortcomings of government mine management.[22]

22 [With the general support of the Prussian government in the late nineteenth century, the German coal industry was increasingly formed into a set of narrow cartels. During World War I, the German coal industry came under greater direct government control in

If Mexico wants to derive from its natural resources all the advantages it can possibly get, it will have to learn that only private enterprise is fit to exploit them.

A special problem is set by the silver mines. The silver market is today manipulated by the purchases on the part of the U. S. Treasury. It is difficult to imagine what the world market price of silver would be if the U. S. abandons its policy of buying and hoarding large amounts.[23]

It is unlikely that the U. S. will continue its very costly silver purchases for a long time; the denunciatory blasts directed against its pursuit become more vehement daily. But on the other hand, it is probable that the U. S. will not sell their enormous stocks of about 3,000 million ounces in a manner adversely affecting market prices. The stopping of the purchases will make many North American silver mines unprofitable and force them to go out of business. But this does not necessarily mean that the Mexican mines will be affected, too. We must disregard conditions of the present moment. The purchase price for Mexican silver was only half of the price paid by the U. S. Treasury for domestic silver. It may be that this lower price will be maintained on the world market even after a withdrawal of the U. S. government from the market. The prospects for an increased silver demand for various industrial purposes are not unfavorable. An improvement of general economic conditions in China and in the East Indies will increase the demand for silver for the coinage of silver token money. There is no reason to be alarmed about the future of the country's silver production.

---

the name of the war effort, with pricing, production, and rationing regulations. Following the abdication of Kaiser Wilhelm II in November of 1918, the new Social Democratic government in Berlin appointed a committee to consider the question of nationalizing the coal industry. In March of 1919, the government also passed the Coal Industry Act, "socializing" the industry and specifying the rules and regulations for government oversight of coal mining activities. In early 1920, the special committee on the socialization of industry was instructed to prepare a report on the status and future of the German coal industry. The majority report read: "We cannot agree to the immediate divestment of private capital. . . . The critical condition of the coal industry" requires that "the strongest and most capable [private] managers remain in charge. The decisive, driving powers of capitalism [private businessmen] were and are the essentials of success. They become active through careful selection, through a high degree of independence, complete authority, social and pecuniary standing, [and] open recognition." See Archibald H. Stockder, *German Trade Associations: The Coal Cartels* (New York: Henry Holt and Co., 1924).—Ed.]

23 [On the U. S. Treasury's silver purchase policy, see Chapter VI, "A Noninflationary Proposal for Postwar Monetary Reconstruction," footnote 24.—Ed.]

B ❧ Oil

It is not necessary to enter into a discussion of whether the unsatisfactory conditions of Mexican oil production have to be charged exclusively to the expropriation of the foreign companies and to the blunders committed on the part of the government-controlled management of the oil wells. At any rate, it is certain that the Mexican experience does not disprove the thesis that public ownership and operation of oil wells is inappropriate and results in mischief.

It is a sad fact that Mexico does not have enough domestic capital for a successful exploitation of its natural resources. By violating foreign property rights, the expropriation not only harmed the evolution of oil drilling, it has also injured the whole nation by frightening foreign capitalists.

The conflict between the Mexican government and the expropriated North American companies has been settled by the accommodating attitude on the part of the U. S. government.[24] But this does not solve the Mexican oil problem; it does not provide the country with the capital needed for a better utilization of its oil deposits. What is needed is a system that makes it attractive for foreign capitalists to invest in Mexican oil production. Nothing but scrupulous respect for the rights of investors, whether foreign or domestic, can achieve this goal.

IV   *Small Business and Distribution*

Some years ago, public opinion was unanimous in the belief that the death knell had sounded for small business. People expected that large-scale enterprise would supplant the independent small shop in the field of distribution in the same way in which it had displaced craftsmanship in the field of production. Department stores, chain stores, and consumers' co-

---

24 [The Mexican Constitution of 1917 gave the government title to all subsurface minerals, including oil. In 1938, the government issued a decree nationalizing all foreign-owned oil properties. The Mexican government agreed to pay financial compensation for the expropriation. The U. S. companies claimed two hundred million dollars in losses. The negotiations were undertaken between the U. S. and Mexican governments; a settlement was reached in 1942, resulting in a payment of twenty-four million dollars to U. S. companies. In 1948, the British and Dutch oil companies received a combined payment of $81.2 million.—Ed.]

operatives would supersede the small shopkeeper and thus absorb the commercial middle class.

A walk through the streets of any North American city clearly demonstrates that this pessimistic outlook has not proved true. In the economically most advanced countries, the small retailers, repair shops, inns and restaurants, and so on still flourish. They compete successfully with the large enterprises.

The reason is obvious. The more the standard of living of the masses improves, the more the demand increases for services that a small shop, managed by the owner, can render in a more "personal" way than a big corporation, whose conduct must necessarily be standardized. The eminence of small business is its adaptability. It adapts itself better and more quickly to local and personal conditions. And its overhead costs are inconsiderable.

The most serious check on the development of small business is obtaining credit. The difficulties that businessmen encounter in this field are due to the structure of present-day banking, namely to the disappearance of the private banker and moneylender.

Whether the owner of a small shop is worthy of credit or not cannot be decided according to the standards applied to medium-sized or large-scale business. The main asset of any small business is the owner's personality. The creditor has to know the man, not only his shop. A decent thrifty man, who shuns drinking, gambling, and expensive hobbies, who is assisted in his work by his wife and other family members, is a more reliable debtor than another whose private life is less irreproachable. The creditor has to pass judgment with much more discretion than in the case of larger-sized debtors. Imponderables must decide the matter, circumstances that the stereotypical rules of a bank's auditing department cannot take into consideration. Such a discretionary power cannot be given to the manager of a bank's branch office. He is an employee who does not risk his own money, but *l'argent des autres.*[25] Only a private banker, who has to bear the loss, can embark upon such deals. He alone can acquire the perfect familiarity with all the local and individual conditions involved.

In Mexico, as in all other countries as well, the spirit of anticapitalism has eliminated the sound and correct local banker. Public opinion disparaged him as a parasitic exploiter profiting from his fellow citizens' em-

---

25 [This French term refers to "another's money." — Ed.]

barrassment. Thus the decent money-lenders went out of business, and reckless usurers had the field to themselves.

Branch banking, mutual loan societies, and government credit institutions are no substitute for the independent small banker. They cannot free themselves from the formalistic viewpoint. They have to look at collateral, guarantees, and pledges, not at the debtor's personal character.

Of course, the rates of interest must be comparatively high in granting credit to small business. But so are the risks, too. To get credit at a comparatively high rate is still better than not to get any credit at all.

Under present conditions, the only source of credit available to small business is the credit granted by his purveyor. This makes him depend on the wholesalers and limits his independence. He cannot freely change his suppliers as he may want to do.

It is doubtful whether the business of small local banking can be revived. Such a reform cannot be achieved by the intervention of the government or the banks. It could only be the outcome of a change in the mentality of all groups concerned. There is little hope that such a change could be achieved in a not-too-distant future.

V   Tourism

The postwar prospects for Mexican tourism are excellent. Traveling abroad is the most popular luxury of our age. The citizens of the U. S. are anxious to visit foreign countries. It is obvious that the country that will attract them most is Mexico.

The public investments needed for an expansion of tourism are comparatively low. The establishment of airfields and the construction of more and better motor roads cannot be considered an investment for tourism only. They are indispensable from any viewpoint. The main investment that tourism requires is modern hotels.

The example of some European countries (Switzerland, France, Italy, Austria) proves what an important role foreign tourists can play in economic evolution. Backward districts were transformed in a few years into the most flourishing areas.

It is a mistake to assume that only the hotel business profits from tourism. In the districts concerned, all branches of craftsmanship, retailing, and farming are also benefited.

No special government interference is needed for the encouragement of tourism. What the government has to provide in this field is simply the elimination of frictions that may hurt the popularity of Mexican resorts and places of interest. It is advisable to make a sufficient number of police and customs officers familiar with the English language, as linguistic misunderstandings are the main source of problems. The rest can be left to private initiative.

VI   Transportation

A ❧ The National Railways

The poor state of the Mexican railways is one of the most serious handicaps to a satisfactory evolution of economic conditions. Putting the railroad system into more perfect shape would necessitate the investment of a huge amount of capital. As a consequence, the capital available for other urgent employment would be perceptibly curtailed.

These financial considerations necessitate recourse to a step of very decisive importance.

The evolution of motoring and of aviation has reduced the role played by the railways in the field of passenger traffic. In a not-too-distant future, the railways probably will be done for as passenger carriers and will, for the most part, act only as freight carriers. Mexico should anticipate this evolution and reorganize its railways accordingly.

But for the two main routes—Mexico City–Vera Cruz and Mexico City–Nuevo Laredo—no money should be wasted for expensive investments designed to improve conditions solely for passenger traffic. All other already existing lines and those to be built or rebuilt in the future should be operated mainly as freight lines. They should not entirely neglect the transportation of passengers, but they should avoid expensive outlays that serve only the improvement of passenger transportation and that are not required from the point of view of the freight business.

The investments and the operating costs of a railway line destined mainly for freight traffic are much lower than those of a line whose ambition is to compete successfully with planes and motorcars in passenger transportation. These considerations have to guide all plans for a reform of the Mexican railways. The money saved by this policy will be spent much more advantageously in the construction of new roads and airfields.

A large and comparatively sparsely populated country like Mexico is especially qualified to anticipate such a transportation reform, which sooner or later all other countries will adopt, too. No drawbacks are to be feared. All those traveling for business or for pleasure prefer the motorcar, the motorbus, or the plane.

Only technical experts can decide which railway lines should be operated by electric power and which by steam power. On those lines, which according to the previous suggestions should primarily be operated as freight carriers, passenger traffic could be best served by rail motorcars (either diesel fuel or gasoline).

There is unanimity with regard to the inexpediency of the present system of the management of the National Railways. All the experiments tried have failed lamentably.

The best solution of the problems involved would be for the sale of the whole system to a corporation. This company would first have to come to an arrangement with the National Railway's creditors and bondholders, which would have to go into effect on the day of the actual transfer of the system on the part of the present management. The arguments once brought forward in favor of railway nationalization have long since lost their power. In this age of motoring and aviation, no transportation monopoly has to be feared. Experience has proved that the governments and their agencies are completely unfit to cope with the tasks of railway management.

However, a realistic appreciation of current prejudices must recognize that public opinion is not ready to endorse such a plan. In view of this fact, a less ambitious reform must be suggested.

The ownership of the National Railways remains with the nation; only the management is handed over to a corporation. This corporation has no obligation toward the creditors whose claims originated before it took over the management. Its only task is to operate the property of the Corporación pública descentralizada ["Decentralized Public Corporation"] for the account of this Corporación and the Mexican nation. In order to avoid confusion, we may call this suggested corporation the "manager" and the Corporación pública descentralizada the "system."

The government and the manager fix by agreement the value of the total system for the first day of the operation of the new scheme and the methods of calculating depreciation to be applied to this asset and to all future investments. All investments have to be paid for by the government, but the manager has to provide the capital needed by lending the money to the government at interest rates and yearly repayment installments fixed in advance. The manager has a free hand in the operation of the system; he alone has to decide how much is to be invested; only the construction of new lines requires the consent of the government. He is free to hire and to dismiss the personnel. The salaries and the wage rates are to be fixed with due regard to the salaries and wages paid for a similar type of work in other branches of Mexican industries. The manager has the obligation to insure all members of the staff against illness and accidents and for pensions with a Mexican insurance institution to be nominated by the government. The premiums have to be deducted from the individual employee's salary or wage.

The financial result of every year's management has to be determined according to a scheme elaborated in accordance with sound principles of railway accountancy. The government and the manager have to agree upon this scheme before beginning the operation. The interest on the capital provided by the manager for the current conduct of business, fixed in advance by an agreement between the government and the manager, has to be considered an operating cost; the same is true of the interest to be paid by the government for the investment credits received from the manager.

The corporation capital of the manager has to be equal to the amount required for the current conduct of business in the first year plus the amount required for the investment of the first two years; it has to be fixed in advance by an agreement between the government and the manager. A profit obtained by a year's management has to be distributed in this way: the first 3 percent to the manager; the next 3 percent in equal parts to the manager and to the employees as a bonus; the surplus in equal parts to the manager, the employees, and the government.

Moreover, for the first three years, the government has to guarantee to the manager a profit of 3 percent of that part of his capital that is destined for the conduct of the current business.

This is, of course, only a tentative scheme, in order to give a picture of the financial construction. The concrete arrangements will depend on capital market conditions at the time of the realization of the plan.

The manager has to be exempt from any taxation and from any restrictions regarding foreign exchange transactions. The equipment imported from abroad is not liable to any import duty.

The government is free to rescind the contract with the manager on three months' notice; in that case, it has to pay back to the manager's account with a New York bank all its debts and the whole amount of capital employed by the manager in the conduct of current business.

All disputes between the government and the manager have to be settled by arbitration.

B ✌ ROADS

Under present conditions, the construction of modern motor roads is more important than the improvement of the railways. Mexico's achievements in making mountain passes practicable are admirable, but there is still a lot to be done.

Some European countries have had some success with highways, whether built by the government or by private enterprise, for whose use motorists (but not horse drivers or pedestrians) are charged a toll. The method may prove expedient in Mexico, too.

C ✌ AVIATION AND SHIPPING

The progress of aviation will revolutionize the country's economic, social, and political conditions. It will not only promote business, it will, moreover, facilitate the operation of the government's apparatus and further the spread of education and enlightenment. One can hardly overrate the moral, intellectual, and political importance of a change that will make it possible for the citizens to reach the remotest parts of their country within a few hours.

It is also highly probable that maritime freight rates will be low in the postwar years. This will encourage foreign trade.

And as modern methods of germ fighting remove the plight of tropical diseases, the country's coastal regions will offer more favorable opportunities for the location of processing industries. It is not unlikely that Vera Cruz may become an important industrial center.

VII *Public Utilities*

One of the major problems of Mexico is the need for better utilization of its water supply, both for the irrigation of arid soil and for the generation of electric power. The problem is not so much technical, as modern engineering has developed methods of dealing with the task in a perfect way; it is, instead, financial, as available capital is scarce.

234 SELECTED WRITINGS OF LUDWIG VON MISES

In view of the fact that the agricultural population is very poor, the main burden of irrigation rests on public funds. But it is different with the construction of power works. The consumers are in a position to pay for the electric current. There is no reason to subsidize them by selling the current at prices that do not cover the total costs of production.

Whether the power plants are operated by the government or by government subsidiaries or by enterprises in which the government holds a large portion of the capital and shares the management with the stockholders or by private enterprise, prices should not be fixed at a level that makes the operation unprofitable. Mexico cannot do without the aid of private capital in the development of its hydraulic power. If the progress of electrification requires sacrifices on the part of the Treasury and is not profitable for private capital because of prices set by the government, it will be delayed and the country will be harmed.

As soon as the war is over, U. S. electric plants will be anxious to resume their regular production and to find new customers. They will provide the capital needed for the construction of new power plants, regardless of whether such plants are built by the government or by free enterprise. It would be a mistake to lose this opportunity by fixing the prices at too low a level.

VIII *Labor Problems*

A ❧ Trade Unions and Wage Rates

The basic idea of trade unionism is the belief that it is possible to raise the income of all wage earners permanently by forcing the employers under duress to pay higher wages and to spend more money for the benefit of the workers (for instance, for housing). Trade unionists consider entrepreneurs and capitalists as parasitic drones whose income—profits and interest—is derived from the exploitation of the wage earners. They aim at a reduction or total annihilation of the unearned revenue.

It is a mistake to confuse trade union doctrine and practice with Marxism. Karl Marx did not believe that trade unions could improve the situation of wage earners within the framework of a capitalist society. He was convinced that the inherent tendency of capitalist evolution is to lower more and more the workers' standard of living and that trade unions are not able to counteract this tendency. Therefore, he recommended to the unions that they change their policies; they should not embark upon futile endeavors to raise wage rates, but should fight for the abolition of private enterprise and the wage system as such.

From the viewpoint of economic doctrines, Marx was consistent in asserting that trade unions cannot raise the standard of living of the wage earners. But he was not consistent in asking the trade unions to fight for socialism. For, according to the Marxian doctrine, there is but one way to bring about the substitution of socialism and communism for capitalism: The evolution of capitalism itself. "Capitalist production begets, with the [inexorable] law of nature, its own negation." It is of no use to speed up this process by political action. For "no social formation ever disappears before all the productive forces are developed for which it has room, and new higher relations of production never appear before the material conditions of their existence are matured in the womb of the old society."[26] It is contrary to purpose to check the evolution of capitalism by government or trade union interference. Such "nonsense" is the characteristic feature of "petty bourgeois" policies. The proletarians, enlightened through their class consciousness, will never embark upon such policies.

Like all other forecasts of Marx, this, too, proved to be erroneous. The workers espoused trade unionism, and their Marxian leaders, unaware of the incompatibility of Marxism and trade unionism, supported this policy.

Wage rates, the price paid for labor, are a market phenomenon. On the unhampered market, prices are set at the point at which the amount of the commodity that the buyer will take is equal to the amount that the sellers will sell. Everyone who is prepared to pay the market price can buy as much as he wants, and everyone who is prepared to take the market price can sell as much as he wants.

The same is true for the market price of labor, [that is,] for wage rates. There is always some amount of voluntary unemployment because there are workers who do not want the jobs that are offered to them and are waiting for better opportunities. But, on the unhampered market, unemployment is more or less a transitory phenomenon. There is no serious problem of unemployment; there is no mass unemployment prolonged year after year.

---

26 [Karl Marx, "Preface to *A Contribution to the Critique of Political Economy*," [1859] reprinted in Robert Tucker, ed., *The Marx-Engels Reader* (New York: W. W. Norton and Co., 1972), p. 5; or in *Karl Marx and Frederick Engels: Selected Works in One Volume* (New York: International Publishers, 1968), p. 183.—Ed.]

It is different if—either by government decree or by trade union pressure and compulsion—wages are fixed at a higher rate than that which the unhampered market would have fixed. Then the demand for labor shrinks and permanent unemployment of a part of the potential labor force results.

The concept of "full employment" is a demagogic slogan if it does not refer to a definite wage rate. There is but one means to obtain full employment: To abstain from the enforcement of minimum wage rates higher than the potential market rates. Mass unemployment is not, as the socialists would have us believe, a phenomenon inherent in capitalism. It is, on the contrary, the result of the endeavors to sabotage capitalism by government or trade union coercion.

In a country that, like Mexico, is at an early stage of its industrialization, the inextricable outcome of trade unionism is disguised. Mexico's unemployed are that rural excess population that could find jobs in industrial factories if trade union action did not put a check on the further progress of industrialization.

It is, of course, a sad fact that market wage rates in Mexico are much lower than in the United States and in Canada. But neither trade unions nor government interference can brush away the conditions that keep wage rates low. There is but one means to raise Mexican wage rates: industrial expansion. Every new factory improves the standard of living of the Mexican masses by creating an additional demand for labor, but industry cannot allow higher wages than such as safeguard the conduct of business. If trade unions are anxious to enforce higher wages, they prevent the establishment of new factories and the expansion of existing factories. They succeed, it is true, in raising wage rates for a comparatively small group of workers, but they force hundreds of thousands to remain in agricultural occupations, in which their income is extremely low, that is, much lower than it would be if they could find industrial jobs.

Mexican trade unionism is led by men familiar with labor conditions in the United States. They cast longing glances at North American wage rates and are convinced that the comparative exiguity, that is, meagerness, of Mexican wage rates is a proof of the soundness of their endeavors to force upon the employers higher wage rates. They do not realize that the only result of their activities is to delay or to hinder the country's industrial progress and, thereby, deprive the greater part of their fellow citizens of the only means available for their material improvement.

It is paradoxical that North American labor leaders lament the lowness of Mexican wage rates and encourage Mexican trade unionism. If the North American trade unions were really sincere in their sympathies with their Mexican "class comrades," they could very efficiently contribute to their well-being. If they were prepared to abolish the immigration barriers and to permit Mexicans to compete freely on the labor market of their own countries, they would create a tendency toward an equalization of wage rates between their own countries and Mexico. Low wage rates in Mexico are a corollary to the raising of wage rates in the United States and in Canada through immigration barriers.

It is impossible to industrialize a country in which trade unions have the power to dictate to the employers the amount of wages to be paid. A businessman planning either a new factory or the expansion of an existing factory will desist from investing if he has to expect troubles with trade unions.

Cheap labor is the only factor that can render Mexican industries profitable. Cheap labor has to compensate for the country's natural disadvantages and the scarcity of domestic capital. But Mexican wage rates, which are considered to be very low when compared with North American conditions, are high when compared with the present income of the bulk of the country's agricultural population. This is what the supporters of Mexican trade unionism do not realize. A true friend of the Mexican poor should oppose every attempt to impose burdens upon an industry that is still in its infancy and that will never develop if menaced by the dictation of demagogic trade union leaders.

The same is true for the efforts of the Mexican government to burden the employers by forcing them to provide housing facilities and so on for the employees. Such measures can benefit those already employed in the existing factory. But they hinder both the expansion of the already existing factories and the establishment of new ones. The capital available for investment is scarce. If a part of it has to be used for the construction of workers' homes, it is lacking for other purposes.

From the viewpoint of the interests of the Mexican masses, both the government's labor policy and the methods of the trade unions must be qualified as detrimental. They constitute the most serious check on the expansion of domestic production. He who pities the unsatisfactory economic conditions of a good deal of the nation has to endorse a quite different system. Only if the government and the workers themselves realize that the best way to improve the worker's lot is not to interfere, by decree or by violent pressure, with industrial relations, can a change toward better conditions be expected.

Low wages, poor housing, long hours of work, and so on are gloomy things. Every Mexican patriot and every foreign friend of Mexico must deplore this state of affairs. However, there is but one means to obtain an improvement: the progress of industrialization. Only profitable business can pave the way for a more satisfactory future. What Mexico needs most is the accumulation of domestic capital and the import of foreign capital. The present policies hinder both.

This is not at all a plea for the abolition of unions or the curtailment of the right of workers to organize labor associations. What is required is the abandonment of violence, coercion, and its threat on the part of labor leaders. No one who is willing to work should be prevented from doing so. He who wants to go on strike may go, but he who wants to work should not be hindered from doing so either.

It is the first duty of government to protect the life, health, and property of everyone against infringement or attack. If the government neglects this obligation, anarchic disorder arises. It was the most serious failure of almost all governments that they denied protection to the entrepreneurs, the executives, and those workers eager to continue their work whenever a union decided to go on strike. This weakness on the part of the police power was the main cause for the deplorable decay of civil liberties and democratic institutions.

Neither should governments resort to arbitration of labor disputes. Recourse to arbitration is all right in cases in which a settlement is required according to the provisions of a law or of a customary law. Then the court has to decide in accordance with a general rule; it has to apply this general rule to the merits of the case in question. But if the workers ask for higher wages than those that the employers are ready to pay, there is no such general rule available. The decision has to be made according to arbitrary standards.

In a labor dispute, there are only two parties represented: the employers and the employees. But in Mexico there is still a third party that, although essentially interested in the outcome, is not heard at all. This is those Mexicans who could find jobs in expanding industries and cannot find such jobs if the progress of industrialization is jeopardized by a rise in wage rates above the level that they would reach in an unhampered labor market. They are the forgotten people.

As a rule, the members of the arbitration court nominated by the employers and those nominated by the unions disagree with regard to the case, and the final decision is made by the chairman appointed by the government. Arbitration thus amounts to fixing wage rates by the government. In its further evolution, it results in complete government control of industrial relations, in freezing employment, and in limiting the mobility of labor. The example of the United States and, still more, of Germany, should be a warning to labor.[27]

B ❧ Social Security and Kindred Measures

The public discussion concerning social security, housing provisions, and similar subjects is misled by erroneous assumptions. People believe that a law forcing upon the employer additional expenditure for the benefit of the employees adds something to the real income of the beneficiaries without any disadvantage to them. This is, however, a bad mistake.

What counts for the employer is not only money in wages paid out to the employee, but also the whole cost of employing a man. In calculating and accounting, he must consider all the outlays incurred by hiring labor, that is, not only wage rates, but all other payments required. The contributions for social security, the cost of housing, medical treatment, and so on are, for the employer, parts of the price to be paid for labor. If he cannot reimburse himself for these outlays in selling the products, business becomes unprofitable and has to be restricted or discontinued altogether. Workers are discharged; unemployment results.

If the law forces the employer to make such outlays, the outcome does not differ from that of a decree forcibly raising wage rates. It comes to a virtual rise in real wage rates. If this raise goes beyond the level that the unhampered market would have fixed, unemployment results, industrial expansion is restricted, and people who could find jobs in industry must remain poor peons.

---

27 [On trade unions and the market economy, see Mises, *Socialism* (Indianapolis: Liberty Fund, [1951] 1981), pp. 432–38; *Human Action: A Treatise on Economics* (Irvington-on-Hudson, N.Y.: Foundation for Economic Education, 4th rev. ed., 1996), pp. 376–77 and 777–79; "Wages, Unemployment, and Inflation," [1958] in *Planning for Freedom* (South Holland, Ill.: Libertarian Press, 4th ed., 1980), pp. 150–61; also Eugen von Böhm-Bawerk, "Control or Economic Law," [1914] in *Shorter Classics of Böhm-Bawerk* (South Holland, Ill.: Libertarian Press, 1962), pp. 139–99; Murray N. Rothbard, *Man, Economy, and State: A Treatise on Economic Principles* (Los Angeles, Calif.: Nash Publishing Co., 1970), pp. 620–32; W. H. Hutt, *The Strike-Threat System: The Economic Consequences of Collective Bargaining* (New Rochelle, N.Y.: Arlington House, 1973). — Ed.]

It is, therefore, not very important whether the employer is entitled to deduct his contributions from the amount to be paid out in cash to the employee or not. The real burden reverts at any rate to the employees. The advantage of the first method lies entirely in the fact that it makes it easier for the employees to grasp the pith of the matter.

Social Security does not increase the total amount of wealth available for consumption. It does not add anything to the employee's real income. It only restricts his freedom to spend his earnings *ad libitum*. It forces him to provide for illness, disability, and old age, to spend a minimum for housing and so on.[28]

The Beveridge Plan is no remedy against the lowering of the British worker's standard of living that will result from this expensive war. It only decrees how the wage earner should spend his reduced income.[29]

What is needed is to make the public understand these facts. It can be left to the decision of the wage earners themselves whether they wish to be forced by law to spend a part of their income for social security.

But the legislators have to realize that to force additional expenditures upon the employer, without giving him the power to reduce correspondingly the amount of wage rates paid out in cash to the worker, only benefits a part of labor. Those discharged on account of the resulting fall in profitability are injured; so are those who cannot find jobs if industrial expansion is prevented.

C ❧ Cooperative Societies

There was a time when reformers considered cooperative societies as the most appropriate means to supplant capitalism and to eliminate the profit motive. The most radical advocate of cooperative combination was Ferdi-

28 [See Mises, "Economic Aspects of the Pension Problem," (1950) in *Planning for Freedom*, pp. 83–93.—Ed.]

29 ["The Beveridge Plan" was the brainchild of Sir William Beveridge (1879–1963), director of the London School of Economics from 1919 to 1937. During the Second World War, at the request of the British government, Sir William prepared a plan for a postwar system of comprehensive government social insurance programs for Great Britain, published as *Social Insurance and Allied Services* (New York: Macmillan Co., 1942). It was widely known, however, as the Beveridge Report.—Ed.]

nand Lassalle.[30] He suggested industrial production by cooperative societies aided by government credits. Other reformers were more cautious. They recommended cooperative stores and farmers' cooperatives, but not workmen's cooperation in industrial production.

Experience with cooperatives in the field of production has proved utterly unsatisfactory. No serious economist believes that a cooperative society could successfully compete with private enterprise. Experiments have resulted in complete failure.

In some European countries, consumers' cooperatives have succeeded fairly well. But this success was frequently due to open or disguised assistance granted to them on the part of the treasury to the disadvantage of the tax-paying public. While the competing private firms—chain stores, department stores, and so on—were heavily taxed or even singled out for discriminatory taxation, the cooperatives enjoyed tax privileges. In many cases, the cooperatives could do business only because the trade unions employed pressure, forcing their members to purchase in these stores.

Conditions are quite different in agriculture. Farmers' cooperatives are not institutions designed to eliminate private ownership and enterprise. They are, on the contrary, auxiliaries of independent farmers who manage their own or rented soil. They are an expedient device for the promotion of the system of private initiative.

A liberal government has to maintain strict neutrality with regard to cooperatives. It must give the cooperatives a fair chance. It must neither hinder their operation by discriminatory measures nor grant them any privileges. Let them compete freely. The consumers, the public, the nation may decide. He who thinks that it is more advantageous to buy in a cooperative store may do so. But the government should neither further these stores by subsidies or tax privileges, nor tolerate pressure against those who shun the cooperative store.[31]

The economic backwardness of a part of Mexico's agricultural popu-

30 [Ferdinand Lassalle (1825–64) was a leading German socialist who advocated universal suffrage and workers' cooperatives over industry as a transition to a full nationalization of economic activity. In the 1860s, he advised Bismarck on social reform in imperial Germany. He was killed in a duel over the affections of a woman.—Ed.]

31 [On the theory and practice of cooperatives and the role of government, see Mises, "Observations on the Cooperative Movement," (1947) in Richard M. Ebeling, ed., *Money, Method, and the Market Process*, pp. 238–79.—Ed.]

lation justifies intervention on the part of the government. It is all right for the government to advise peons on how to establish and run cooperatives. Even small subsidies for newly formed cooperatives may be advocated. But it would be a mistake to subsidize them permanently or to grant them tax privileges. It does no good to mask the failure of any institution by such measures. Mexico is not rich enough to indulge in the luxury of waste.

IX Currency and Banking

A ❧ Currency

Mexico's monetary history is, like that of all other nations, a record of failures and disasters.[32] But these events of the past do not in any way restrict the country's freedom to adopt in the future that policy that best serves its interests.

Monetary troubles are never the inextricable outcome of conditions beyond the control of a country's government. They are always the result of a deliberate policy. This policy is sometimes the result of erroneous monetary doctrines. But sometimes even a government that is imbued with perfectly sound ideas may prefer monetary troubles as the lesser evil.

Let us recapitulate some fundamental facts concerning currency and credit.

1. Every country, whether rich or poor, can enjoy the advantages of a stable currency and of stable foreign-exchange rates. Every country is free to stabilize its own currency system with respect to gold and to maintain permanently the gold parity of its monetary unit, provided that it abstains from domestic credit expansion and inflation. Those backward countries that never succeeded in launching a circulation of paper money and of bank notes and never tried coinage debasement never experienced any monetary worries. Monetary troubles are a disease affecting only nations enjoying some bank credit.

2. An unfavorable balance of trade or of payments never brings about a monetary impasse. The outflow of money that they effect is self-liquidating. A domestic shortage of money tends to lower domestic prices

---

32 [For a brief account of Mexico's monetary history in the nineteenth and early twentieth centuries, see J. Laurence Laughlin, *A New Exposition of Money, Credit, and Prices*, Vol. I: *The Evolution of the Standard* (Chicago: University of Chicago Press, 1931), pp. 429–40. — Ed.]

and to raise domestic interest rates. The former increases exports and re-stricts imports; the latter attracts short-term funds from abroad and stops the withdrawal of funds from the country.

3. A permanent, not self-liquidating, outflow of money is always the re-sult of the working of the forces that Gresham's Law describes. If a gov-ernment endows money of different value with the same legal tender, the overvalued money drives the undervalued out of circulation.[33]

All means for hindering a rise of domestic prices and foreign-exchange rates are useless. If there is no inflation and credit expansion, they are su-perfluous; if there is such a policy, they remain ineffective.

4. In the years between the two world wars, inflation and credit ex-pansion became very popular. (This popularity was mostly due to the fal-lacious doctrines of Lord Keynes. But Keynes has changed his mind; he nowadays no longer considers stability of foreign-exchange rates an evil but a blessing; the proof is in his proposals for an International Clearing Union.)[34] Age-old errors, long since unmasked as such in an irrefutable way by economic science, were revived and publicized as a "modern ap-proach." The advocates of inflation, credit expansion, currency devalua-tion, and foreign-exchange control arrogantly ridiculed the supporters of monetary stability by calling them "orthodox" and "economic royalists."[35] But they never made any serious attempt to refute the theories that they disparaged.

The simple truth was that these allegedly new doctrines were but a ra-tionalization of policies to which governments were forced to take recourse on account of their political weakness. Powerful pressure groups had suc-ceeded in making prices of many items rigid. This rigidity paralyzed the working of the market mechanism and thereby brought chaos into the eco-

---

33 [On Gresham's Law, see Chapter VI, "A Noninflationary Proposal for Postwar Mone-tary Reconstruction," footnote 26.—Ed.]

34 [On Keynes's International Clearing Union proposal, see Chapter VI, footnote 18. —Ed.]

35 [For an overview of some aspects of the monetary mismanagement in the period be-tween the two world wars, see Melchior Palyi, *Managed Money at the Crossroads: The Eu-ropean Experience* (Notre Dame: University of Notre Dame Press, 1958), and *The Twilight of Gold, 1914–1936: Myths and Realities* (Chicago: Henry Regnery Co., 1972); also Mur-ray N. Rothbard, *What Has Government Done to Our Money?* (Auburn, Ala.: Ludwig von Mises Institute, 1990), pp. 90–99, and "The Gold-Exchange Standard in the Interwar Years," in Kevin Dowd and Richard H. Timberlake, Jr., eds., *Money and the Nation-State* (New Brunswick, N.J.: Transaction Publishers, 1998), pp. 105–65.—Ed.]

nomic system. The outstanding case was that of wage rates rigidity. Trade unions frustrated all attempts to adjust wage rates to the amount that would make it possible to employ all those anxious to find jobs; their intransigent attitude resulted in mass unemployment prolonged year after year. The governments lacked both the courage and the might to attack trade union policies. They preferred to employ cunning. They expected that currency devaluation would result in raising prices of consumer goods without raising nominal wage rates, that is, in reducing real wage rates. Devaluation was considered as a means to do away with mass unemployment in spite of the resistance of unionized labor.[36]

A government, weighing in its mind these five fundamental principles, would never have any doubts concerning its monetary and credit policy. It would resist all temptations to evade monetary embarrassments by inflationary measures. It would unswervingly cling to the gold standard and would not venture to strive after illusory advantages by reducing the gold content and the purchasing power of its currency unit.

However, the course of world events has brought about peculiar conditions that require a special policy and raise the question whether it is not expedient to take recourse to measures that would have to be qualified as detrimental under other circumstances.

The world's paramount nations—the United States and Britain—have sold themselves to an inflationary policy. In dealing with Mexican problems, we do not have to question the expediency of their procedure; we have simply to acknowledge the fact and to ask what are its consequences for Mexico.

On account of the strategic situation, the United States is at the moment the only big and rich country with which Mexico can do business. Mexico's foreign trade is today mostly with the United States. This situation changes the aspect of the monetary problems.

If Mexico keeps to a policy of monetary stability, the exchange ratio between the two currency systems will result in a continuous appreciation of the Mexican peso and in a corresponding fall of the price to be paid in pesos for one dollar. The Mexican exporter will obtain a smaller number of pesos for the dollar than previously. It is true that he will profit from the rise in North American prices and earn more dollars than

36 On the problem of money-wage rigidity and government policies that prolonged the Great Depression, see Chapter V, "Aspects of American Trade Policy," footnote 6.—Ed.]

before. But the time lag between the rise of domestic prices (in the U. S.) and the fall of the dollar price (in terms of pesos) may result in a reduction of the amount of pesos obtained for the unit sold and exported. This would bring hardship to an important part of Mexican production.

Faced with this problem, the Banco de Mexico has decided to maintain the exchange rate of the dollar. (The slight fall from 4.859 pesos in December of 1941 to 4.851 pesos in December of 1942 is of no consequence.) This means that Mexico joins in North American inflation. Conditions being as they are, it would be preposterous to adopt another policy. But it is obvious that this procedure can only be continued if the United States succeeds in checking its inflation soon. It would be absurd to expose Mexico to the pernicious consequences of a catastrophic inflation. But fortunately there is no danger of such an inflation in the United States.

The announcement that the Banco de Mexico will soon allow the free purchase of gold is proof that responsible men are fully aware of the advantages of monetary stability. If Mexico reestablishes domestic gold circulation, it will not only effectively further the evolution of its national economy; it will, at the same time, set a good example for the rest of the world.

B ❧ COMMERCIAL BANKING

The main task of commercial banking is to stimulate savings and the accumulation of capital and thus to provide the funds for an expansion of business. This process is in progress in Mexico. Nothing but an inflation could wreck it.

Monetary stability is, of course, an indispensable requirement for the formation of capital. Saving is discouraged if the thrifty man realizes that the purchasing power of his savings is shrinking and if the spendthrifts contracting debts are constantly favored by the alleviation of their burden.

A lot of nonsense has been written about an alleged propensity of some nations for prodigality. The truth is that the immense majority of all peoples are ready to turn toward parsimony if conditions are such that they can expect to enjoy the fruits of their saving. The Swiss, the Germans, the English, the French, and other Europeans became thrifty because their countries did not experience inflation in the course of the nineteenth century or, if there was temporary inflation (as in Great Britain during the Napoleonic wars or in France in 1871), the country very soon went back to the gold parity of the preinflation period.[37] The Austrians, the Russians, and the Balkanese were less thrifty because they had to go through inflationary experiences. If Mexico clings in the future to the sound monetary policy it has inaugurated, it will promote domestic saving and will not be harassed by "capital flight."[38]

Commercial banking in Mexico is rather sound. It will expand in a very propitious way and play a very important role in the building up of a prosperous industry.

Under present conditions, the Mexican exporter earns North American dollars that exceed the amount of Mexican purchases in the U. S. It is difficult to import from producers U. S. goods. The replacement of worn-out industrial equipment and new investments often have to be postponed. This involves considerable risk, as the future evolution of the dollar's purchasing power is uncertain.

The obvious solution to this problem is provided by announced changes in the country's gold policy. If the Mexican businessman is in a position to keep his funds in gold coins or in bullion or in gold balances with Mexican banks, he is safe against a further fall in the dollar's purchasing power. Of course, funds of this type do not bear interest. But this does not count very much under present money market conditions.

It will be very advantageous for Mexico to own large gold reserves at the time of the return to peace.

It would be advisable to make this mode of saving accessible to the

---

37 [Because of the heavy costs of financing its war with France, the British government entered into a special relationship with the Bank of England to obtain loans at below-market rates of interest in 1793. By 1795, heavy demands were being made on the Bank for specie redemption of outstanding notes issued in great excess of available gold reserves. In May of 1797, Parliament passed the Bank Restriction Act, freeing the Bank of England from payments in gold for its notes. Bank of England notes in circulation increased from 9.7 million in 1797 to 28.4 million in 1814. And bank deposits increased from 4.9 million in 1797 to 14.8 million in 1814. In terms of Bank of England pound notes, prices increased by 36.4 percent between 1797 and 1813. In 1819, Parliament passed the Resumption Act, and in May of 1821, redemption of Bank of England notes on demand in gold was fully restored. See Edwin W. Kemmerer, *Money: The Principles of Money and Their Exemplifications in Outstanding Chapters of Monetary History* (New York: Macmillan Co., 1935), pp. 198–229. — Ed.]

38 ["Capital flight" refers to the attempt to withdraw financial resources invested in one country and shift them to another country and currency expected to be more secure and stable; see Fritz Machlup, "The Theory of Capital Flight," *Weltwirtschaftliches Archiv*, Vol. XIV (1932), pp. 512–29. — Ed.]

Mexican workers, both to those at home and to those working in the U. S. In their activities on North American farms, the Mexican agricultural workers become familiar with more advanced methods of management than those they knew. They will be anxious to apply similar procedures in their own country, to buy modern tools, to utilize fertilizers, and so on. Their savings will facilitate such plans.

C ❧ FOREIGN CAPITAL

Like all other nations, Mexico, too, embarked in the last decades upon a policy of fanatical anticapitalism. Like all other debtor nations, in Mexico, this hostility was directed principally against foreign capital.

It is usual in Latin America to brand foreign capital as a variety of "colonialism" and to view its expropriation as a continuation of the glorious fight for national liberation and independence. However, this viewpoint is quite unsatisfactory. It has done a lot of harm in Central and South America.

The colonial system of mercantilism, as applied by the European powers to their American possessions in the first three centuries after the discovery of the New World, was a political scheme of monopolistic exploitation. The mother country enjoyed monopolistic privileges in trade and shipping. The colonists were second-class citizens. The government did not care for their well-being but for the maintenance of their subjugation. The colonies were considered a source of revenue for the motherland and its citizens. The merchants of the motherland derived profits from the sale of colonial products that the colonists were forbidden to sell directly to European consumers.[39]

None of these features is present in foreign investments and foreign loans. International capital transactions are regular business; they benefit both parties equally.

The development of the international capital market was one of the most admirable achievements. Thanks to this enormous capital transfer, the nations that had been slow in accumulating domestic capital were provided the means necessary for the exploitation of their natural resources

---

39 [For a recent account of Spanish mercantilist policies in colonial Central and South America and their lingering influence on Latin American culture and politics, see Paul Craig Roberts and Karen Lafollette Araujo, *The Capitalist Revolution in Latin America* (New York: Oxford University Press, 1997).—Ed.]

and their industries. But for foreign capital, neither Germany nor the United States would have succeeded in developing, in only a few decades, their marvelous industrial systems. The capitalists of Western Europe—and later those of the United States, too—supplied all other nations with the means needed for the adjustment of their apparatus of production and transportation to modern standards.

The repudiation of foreign debts and the expropriation of foreign investors on the part of the debtor nations was a serious blunder. Its sinister consequences are today, and for many years to come, a check on the development of these countries' material well-being.

The pace of Mexico's economic progress would be slowed down significantly if the country would not be in a position to obtain foreign capital. The most advantageous way to import capital was the system of bonds and of investments on the part of foreign capitalists. It did not interfere with the nation's sovereignty and did not bring the country into dependence on foreign governments.

In the 1860s, Mexico had a very unfortunate experience, but that invasion was not truly motivated by the interests of foreign capital. The adventurous emperor of France could not keep the peace; he was anxious to attack every country that seemed to offer the opportunity for the acquisition of military glory. He chose Mexico because he expected—erroneously, of course—that it would be easy to conquer it.[40]

All the arguments brought forward for the justification of the repudiation of foreign debts and for the expropriation of foreign investments would justify confiscation of domestic capital, too.

---

40 [Finding itself with an empty treasury in 1861, the Mexican government suspended payments on all foreign debts to France, Spain, and Britain. The three nations sent troops to the port of Veracruz to occupy the customs house, but soon had a falling out because of France's financial claims. Emperor Napoleon III used this as an excuse to try to establish an empire in Central America; he sent a large contingent of French forces to occupy the country in 1862, and Mexico City was conquered in 1863. He appointed Archduke Maximilian of the Austrian House of Hapsburg as emperor of Mexico. However, continuing resistance by Mexican forces placed a heavy drain on France, both in terms of men and money. Finally, under domestic and foreign pressure (including from the United States), Emperor Napoleon III agreed to withdraw his forces by November of 1867. As the French withdrew, Mexican resistance increased; the Mexicans laid siege to the city of Queretaro, where Emperor Maximilian had chosen to make a stand. In May the city surrendered, and Maximilian was captured. In June he was put on trial, found guilty of treason, and executed by firing squad. Thus the Mexican republic was reestablished.—Ed.]

Mexico badly needs capital for its industrialization and for a more intensive exploitation of its domestic resources. It has, therefore, to abstain from measures that could deter the foreign capitalist and hinder the accumulation of capital by its own citizens.

X   Fiscal Problems

A ❧ GOVERNMENT SPENDING

The fallacious doctrine maintaining that heedless government spending is a blessing can easily be disposed of. With a balanced budget, the government can only spend what it has collected by way of taxation. Government expenditure does not add anything to the means available. When the government spends more, the individual citizens spend less. The poor have to restrict their consumption; saving and capital accumulation on the part of the well-to-do is curtailed.

With an unbalanced budget, additional government spending means either inflation or borrowing from the capital accumulated by the citizens. We can abstract from the first eventuality. The second curtails the citizens' capacity to invest by the same amount that it increases the government's capacity to spend.

If some Mexican capitalists prefer to invest a part of their funds abroad or to deposit them with foreign banks, the nation's interests do not suffer harm. The income derived from these funds increases Mexico's capacity to pay for imported merchandise.

The government does not have the power to repatriate these funds forcibly. The capitalists concerned avoid an expansion of their domestic investments because they are frightened, whether rightly or wrongly, by the government's anticapitalist measures. If they are prevented from investing abroad, they will increase their consumption. A man believing that he will not be free to reap the fruits of his fortune sees no fault in consuming the principal of his capital.

If the government is anxious to induce its citizens to invest their means at home, it must inspire confidence. It must avoid open expropriation and confiscatory taxation.

If the government has a good reputation, it can borrow money abroad. A foreign loan temporarily increases its spending capacity. But borrowing abroad is a sound policy only insofar as the government uses the proceeds in a way that increases, for the future, citizens' earning capacity and, thereby, their ability to pay taxes.

B ❧ TAXATION

The rich nations, foremost among them Great Britain and the United States, have espoused the principle of confiscatory taxation. Income taxes absorb in some countries 80 percent, 90 percent, and more of high incomes; inheritance taxes, in the higher brackets, absorb the greater part of an estate.

Such a policy cannot last. It must be abandoned altogether either by a return to reasonable rates or by a wholesale nationalization of private property. It works for the moment because the entrepreneurs and capitalists believe that it is only makeshift and that a radical change will occur as soon as the war is over.

These taxes paralyze the spirit of entrepreneurship. No capitalist embarks upon a risky undertaking if he cannot expect sufficient compensation for the risk of losing. The system of private enterprise cannot work if there is no reward for success, only a penalty for malinvestment. It would have been impossible for Mr. Ford to expand his automobile factories if the government had appropriated the greater part of his yearly earnings. Modern taxation expropriates the rich and prevents newcomers from acquiring wealth. It is an obstacle to economic progress. It disintegrates the structure of industry and trade.

A country suffering from an insufficient supply of capital, like Mexico, must not adopt such suicidal policies. The first principle of Mexican taxation has to be the aim not to discourage saving and capital accumulation. Income taxes have to be kept, even in the upper income brackets, at a moderate level. Besides, that part of a man's income which is not consumed, but invested, has to be subject to an even lower rate. Moderation should be applied with regard to all other taxes, too, especially corporate and inheritance taxes.

After the war, competition on the world market will be very sharp. It will probably be impossible for Mexico to levy special taxes on industrial production and on mining. Prudence would require anticipating these conditions and avoiding any unnecessary increase in expenditure in order to balance the budget when the abolition of these taxes becomes unavoidable.

It is an obvious fact that the burden of public expenditure must revert to the bulk of the population. Confiscatory taxation of the wealthy citizens —a small group in every country, a very small group indeed in Mexico— and of corporations by preventing capital accumulation does more harm than good to the masses.

XI   *Education*

Mexico is a country rooted in an old civilization. Its universities are notable seats of teaching and research. It has succeeded in the last decades in the establishment of an efficient system of primary education for the masses. It is anxious to further vocational and technical schools. All foreign experts are unanimous in the praise of Mexican achievements in this field.

However, the economist must warn of the dangers of some trends in contemporary education. Germany and France were paramount in the development of teaching and instruction. But the results did not come up to expectations. Germany is today a nation of barbarians; Germany, once styled as a nation of poets and thinkers, is now a nation of gangsters. The high state of French education did not prevent a moral and political collapse.

The truth is that the French and the German schools instilled in their pupils a pernicious mentality. The students were imbued with the religion of *étatism*.[41] They were taught that the state is God, that nothing counts but its power, greatness, and glory. And they were also taught to despise and to hate all other peoples. Graduates looked down upon the business of private citizens. Their only aim was to obtain jobs in the service of the government. The ideal of the Frenchman was to be a *fonctionnaire*,[42] that of the German to be a *Beamter*.[43] They were not eager to work; they wanted to

---

41 [*Étatism* is a French term for "statism." See Mises, *Omnipotent Government: The Rise of the Total State and Total War* (Spring Mills, Pa.: Libertarian Press, [1944] 1985), pp. 5 & 46: "Étatism appears in two forms: socialism and interventionism. Both have in common the goal of subordinating the individual unconditionally to the state. . . . Étatism assigns to the state the task of guiding the citizens and of holding them in tutelage. It aims at restricting the individual's freedom to act. It seeks to mold his destiny and to vest all initiative in the government alone."—Ed.]

42 [This is a French term for "state functionary."—Ed.]

43 [This is a German term for "civil servant."—Ed.]

give orders and to be paid out of funds collected by taxation. They preferred the parasitic life of a bureaucrat to the industrious life of a plain citizen. They did not care for anything other than a career in the daily increasing body of state employees.

Corrupt politicians and unprincipled civil servants have ruined the glorious civilization of Western Europe. The institutions of learning and of education were instrumental in creating the vicious mentality that led to this disaster. It is a characteristic fact that many of the most eminent harbingers of the new barbarism were professors of the German universities or members of the Académie Française.[44] Intellectuals have built the houses in which Hitler, Mussolini, and Laval[45] lived at their ease. It was a real *trahison des clercs*, as Julien Benda[46] stigmatized it in his well-known book.

A nation that would guard itself against such a catastrophe has to watch its educational institutions. The youth have to be protected against the arrogant self-conceit that makes them disparage ordinary business activities. It is true that one goal of higher learning is to train people for the correct fulfillment of duties in the civil service. But the first requirement of a government employee is due regard for the individual citizen, for the man whose work produces the means of supporting the nation and the state.

The worst outcome of the *étatist* superstition is the habit of considering the "state" as a mythical being, commanding inexhaustible treasures that it can lavishly spend. The "state" should do this and this, they say; it should pay more and more for various purposes. It never occurs to the *étatist* mind that the state cannot spend except by collecting taxes or by incurring debts or by embarking upon inflation. They do not realize that "the state" that pays is the citizenry itself and not some mythical Midas.

44 [This is the name of France's Academy of Science.—Ed.]

45 [Pierre Laval (1883–1945) was a French politician who led the Vichy French government in collaboration during the German occupation of France. He was a prominent member of the French Socialist Party until 1920, and he served in various ministerial positions during the interwar period. He became head of the Vichy government in 1942 and publicly advocated a German victory. In July of 1945, he was found guilty of treason and was executed.—Ed.]

46 [Julien Benda (1867–1956) was a French novelist and philosopher who strongly defended reason and the intellect against antirationalist movements in Europe in the period between the world wars. His most famous work was *The Treason of the Intellectuals* (New York: W. W. Norton and Co., [1927] 1969), in which he criticized as moral traitors those who betrayed truth for racial and nationalist goals.—Ed.]

The problems of a balanced budget and of an equilibrated economic system are not political and technical; they are moral and intellectual. If public opinion is convinced that the state has never-failing sources of income, and that the only decent way to make a living is to get salaries or subsidies from the treasury, then even a well-intentioned government and parliament cannot succeed in making both ends meet.

One of the main purposes of education must be to dispel the superstitions of *étatism*.

Conclusion

It is a common mistake of our contemporaries to view a country's economic problems primarily as a matter of "material" factors and of technical changes. The main issue is intellectual and moral; the spirit is supreme in this field, too.

It is necessary to realize the following fundamental principles:

A. A nation's civilization depends on its material well-being. The richer a nation is, the easier it becomes for its most gifted sons to achieve great things in every field of human activity. The richer a nation is, the more it can spend for an improvement of education and for the fight against disease.

B. There is but one means to make a nation richer: an increase in production. A man who succeeds in producing more, better, and cheaper goods renders his fellow citizens a far more valuable service than all the promoters of spurious plans for utopian reforms.

C. The accumulation of private capital is not a mischief but a blessing for the community. The greater the amount of capital available, the greater—other conditions being the same—is the productivity of labor and thereby wage rates. A policy resulting in capital consumption or in preventing or delaying the accumulation of capital seriously hurts the interests of the wage earners.

D. Private ownership of the means of production and free enterprise are the foundations of our civilization and of political democracy. The profit motive is the vehicle of progress. Modern science and engineering and modern capitalism are linked together. Neither aprioristic reasoning nor historical experience can justify the assumption that a totalitarian system of economic management could initiate technical improvements.

The acceptance of these principles in the nineteenth century made

Great Britain and the United States the richest nations of the world. Mexico has no other way open.

The task of civil government is to provide the security needed for the steady and continuous operation of private business. British and French eighteenth- and nineteenth-century liberals were not secluded armchair doctrinarians when they recommended *laissez-faire*. It was unhappy experience with the authoritarian direction of business that prompted their teachings. Today, after half a century of government interference with business and public control, we cannot help but approve of their free trade principles.

The German socialist and harbinger of National Socialism, Ferdinand Lassalle, sneered disparagingly at liberal government as a "nightwatchman" and proclaimed, "The state is God."[47] It is this superstitious belief in the omnipotence of government that has brought about the present crisis of civilization.

---

47 [The phrases are from Lassalle's 1863 "Open Letter" advocating a program based on cooperatives and state power. He saw these as the main instruments for the cultural improvement of workers. See Alexander Grey, *The Socialist Tradition: From Moses to Lenin* (New York: Harper and Row, [1946] 1968), pp. 340–41.—Ed.]

Index

Note: Page numbers followed by *(n)* indicate material in footnotes.

Business interests: of government, 254; government divestiture, 152; lack of uniformity of, 65; Marxian view of, 62–63; protectionism and, 68–69
Business taxes, xxxiv–xxxv

Campbell, Colin D., 69(n)
Capital, 107, 219. See also Foreign investment: accumulation of, 204, 204(n), 253; Austrian economy and, 138(n), 138–39; consumed by inflation, 104–5, 105(n); consumed by war, 34–35, 35(n); foreign capital in Mexico, 247–49; migration from Europe, 22–23; postwar shortage of, 24, 24(n), 25–26; for railroad improvements, 230; scarcity of, 191, 208, 209; taxation policy and, 144(n), 144–45, 145(n); of United States, 51, 56
Capital flight, 246, 246(n)
Capital gains taxes, 151
Capitalism. See also Free markets; Market economy: anticapitalist bias and, 221–22, 247–49; economic freedom and, 206–9; European, 33; evolution into socialism, 235; reconstruction and, 29; stereotype of, 207
Capitalist economy. See Market economy
Carnap, Rudolf, 148(n)
Cassel, Gustav, 131(n)
Cassidy, Ralph, 45(n)
Central banks, 96–97, 99(n), 99–100
Central Europe: industrial countries of, 34; national self-determination in, xxviii; unique problems of, xxxiv–xxxv
Central government: authority of, 153; for EDU, 186–88, 194
Chamberlain, Houston Stewart, 174, 174(n)
Chamberlin, William Henry, xxii(n), 22(n), 39(n)
Charles, Prince of Mecklenburg-Strelitz, 177(n)
Charles V, Holy Roman Emperor, 151, 151(n)

Cheap labor: in Mexico, 215, 237
Churchill, Winston, 24(n), 200(n)
Citizen(s): advantage of war to, 4, 6, 170; burden of war on, 79; in Eastern European union, xxxvi; free society and, xxx; initiative of, 30; as national asset, 205; self-determination of, xxxv; state interventionism and, 11
Citizen organizations, 156
Citizenship: equality of, 44–45, 46–47
Civilization, 1, 68, 253
Civil service: competitive examinations for, 156; education and, 251(n), 251–52
Clearing countries, 36, 36(n)
Closed-door method of industrialization, xxxvii–xxxviii, 216(n), 216–19
Cobden, Richard, 5, 5(n)
Cold War: effects of, xxv
"Colonization of the East," 177, 177(n)
Colton, Joel, 219(n)
Commercial banking, 245–47
Commodities: changes in, 120–21
Communism: demise of, xxv–xxvi
Comparative advantage, x
Comparative costs: law of, 56–57
Compulsory organizations, 156
Condliffe, J. B., xxi(n), xxii(n), xxiv(n)
Congress of Berlin (1878), 176, 176(n)
Congress of Paris (1856), 176, 176(n)
Congress of Peace in Paris (1919), 176, 176(n)
Congress of Vienna (1814–1815), 175(n), 175–76
Conquest: annexation of territory, xxxv, 146, 146(n), 148, 176, 176(n); lasting peace and, 17
Conquest, Robert, 161(n)
Consumer goods: French, 38; luxury goods, 98, 149, 151; prices of, 55
Consumer-oriented policy, xxix–xxx
Consumers' cooperatives, 241
Consumers' sovereignty, 63–64, 64(n)
Continental currency, 81, 81(n)
Cooperative societies: agricultural, 213, 241; effects of, 240–42, 241(n)